A 'Stepped Approach' to Disputes on International Watercourses

International Water Law Series

VOLUME 13

The titles published in this series are listed at *brill.com/iwl*

A 'Stepped Approach' to Disputes on International Watercourses

By

Riley T. Denoon

BRILL | NIJHOFF

LEIDEN | BOSTON

Library of Congress Cataloging-in-Publication Data

Names: Denoon, Riley T., author.
Title: A 'stepped approach' to disputes on international watercourses / by Riley T. Denoon.
Description: Leiden ; Boston : Brill/Nijhoff, 2025. | Series: International water law series, 2351-9606 ; volume 13 | Includes bibliographical references and index.
Identifiers: LCCN 2025018142 (print) | LCCN 2025018143 (ebook) | ISBN 9789004736764 (hardback) | ISBN 9789004736771 (ebook)
Subjects: LCSH: Water resources development—Law and legislation. | Water rights (International law) | Dispute resolution (Law)
Classification: LCC K3498 .D46 2025 (print) | LCC K3498 (ebook) | DDC 346.04/691—dc23/ENG/20250415
LC record available at https://lccn.loc.gov/2025018142
LC ebook record available at https://lccn.loc.gov/2025018143

Typeface for the Latin, Greek, and Cyrillic scripts: "Brill". See and download: brill.com/brill-typeface.

ISSN 2351-9606
ISBN 978-90-04-73676-4 (hardback)
ISBN 978-90-04-73677-1 (e-book)
DOI 10.1163/9789004736771

Dedicated to Margot

Contents

Acknowledgements

With thanks to Marguerite de Chaisemartin, Prof. Stephen C. McCaffrey, Prof. Jarrod Wong, Prof. Mike Vitiello, Richard K. Paisley, Linda J. Payne, Prof. Emeritus John Humphrey, Dr. Laura McLeod, Beth Powers, and Maya Motyka for their insights and feedback on this work. The views expressed in this work are those of the author.

Tables

Terms

Adjudicative level – A phase or 'Step' primarily concerned with judicial/legal issues, rights or mechanisms or dominated by judicial/legal experts such as lawyers or judges, examples of this level are arbitration or litigation before an international tribunal such as the International Court of Justice.

Boundary Waters Treaty – *Treaty Relating to Boundary Waters, and Questions Arising Between the United States and Canada, Great Britain and United States*, 11 January 1909, UKTS 1910 No 23 (*Boundary Waters Treaty*).

Dispute – "[A] disagreement on a point of law or fact, a conflict of legal views or of interests between two persons."[1]

Diplomatic level – A phase or 'Step' primarily concerned with diplomatic issues or mechanisms (such as negotiation, mediation or good offices) or dominated by diplomatic decision makers such as diplomats, envoys or other State representatives.

FAO – Food and Agricultural Organization of the United Nations ('FAO')

International watercourse – "[A] watercourse, parts of which are situated in different States".[2]

Indus Waters Treaty – *The Indus Waters Treaty 1960 (with annexes)*, 19 September 1960, 419 UNTS 125 (*Indus Waters Treaty*).

ICJ – International Court of Justice

IJC – International Joint Commission between Canada and the United States of America under the Boundary Waters Treaty of 1909.[3]

ILA – International Law Association

ILC – International Law Commission

IDI/IIL – Institut de Droit International (IDI)/Institute of International Law (IIL)

Law of international watercourses / International watercourse law – The law of the non-navigational uses of international watercourses.[4]

---

1 *Case of the Mavrommatis Palestine Concessions* (*Greece v Great Britain*), (1924) PCIJ (Ser A) No 2 at 11. (the "*Mavrommatis Case*").

2 *Convention on the Law of Non-Navigational Uses of International Watercourses, 21 May 1997, 2999 UNTS 77, 36 ILM 700* (*Watercourses Convention*) at 122 art 2(b) (*entered into force 17 August 2014*).

3 *Treaty Relating to Boundary Waters, and Questions Arising Between the United States and Canada, Great Britain and United States*, 11 January 1909, UKTS 1910 No 23 (*Boundary Waters Treaty*).

4 This excludes the law concerning the navigational uses of international watercourses which would also normally fall under the term of "Law of International Watercourses/International Watercourse Law", this has been done for ease of use for the purposes of this work.

PCA – Permanent Court of Arbitration

RBO – River Basin Organization

Technical level – A phase or 'Step' primarily concerned with factual and technical issues, systems or functions or dominated by technical experts such as scientists or engineers.

TFDD – Transboundary Freshwater Diplomacy Database ('TFDD') at Oregon State University's Program in Water Conflict Management and Transformation.

UN – United Nations

UN Watercourses Convention – *Convention on the Law of Non-Navigational Uses of International Watercourses*, 21 May 1997, 2999 UNTS 77, 36 ILM 700 (*UN Watercourses Convention*) (entered into force 17 August 2014).

UNECE ***Water Convention*** – *Convention on the Protection and Use of Transboundary Watercourses and International Lakes*, 17 March 1992, 1936 UNTS 269 (*UNECE Water Convention*).

Watercourse – "[A] system of surface waters and groundwaters constituting by virtue of their physical relationship a unitary whole and normally flowing into a common terminus".[5]

5 *Convention on the Law of Non-Navigational Uses of International Watercourses*, 21 May 1997, 2999 UNTS 77, 36 ILM 700 (*Watercourses Convention*) at 121 art 2(a) (*entered into force* 17 *August* 2014).

Introduction

> Be formless, shapeless, like water. Now if you put water into a cup, it becomes the cup. Put it into a teapot, it becomes the teapot. Now water can flow, or creep or drip or crash. Be water my friend.[1]

∵

It is important in thinking about disputes in regard to international watercourses that we look for this type of flexibility and adaptability. "Disputes concerning fresh water are varied. They reflect the many values of water, be they social, ecological, cultural, or economic."[2] This work will look for a framework that can address diverse types of disputes using multiple dispute resolution and avoidance mechanisms at different 'Steps' in a progressive process, exploring the idea of what has been termed here a 'Stepped Approach' to disputes in the law of the non-navigational uses of international watercourses. While a 'Stepped Approach' has been discussed in some form or another for some time it has remained relatively general in its definition.[3] For our purposes a 'Stepped Approach' to disputes on international watercourses encompasses a dispute resolution and avoidance system dealing with an international watercourse and composed of a set of graduated discrete 'Steps', phases, or echelons of limited scope or duration with a relatively clear progression from one 'Step'

---

1 Bruce Lee, *Longstreet: The Way of the Intercepting Fist*, 1971, TV Series (American Broadcasting Company (ABC), 1971).

2 Laurence Boisson de Chazournes, *Fresh Water in International Law*, 2nd ed (Oxford University Press, 2021) at 276.

3 "[E]chelon" Stephen M. Schwebel, "Third report on the law of the non-navigational uses of international watercourses" (UN Doc A/CN.4/348) in *Year Book of the International Law Commission 1982 vol 2 part 1 (1984)* 65 at 182 (UN Doc A/CN.4/SER.A/1982/Add.1(Part 1)); "[S]tepwise dispute-resolution system" Stephen C. McCaffrey, *The Law of International Watercourses*, 3rd ed (Oxford University Press, 2019) at 577; "[S]taged procedure for the avoidance and resolution of disputes" Stephen C. McCaffrey, *The Law of International Watercourses*, 3rd ed (Oxford University Press, 2019) at 578–579; "[S]eries of stages, or echelons" Stephen C. McCaffrey, "Sixth report on the law of the non-navigational uses of international watercourses" (UN Doc A/CN.4/427 and Add.1) in *Yearbook of the International Law Commission 1990*, vol 2, part 1 (1993) 41 at 72 para 75 (UN Doc A/CN.4/SER.A/1990/Add.1 (Part 1)); "[P]hased approach" Sergei Vinogradov, Patricia Wouters and Patricia Jones, *Transforming Potential Conflict into Cooperation Potential: The Role of International Water Law* (UNESCO-IHP, PCCP, 2003) at 63.

 | DOI:10.1163/9789004736771_002

to another. This work will look at scholarly contributions, existing dispute resolution mechanisms in the field, as well as state practice through treaties and international organizations. This work will also put forward an analytical framework of nine (9) criteria to help identify the presence of an ideal 'Stepped Approach' in existing international agreements and to analyze those 'Stepped Approaches'.

This work will first attempt to position its proposed 'Stepped Approach' in the broader context of international dispute resolution and the law of international watercourses by looking at the growing trend of water stress in today's world, the framework of the law of the non-navigational uses of international watercourses and finally the major existing mechanisms of dispute resolution in the field today.

Next this work will explore the idea of the resolution and avoidance of disputes at a 'Technical Level'. In advocating for the desirability of 'Technical Level' dispute resolution and avoidance this work will attempt to describe what is meant for a dispute to be dealt with at such a 'Level' and provide examples of such dispute resolution and avoidance mechanisms.

Thirdly this work will explore the concept of a 'Stepped Approach' to disputes on international watercourses. It will attempt to show what is meant by a 'Stepped Approach' while providing examples of what such an approach would look like in practice, highlighting particular characteristics and traits that the approach should possess and arguing for the merits of employing such an approach. This discussion will be concluded by examining two recent international disputes before the International Court of Justice (the 'ICJ') and the Permanent Court of Arbitration (the "PCA") to see what these cases could illustrate about the importance and usefulness of employing a 'Stepped Approach' to disputes involving international water resources. Beyond this, the discussion will use treaties and reference existing disputes to illustrate the importance of various components of a 'Stepped Approach'.

Much ink has been spilled on dispute resolution and avoidance on international watercourses from other disciplines such as geography, mathematics, hydrology and the social sciences, particularly in regard to alternative dispute resolution ('ADR') and negotiation theory or dispute avoidance.[4] This work will generally focus on the legal mechanisms for dealing with disputes on international watercourses. In this work the author has taken a rather broad interpretation of what qualifies as a "dispute" or "dispute resolution" often

4 For example, and further reference see Heather L. Beach et al, *Transboundary freshwater dispute resolution: Theory, practice, and annotated references* (United Nations University Press, 2000).

encapsulating what would often be termed as "dispute avoidance" or cooperative/preventative actions particularly under the discussion around 'Technical Level' dispute resolution and joint mechanisms.

"Water is a challenging issue for international law, even if it has been addressed for many decades by a large body of rules in the form of global and regional treaties and other rules and soft law instruments."[5] Indeed the law of international watercourses is a specialized and very important area of international law and particular attention should be given to articulating relevant dispute resolution and avoidance frameworks. "While 'dispute settlement' is itself a large and traditional topic in international law, settlement of disputes over the use of international watercourses has long received unusually close attention by States and commentators."[6]

The importance of this area of law is underscored by the work of the International Law Commission (the 'ILC') on the subject of the non-navigational uses of international watercourses. In his sixth report to the ILC at its forty-second session, the then Special Rapporteur on the subject of the law of the non-navigational uses of international watercourses, Stephen McCaffrey, suggested a "process for the avoidance and settlement of watercourse disputes that consist[ed] of a graduated series of stages."[7] He appears to be the third special rapporteur on the subject to suggest dispute-settlement procedures entailing stages.[8] The work undertaken by the ILC on this subject ultimately became the draft articles on the law of the non-navigational uses of

---

5 Philippe Sands Q.C., "Water and international law: science and evidence in international litigation" (2010) 22 Environmental Law & Management 151, at 151.

6 Stephen M. Schwebel, "Third report on the law of the non-navigational uses of international watercourses" (UN Doc A/CN.4/348) in *Year Book of the International Law Commission 1982* vol 2 part 1 (1984) 65 at 181 (UN Doc A/CN.4/SER.A/1982/Add.1(Part 1)).

7 "[T]he Special Rapporteur proposes in the present chapter a process for the avoidance and settlement of watercourse disputes that consists of a graduated series of stages. The proposals are based on several propositions: first, that it will often be necessary in this field to rely heavily on technical expertise; secondly, that a non-binding expert report, possibly accompanied with a recommended course of action, will frequently result in resolution of an actual or potential dispute without the need to have recourse to a procedure that results in a binding settlement; and thirdly, that procedures of the latter kind should be resorted to only after attempts to settle differences at the technical level have failed." Stephen C. McCaffrey, "Sixth report on the law of the non-navigational uses of international watercourses" (UN Doc A/CN.4/427 and Add.1) in *Yearbook of the International Law Commission 1990*, vol 2, part 1 (1993) 41 at 66 para 42 (UN Doc A/CN.4/SER.A/1990/Add.1 (Part 1)).

8 Stephen C. McCaffrey, "Sixth report on the law of the non-navigational uses of international watercourses" (UN Doc A/CN.4/427 and Add.1) in *Yearbook of the International Law Commission 1990*, vol 2, part 1 (1993) 41 at 75 para 85 (UN Doc A/CN.4/SER.A/1990/Add.1 (Part 1)).

international watercourses, which became the *Convention on the Law of Non-Navigational Uses of International Watercourses*, 21 May 1997, 2999 UNTS 77, 36 ILM 700 (the '*UN Watercourses Convention*').[9] Others have also observed a 'Stepped Approach' to disputes in the context of international watercourses: "[i]f a dispute or a disagreement arises, most international watercourse legal regimes tend to gradually elevate it from one level of dispute settlement procedure to another: from using technical experts within a joint institution to diplomatic negotiations and, eventually, to binding resolution by the impartial third party."[10]

The idea of seeking out alternative dispute resolution mechanisms when another mechanism has failed to produce a settlement is not a revolutionary idea by any stretch. "In the event of failure of the parties to a dispute to reach an early solution by any of the above means of settlement, they shall continue to seek a peaceful solution and shall consult forthwith on mutually agreed means to settle the dispute peacefully."[11] In this work we discuss a 'Stepped Approach' which formalizes the relationship and interaction of the various mechanisms in a progressive framework of ordered 'Steps'. This is supported in State practice outside the realm of international watercourses. "[T]he dispute settlement clauses of many multilateral treaties provide that disputes which cannot be settled by negotiations shall be submitted to another peaceful settlement procedure. Various patterns of successive steps can be found in practice [...]."[12] In this work we will generally focus on international watercourse agreements for our analysis. "An integrated approach to watercourse disputes that takes all of the existing means and procedures for conflict resolution, including adjudication and arbitration, into account finds support in basic international law."[13]

In dealing with conflicts over scarce freshwater resources at the international level Tjaco T. van den Hout, the then Secretary-General of the Permanent Court of Arbitration, wrote that "[t]he dispute resolution provisions in the

---

9 *Convention on the Law of Non-Navigational Uses of International Watercourses*, 21 May 1997, 2999 UNTS 77, 36 ILM 700 (*UN Watercourses Convention*) (entered into force 17 August 2014).

10 Sergei Vinogradov, Patricia Wouters and Patricia Jones, *Transforming Potential Conflict into Cooperation Potential: The Role of International Water Law* (UNESCO-IHP, PCCP, 2003) at 62–63.

11 *Manila Declaration on the Peaceful Settlement of International Disputes*, GA Res 37/10, UNGAOR, 37th Sess, SUPP NO 51, UN Doc A/37/51, (1982) 261 at 262 Annex Section I para 7.

12 United Nations, *Handbook on the Peaceful Settlement of Disputes* (UN, 1992) at 21.

13 Attila Tanzi, *The Economic Commission for Europe Water Convention and the United Nations Watercourses Convention: An analysis of their harmonized contribution to international water law*, Water Series No 6 (UN, 2015) at 73 [footnote omitted].

UN Watercourses Convention are of course a vital step in this direction, but the next step is to continue to develop an appropriate framework for dispute resolution – one which is capable of dealing with complex water disputes rapidly and with a final and binding outcome."[14] This work attempts to articulate just such a framework by addressing the question: What is a 'Stepped Approach' to disputes on international watercourses and what is its utility to resolving disputes under the law of the non-navigational uses of international watercourses?

---

14 Tjaco T. van den Hout, "Introduction" in The International Bureau of the Permanent Court of Arbitration, ed, *The Permanent Court of Arbitration/Peace Palace Papers Resolution of International Water Disputes* (Kluwer Law International, 2003) xi at xiii.

Methodology

In addition to reviewing the relevant legal scholarship, the work of learned societies of international law, decisions of international (judicial, arbitral and general dispute resolution) organs as well as the work of International River Basin Organisation(s) ('RBO(s)') this work has also analysed existing international agreements and instruments.

In analysing international agreements and instruments this work has made use of the International Freshwater Treaties Database (current as of 2018) maintained by the Transboundary Freshwater Diplomacy Database ('TFDD') at Oregon State University's Program in Water Conflict Management and Transformation.

Using the TFDD's International Freshwater Treaties Database this work identified five hundred and ninety-five (595) treaties or international instruments that pertained to international water resources.[1] This number excluded minor treaties or instruments, as determined by the TFDD program, that had "components related to water as a resource but whose water component is believed insignificant and with little relation to international water management issues (e.g. a clause allowing border guards to access drinking water on adjacent territory). Essentially, the agreement's focus, subjectively, is not or has little to do with water".[2]

One hundred and eighty-eight (188) treaties or international instruments that were identified contained a conflict resolution mechanism. Two hundred and twenty (220) treaties or international instruments did not contain a specific conflict resolution mechanism. One hundred and eighty-seven (187) treaties or instruments were uncoded or unavailable in regard to information on specific conflict resolution mechanisms on the database.

1 Four (4) instruments were later removed as two (2) were deemed to be draft agreements, one (1) was a duplicate with a different conclusion date, and one (1) was domestic legislation enacting a treaty already in the database. The number of treaties would therefore be five hundred and ninety-one (591). These four (4) treaties were removed from the final total that was ultimately reviewed for this work.

2 Oregon State University, *Transboundary Freshwater Disputes Database*, "International Freshwater Treaties Database – Codebook and Description for Excel" (Updated January 2023), online: International Freshwater Treaties Database <https://transboundarywaters.ceoas.oregonstate.edu/sites/transboundarywaters.ceoas.oregonstate.edu/files/2024-02/TreatyCodeBook_v29%20%281%29.pdf>.

 | DOI:10.1163/9789004736771_003

Next these treaties were cross-referenced against a table of two hundred and nineteen (219) treaties compiled by Dr. Christina Leb,[3] her table identified one hundred and fifteen (115) treaties with dispute resolution provisions. By cross-referencing these two data sets two hundred (200) treaties were identified with dispute resolution provisions. Several treaties were found to not contain dispute resolution provisions between State parties to the agreement and these were removed and a few treaties were also removed that were concluded before 1900. Additional treaties were added using the authors own knowledge. The FAOLEX database[4] by the Food and Agriculture Organization of the United Nations (FAO), the ECOLEX Database[5] operated jointly by the FAO, The International Union for Conservation of Nature (IUCN), and the United Nations Environment Programme (UNEP), as well as the International Environmental Agreements (IEA) Database Project hosted by the Université Laval[6] were also reviewed for additional treaties particularly from 2009 to the present.[7]

In the end six hundred and seven (607) international water resources treaties since 1900 AD were analyzed, two hundred and twenty-five (225) of which were identified containing distinct dispute resolution provisions between State actors.[8] These two hundred and twenty-five (225) treaties were then reviewed and scored based on the presence of nine (9) criteria,[9] identified by the author after a review of relevant treaties. These criteria were:

– **The presence of three (3) or more 'Steps'** – three (3) or more distinct 'Steps' were looked for in the specific provision(s) dealing with the resolution of

3 Christina Leb, *Cooperation in the Law of Transboundary Water Resources* (Cambridge University Press, 2013) at 263–298.

4 Food and Agriculture Organization of the United Nations: FAOLEX Database (last visited 29 August 2024), online: FAOLEX Database <https://www.fao.org/faolex/en/>.

5 The Food and Agriculture Organization of the United Nations (FAO), The International Union for Conservation of Nature (IUCN) and the United Nations Environment Programme (UNEP): ECOLEX: Home (last visited 29 August 2024), online: ECOLEX <https://www.ecolex.org>.

6 Université Laval: International Environmental Agreements (IEA) Database Project (last visited 29 August 2024), online: International Environmental Agreements (IEA) Database Project <https://www.iea.ulaval.ca/en>.

7 In total forty-two (42) treaties were added based on this additional search.

8 It is important to note that only distinct provisions addressing disputes between State parties were reviewed. The author attempted to differentiate these from compliance and management mechanisms in the agreements, unless these mechanisms were specifically mentioned in the dispute resolution provisions as applying to disputes between State actors.

9 The percentages provided in five (5) tables in the text of this book are rounded to the nearest full percentage meaning they will not necessarily equal one hundred percent (100%).

disputes between State parties to an agreement during the implementation of the treaty;

- **Steps of limited scope or duration** – agreements were assessed for either subject-matter or time-period limitations in the provision(s) dealing with the resolution of disputes between State parties to an agreement;
- **A clear progression through the 'Steps'** – this criterion assessed whether there was an obvious and clearly articulated progression through the various 'Steps' dealing with the resolution of disputes between State parties to an agreement. For example, provisions which provided parties to a dispute with a series of choices were regarded as a single 'Step';
- **Recourse to technical expertise and decision making** – for this criterion dispute resolution provisions were assessed to see if parties to a dispute had explicit recourse to specific technical expertise in the process, for example, the ability to have a technical report made or to consult with an engineer;
- **A distinct technical 'Step'** – this criterion is distinct from the preceding criteria in that it looks for a specific technical 'Step', separate from juridical, political or diplomatic mechanisms; in some cases it was not always apparent if a mechanism or body was exclusively technical in its composition or work, here the function and makeup of a mechanism or body was analysed based on the surrounding provisions of the treaty to assess if it had predominantly technical functions or composition;
- **A distinct diplomatic 'Step'** – agreements were analysed to see if there was a clearly diplomatic 'Step', i.e. negotiation, mediation, good offices, 'by agreement' etc., parties arguably always have recourse to diplomatic means of dispute resolution but unless it was specifically mentioned in the dispute resolution provision(s) it was not counted as such for our purposes here;
- **A distinct adjudicative 'Step'** – this criterion looked at whether a dispute resolution provision in an agreement provided a distinct 'Step' for adjudicative means of resolving the dispute, such as arbitration or recourse to an international court or tribunal of a distinctly juridical nature;
- **At least one compulsory 'Step'** – agreements were reviewed to see if they had at least one clearly compulsory dispute resolution 'Step' that obligated a party or the parties to participate, regardless of their consent; the use of the language 'must' or 'shall' or the presence of a 'Step' that could be instigated by only one of the parties were determined to indicate such a compulsory 'Step'; and
- **A binding ultimate 'Step'** – agreements were looked at to see if the final 'Step' in their dispute resolution process had the power to impose a 'binding'

or 'final' determination of the dispute regardless of any agreement or lack of agreement of the parties to the dispute.[10]

There are obvious shortcomings with this methodology. For instance, any weakness shared by the TFDD and Dr. Leb's data sets will be reflected in the data used here. The legal mechanisms embodied in the provisions of international agreements are analysed, but quite often the treaty provisions differ from the practice of the State parties under the treaty, although an effort has been made to discuss the real practice of States under these treaties, in the instances where this work deals with the treaties in more detail. There is also a subjective element to the assessments made here by the author, despite best efforts being made to fix on objective provisions. In some cases, it can be difficult to draw a clear line between dispute resolution, dispute avoidance, compliance, or governance mechanisms.[11] In fact, these various mechanisms can often have overlapping functions in regard to dispute avoidance and settlement. As observed by Dr. Leb "It is common that treaties establish an obligation to first attempt to settle any disagreement by negotiation. If a treaty also provides for the establishment of a joint mechanism, the task of dispute settlement by negotiation is frequently assigned to those institutions."[12] In this work distinct 'Steps' were measured, where a provision allowed for a suite of options such as in article 33(2) of the *UN Watercourses Convention*,[13] these were not measured. Meaning that an agreement could provide for several mechanisms in a 'menu' for the parties that are not accounted for. This work also did not count general provisions that allowed parties to consent to the jurisdiction of the ICJ or another international court or tribunal as a distinct 'Step'. Despite these shortcomings it is felt that the data and conclusions gathered from this broad analysis of treaty provisions can give a useful overview of the practice in

10 In some cases, where it was not stated, the binding nature of the mechanism was assumed i.e. the ICJ or arbitration being deemed to be binding. Other mechanisms, such as diplomatic means, were deemed to be non-binding.

11 Christina Leb, *Cooperation in the Law of Transboundary Water Resources* (Cambridge University Press, 2013) at 193; see also Salman Salman, "Evolution and Context of International Water Resources Law" in Laurence Boisson de Chazournes and Salman Salman, eds, Les resources en eau et le droit international – Water resources and International Law (Martinus Nijhoff Publishers, 2005) 45 at 89.

12 Christina Leb, *Cooperation in the Law of Transboundary Water Resources* (Cambridge University Press, 2013) at 194.

13 *Convention on the Law of Non-Navigational Uses of International Watercourses, 21 May 1997, 2999 UNTS 77, 36 ILM 700* (*Watercourses Convention*) at 136–138 art 33(2) (*entered into force 17 August 2014*).

the field and indicate either the relative prevalence or obscurity of a 'Stepped Approach' to disputes in the law of international watercourses.

It is important to keep in mind that treaties will exist on a spectrum regarding this conceptual 'Stepped approach'. It is not a failure for a treaty to only have one or two of the criteria provided or to have multiple 'Steps' function concurrently or as a suite of options. The nine (9) criteria put forward largely represent an idealized 'Stepped Approach' and the absence of any particular criteria generally should not be seen as a failure of such a framework in terms of qualifying as a 'Stepped Approach'.

It is also important to note that this work does not seek to "prove" the superiority of a 'Stepped Approach' for all disputes in regard to international watercourses, it simply seeks to provide a conceptual framework to articulate what is a 'Stepped Approach', a set of criteria to allow us to evaluate it, a database to understand its use in international watercourse agreements, and to illustrate some of the possible benefits in utilizing such a 'Stepped Approach'. This is not to say that a 'Stepped Approach' will always be the best approach for any situation, but it should be viewed as a useful tool that parties can adopt when drafting a treaty, or practitioners can use to evaluate or view a dispute resolution mechanism, depending on their needs. In some specific examples a 'Stepped Approach' may not be best adapted to a particular basin, dispute, or group of riparians. This work has taken a fairly macro and generalized perspective on international watercourse dispute mechanisms. As is true of the *UN Watercourses Convention* the approach here needs to be tailored to the specific needs of a particular basin.

CHAPTER 1

Disputes and the Law of the Non-navigational Uses of International Watercourses

In this chapter we will explore dispute resolution in the law of the non-navigational uses of international watercourse to provide some general context for the 'Stepped Approach' discussed in this work. Time will be dedicated to understanding the important need for dispute resolution mechanisms in the field and the specific mechanisms available that may comprise the various 'Steps' of the 'Stepped Approach' put forward here. This discussion will be put in the context of the survey of agreements in the field conducted for this work to give the reader some context to the practice in the field and an argument will be made for an integrated approach incorporating various, complementing, mechanisms of dispute resolution in the field.

We will first look at the increasing water stress on vital water resources and the resulting increase in conflict on international watercourses for these precious resources. We will then look at the law of the non-navigational uses of international watercourses, including the major multilateral treaties in the field, to give the reader the legal context of our discussion. Finally, we will look at inter-State dispute resolution regarding the non-navigational uses of international watercourses.

1 Increasing Water Stress and Conflict

1.1 *Growing Demand in a Fixed System*

Water is vital for the ecological well-being of our planet as well as human life and economic activity. The amount of this vital resource on Earth has remained fixed, generally, for the duration of human history. At the same time human population growth as well as increased industrialization and economic growth have placed ever greater demands on our planet's finite water resources.[1]

1 Peter H. Gleick, "An introduction to global fresh water issues" in Peter H. Gleick, ed, *Water in Crisis A Guide to the World's Fresh Water Resources* (Oxford University Press, 1993) 3; see also Aaron T. Wolf, "Shared Waters: Conflict and Cooperation" (2007) 32 Annual Review of Environment and Resources 241.

 | DOI:10.1163/9789004736771_004

In 2019 the global population was estimated to be roughly 7.7 billion people,[2] by 2050 it is estimated that there will be 9.7 billion humans on this planet.[3] This increased population will have major ramifications for the pressure on global water supplies. Global water demand is expected to increase by 55% with an estimated 40% of the world's population, or 3.9 billion people, anticipated to be living in water basins experiencing severe water stress by 2050.[4]

Most water resources on Earth are not readily available for human use. Ninety-seven and a half percent (97.5%) of Earth's water resources are saltwater, freshwater makes up a miniscule two and half percent (2.5%) (of which roughly sixty-nine percent (68.9%) is captured in glaciers and permanent snow cover), roughly thirty-one percent (30.8%) is found in groundwater (including soil moisture, swamp water and permafrost), leaving only point three percent (0.3%) in Earth's rivers and lakes.[5] Pollution and the contamination of freshwater resources puts even greater stress and pressure on this already scarce resource, and, as such, "disputes over freshwater will pose an ever greater threat to the peace and security of our planet."[6]

Currently we experience an uneven distribution of water resources on earth, by both geography and time, with geographic regions and certain seasons experiencing abundance while other areas or times of year struggle with scarcity.[7] It is often observed that water is often not where it is needed.[8] Many people around the world today are experiencing inadequate quantity and

---

2 United Nations Department of Economic and Social Affairs, Population Division, *World Population Prospects 2019: Highlights* (UN, 2019) at 1, 5.

3 *Ibid.*

4 Organisation for Economic Co-operation and Development (OECD), *Environmental Outlook to 2050* (OECD Publishing, 2012) at 208, 218.

5 Igor A. Shiklomanov, *World Water Resources a New Appraisal and Assessment for the 21st Century* (UNESCO, 1998) at 4; NASA states "Of all of the water on Earth, 97% is saltwater, leaving a mere 3% as freshwater, approximately 1% of which is readily available for our use. The world's population is becoming more and more reliant on this precious resource for power, irrigation, industrial practices, and daily consumption." NASA, "freshwater availability" (8 September 2021), online: *NASA Earthdata open access for open science* <earthdata.nasa.gov/learn/toolkits/freshwater-availability>.

6 Tjaco T. van den Hout, "Introduction" in The International Bureau of the Permanent Court of Arbitration, ed, *The Permanent Court of Arbitration/Peace Palace Papers Resolution of International Water Disputes* (Kluwer Law International, 2003) xi at xii.

7 Peter H. Gleick, "An introduction to global fresh water issues" in Peter H. Gleick, ed, *Water in Crisis A Guide to the World's Fresh Water Resources* (Oxford University Press, 1993) 3 at 3–4.

8 Stephen C. McCaffrey, *The Law of International Watercourses*, 3rd ed (Oxford University Press, 2019) at 12.

quality in regard to their water supply[9] and "[w]ithout major policy changes and considerable improvements in water management processes and techniques, by 2050 the situation is likely to deteriorate, and will be compounded by increasing competition for water and increasing uncertainty about water availability."[10]

This is to say nothing of the growing threat climate change poses to human reliance on these unevenly distributed global water resources. Climate change threatens to disrupt freshwater ecosystems by altering stream flow, causing arid regions to become even drier, reducing water quality, and altering seasonal streamflow by reducing snowfall and glaciers; all of these changes will have the effect of increasing competition over scarce global freshwater resources.[11]

When the UN General Assembly instructed the ILC to begin work on the progressive development and codification of the law of non-navigational uses in 1970, the Assembly acknowledged that "water, owing to the growth of population and the increasing and multiplying needs and demands of mankind, is of growing concern to humanity, that the available fresh water sources of the world are limited and that the preservation and protection of those resources are of great importance to all nations".[12]

International water resources are of incredible significance with roughly 40% of the world's population residing in an international drainage basin.[13] These international basins cover more than half of the Earth's land surface, with one hundred and fifty-three (153) countries sharing international water

9 1.6 billion people worldwide in 2000 were living in water stressed basins. Organisation for Economic Co-operation and Development (OECD), *Environmental Outlook to 2050* (OECD Publishing, 2012) at 208, 218; see also United Nations Children's Fund (UNICEF) and World Health Organization (WHO), *Progress on household drinking water, sanitation and hygiene 2000–2017: Special focus on inequalities* (UNICEF and WHO, 2019).

10 Organisation for Economic Co-operation and Development (OECD), *Environmental Outlook to 2050* (OECD Publishing, 2012) at 208.

11 Blanca E. Jiménez Cisneros et al, "Freshwater Resources" in IPCC, Christopher B Field et al, eds, *Climate Change 2014: Impacts, Adaptation, and Vulnerability Part A: Global and Sectoral Aspects Contribution of Working Group II to the Fifth Assessment Report of the Intergovernmental Panel on Climate Change* (Cambridge University Press, 2014) 229 at 232–233; see also Stephen C. McCaffrey, *The Law of International Watercourses*, 3rd ed (Oxford University Press, 2019) at 8–10.

12 *Progressive development and codification of the rules of international law relating to international water courses*, GA Res 2669 (XXV), UNGAOR, 25th Sess, Supp No 28, UN Doc A/8028 (1970) 127 at 127.

13 United Nations Educational, Scientific and Cultural Organization (UNESCO) and United Nations Economic Commission for Europe (UNECE), *Progress on Transboundary Water Cooperation, Global Baseline for SDG Indicator 6.5.2* (UNESCO, 2018) at 7.

resources, and accounting for approximately 60% of global freshwater flows.[14] There are three hundred and ten (310) international river and lake basins[15] and five hundred and ninety-two (592) transboundary aquifers on earth.[16] It is therefore increasingly important that States are able to cooperate over shared water resources and have recourse to resolve disputes quickly, peacefully and efficiently regarding these resources.

1.2 *Cooperation Is the Rule rather than the Exception*

Even while shared international watercourses can lead to "tensions, threats, and even to some localized violence"[17] over competition for scarce water resources, the general norm is of cooperation between riparians of shared international watercourses.[18] The idea that internationally shared water resources could be a source of international cooperation rather than just a point of international competition and conflict was famously espoused by, then Secretary-General of the United Nations, Kofi Annan, "[T]he water problems of our world need not be only a cause of tension; they can also be a catalyst for cooperation [...] [i]f we work together, a secure and sustainable water future can be ours."[19]

The fact that cooperation seems more the rule than conflict in terms of international water resources seems to be borne out by the many treaties in the field, "The numerous treaties on international drainage basins makes it clear that states have usually managed to resolve their problems by agreement".[20] There have been thirty six hundred (3,600) international water treaties between 805 AD and 1984 AD identified by the Food and Agricultural

14 *Ibid*; United Nations Environment Programme (UNEP), *Atlas of International Freshwater Agreements* (UNEP, 2002) at 2.

15 Melisa McCracken and Aaron T. Wolf, "Updating the Register of International River Basins of the world" (2019) 35: 5 International Journal of Water Resource Development 732.

16 IGRAC (International Groundwater Resources Assessment Centre), UNESCO-IHP (UNESCO International Hydrological Programme), "Transboundary Aquifers of the World Map 2015 1:50 000 000" (Map Special Edition for the 7th World Water Forum 2015) (IGRAC, 2015), <https://www.un-igrac.org/resource/transboundary-aquifers-world-map-2015>.

17 Aaron T. Wolf, "Shared Waters: Conflict and Cooperation" (2007) 32 Annual Review of Environment and Resources 241 at 243.

18 *Ibid* at 260.

19 United Nations, Press Release, SG/SM/8139-OBV/262, "World's Water Problems Can be 'Catalyst for Cooperation' says Secretary-General in Message on World Water Day" (26 February 2002) online: UN Meetings Coverage and Press Releases https://www.un.org/press/en/2002/sgsm8139.doc.htm.

20 C.B. Bourne, "Mediation, Conciliation and Adjudication in the Settlement of International Drainage Basin Disputes" (1971) 9 Canadian Yearbook of International Law 114, at 142.

Organization of the United Nations ('FAO').[21] The TFDD identifies "more than 600 international, freshwater-related agreements, covering the years 1820 to 2007."[22] There are also at least 119 river basin organizations RBO's around the world between riparian states sharing international watercourses.[23] "There is also an extensive history of water cooperation between nations from 1948 to 2000, [showing] that cooperative events outnumbered conflictive events by over two to one."[24] All of this is to say that cooperation by States in regard to international watercourses is both important and frequent.

Disputes over international watercourses still occur, "[d]espite the fact that the only recorded war with water as its principal cause happened some 4,500 years ago, disputes over international waters are both common and current."[25] As competition for global freshwater resources becomes more acute these disputes may become more frequent and take on even greater importance to States. The law of international watercourses and international dispute resolution mechanisms can play an important role in resolving or minimizing these disputes.

---

21 United Nations Environment Programme (UNEP), *Atlas of International Freshwater Agreements* (UNEP, 2002) at 6. Note that these treaties include agreements on the navigational uses of international watercourses.

22 Oregon State University: Transboundary Freshwater Diplomacy Database, International Freshwater Treaties Database: Home (last visited 13 November 2021), online: International Freshwater Treaties Database <transboundarywaters.science.oregonstate.edu/content/international-freshwater-treaties-database>; "There is also an extensive history of formalized water cooperation; over 650 treaties related to water have been signed since 1820 [...]." [footnote omitted] Jacob D. Petersen-Perlman, Jennifer C. Veilleux and Aaron T. Wolf, "International water conflict and cooperation: challenges and opportunities" (2017) 42:2 Water International 105 at 107.

23 Susanne Schmeier, *Governing International Watercourses: River Basin Organizations and the sustainable governance of internationally shared rivers and lakes* (Earthscan, 2013) At 65. Currently the TFDD has catalogued more than a 120 RBOs on their database. Oregon State University: International River Basin Organization (RBO) Database, International River Basin Organization (RBO) Database: Home (last visited 7 May 2025), online: International Freshwater Treaties Database <https://transboundarywaters.ceoas.oregonstate.edu/international-river-basin-organization-database>.

24 Jacob D. Petersen-Perlman, Jennifer C. Veilleux and Aaron T. Wolf, "International water conflict and cooperation: challenges and opportunities" (2017) 42:2 Water International 105 at 107.

25 Sergei Vinogradov, Patricia Wouters and Patricia Jones, University of Dundee, *Transforming Potential Conflict into Cooperation Potential: The Role of International Water Law* (UNESCO-IHP, PCCP, 2003) at 22.

> [D]espite the emerging trend towards cooperation over shared watercourses, disputes do exist and are emerging. Those disputes are compounded by an upsurge in the competing demands over the waters of such watercourses, and by the different, and oftentimes contradictory, perceptions about water rights, and the basic principles of international law in this regard.[26]

2 The Law of the Non-navigational Uses of International Watercourses

2.1 *The Structure of the Law of International Watercourses*

Public international law is primarily concerned with Westphalian State actors, co-equal sovereign States possessing territorial integrity. Both the *UN Watercourses Convention*[27] and customary public international law, discussed below, are generally focused on States and other actors with international personality.[28]

The law of international watercourses has developed, thanks to the contributions from diverse sources that have sought to codify or create norms governing this unique area of law. For instance, the 1966 ILA *Helsinki Rules on the Uses of the Waters of International Rivers* (the '*Helsinki Rules*') and the IDI/IIL's 1911 *Madrid Declaration*[29] *on International Regulations Regarding the Use of international watercourses for Purposes other than Navigation* (the '*Madrid Declaration*'), are two examples which have articulated concepts that have been integrated into both customary international law and the *UN Watercourses Convention.*[30]

---

26 Salman M.A. Salman, "Good Offices and Mediation and International Water Disputes" in The International Bureau of the Permanent Court of Arbitration, ed, *The Permanent Court of Arbitration/Peace Palace Papers Resolution of International Water Disputes* (Kluwer Law International, 2003) 155 at 168.

27 *Convention on the Law of Non-Navigational Uses of International Watercourses, 21 May 1997, 2999 UNTS 77, 36 ILM 700 (Watercourses Convention) (entered into force 17 August 2014).*

28 Article 32 of the *UN Watercourses Convention* extends recourse to national courts to the private sphere, regardless of nationality, to address transboundary harm on an international watercourse, where harm is experienced by private individuals, either natural or juridical, in another riparian state. *Ibid.*

29 "The first important enunciation of rules regulating the non-navigational uses of international waters is found in the 1911 Madrid Declaration". C.B. Bourne, "Mediation, Conciliation and Adjudication in the Settlement of International Drainage Basin Disputes" (1971) 9 Canadian Yearbook of International Law 114, at 115.

30 Stephen C. McCaffrey, *The Law of International Watercourses*, 2nd ed (Oxford University Press, 2007) at 376.

Various judicial and arbitral decisions have also led to the development of the law of international watercourses; such as *the River Oder Case*,[31] the *Lac Lanoux* arbitral decision,[32] *The Trail Smelter* case,[33] *The Corfu Channel* case,[34] the *Pulp Mills* case, the *Road* case[35] and the *Gabčíkovo-Nagymaros Project* case.[36]

Much of public international law centers around the ability of sovereign states to enter into binding international agreements, as outlined in the *Vienna Convention on the Law of Treaties*.[37] The law of international watercourses by its nature tends to predominantly feature bilateral or regional agreements that focus on a particular shared watercourse or watercourses. These agreements take precedence, to the extent they are inconsistent with otherwise applicable international norms, when interpreting legal rights regarding the use of international watercourses under the principle of *lex specialis derogate legi generali*,[38] although usually these agreements will be interpreted and function in conjunction with international customary law. It is, however, also important

31 *Territorial Jurisdiction of the International Commission of the River Oder* (1929) PCIJ, (Ser A) No 23; *For a discussion of this case* see Stephen C. McCaffrey, *The Law of International Watercourses*, 2nd ed (Oxford University Press, 2007) at 204–206.

32 *Affaire du Lac Lanoux* (*France v Spain*) (1957), Judgment, 12 RIAA 281.

33 *Trail Smelter Arbitration* (*United States v Canada*) (1941), 3 RIAA 1911.

34 *Corfu Channel case* (*United Kingdom v Albania*), Judgment of April 9 1949, [1949] ICJ Rep 4.

35 *Certain Activities Carried Out by Nicaragua in the Border Area* (*Costa Rica v Nicaragua*) *and Construction of a Road Along the San Juan River* (*Nicaragua v Costa Rica*), Judgment of 16 December 2015, [2015] ICJ Rep 665.

36 *Gabčíkovo-Nagymaros Project* (*Hungary v Slovakia*), Judgment of September 25 1997, [1997] ICJ Rep 7.

37 Article 2(1)(a) of the VCLT defines a treaty as: "… an international agreement concluded between States in written form and governed by international law, whether embodied in a single instrument or in two or more related instruments and whatever its particular designation". *Vienna Convention on the Law of Treaties*, 23 May 1969, 1155 UNTS 331, art 2(1)(a) (entered into force 27 January 1980).

From this we can extract a set of rules for the creation of a treaty under the VCLT. For the creation of a treaty there must be:

1. a written agreement;
2. the agreement must be between States; and
3. the parties to the agreement must intend that the agreement is to be governed by international law.

38 The principle that the more specific norm governs over the more general, where the two concern the same subject matter, which is often cited as an example of a general principle of international law. The Court found that the 1977 treaty governed the relationship between the parties, under *lex specialis*, in the *Case concerning the Gabčíkovo-Nagymaros Project* (*Hungary v Slovakia*), Judgment of September 25 1997, [1997] ICJ Rep 7 at 76 para 133.

to note that courts and tribunals have drawn on custom to interpret and even update treaties.[39]

2.2 *The Major Multilateral Treaties*

2.2.1 The 1997 UN Watercourses Convention

The *UN Watercourses Convention* is recognized as an authoritative instrument in the field and a significant milestone in the development of the law of international watercourses. The *UN Watercourses Convention* was adopted May 21, 1997 and is largely a product of work performed by the International Law Commission (ILC) at the request of the UN. On August 17, 2014 the *UN Watercourses Convention* finally entered into force,[40] and has been ratified by 36 parties. The *UN Watercourses Convention* itself would not bind the many countries that have not yet ratified it, except to the extent that the *UN Watercourses Convention* reflects customary international law. States that are not parties to the *UN Watercourses Convention* would arguably still be bound by many of the tenets of the *UN Watercourses Convention* in so far as those tenets reflect customary international law. Customary international law binds international actors generally. Customary international law is established through widespread and consistent practice amongst states, out of a sense of legal obligation, or *opinio juris*.

There is "general agreement among experts in th[e] field that the provisions of the [*UN Watercourses Convention*] reflect the basic principles of customary international water law,"[41] a sentiment shared by the Court in the *Gabčíkovo-Nagymaros Project* case.[42] Thus many of the key provisions of the *UN Watercourses Convention* largely embody the codification of

---

39 See *Case concerning the Gabčikovo-Nagymaros Project* (*Hungary v Slovakia*), Judgment of September 25 1997, [1997] ICJ Rep 7; *Case Concerning Pulp Mills on the River Uruguay* (*Argentina v Uruguay*), Judgment of April 20 2010, [2010] ICJ Rep 14.; *Indus Waters Kishenganga Arbitration* (*Pakistan v India*) (20 December 2013), Final Award, 31 RIAA 309, (Permanent Court of Arbitration).

40 UN Secretary General, *UN Convention on the Law of the Non-Navigational Uses of International Watercourses, Entry into Force*, UN Doc C.N.271.2014.TREATIES-XXVII.12 (Depository Notification), 21 May 1997, (last visited November 15, 2021) Online: United Nations Treaty Collection <treaties.un.org/doc/Publication/CN/2014/CN.271.2014-Eng.pdf>.

41 Salman M.A. Salman, *The World Bank Policy for Projects on International Waterways: An Historical and Legal Analysis* (World Bank, 2009) at 54–57.

42 Stephen McCaffrey, "The contribution of the UN Convention on the law of the non-navigational uses of international watercourses" (2001) 1:3/4 International Journal of Global Environmental Issues 250 at 259–260; *Case concerning the Gabčikovo-Nagymaros Project* (*Hungary v Slovakia*), Judgment of September 25 1997, [1997] ICJ Rep 7 at 76 para 133, 56 para 85.

existing international customary law.[43] The dispute resolution provisions embodied in Article 33 of the *UN Watercourses Convention* cannot be said to have received sufficient acceptance to be viewed as a codification of customary international law.

The *UN Watercourses Convention* was designed as a 'framework agreement' with the intent that it would be supplemented by more specific agreements tailored to the particular characteristics of a specific watercourse,[44] as States sharing watercourses are encouraged to adopt and adjust the *UN Watercourses Convention*'s provisions into specific agreements between them and harmonize existing agreements with the principles of the *UN Watercourses Convention*.[45] The *UN Watercourses Convention* deals with several elements containing substantive and procedural obligations while also dealing with groundwater, dispute avoidance and settlement, notification of planned works, data and information exchange, to name some of the key provisions.

The term 'international watercourses' was used throughout the ILC led process by successive rapporteurs before being incorporated into the *UN Watercourses Convention*[46] and is the original language from the UN General Assembly resolution requesting the ILC commence work on the topic.[47] The *UN Watercourses Convention*, in Article 2, defines the term 'watercourse' as "a system of surface waters and groundwaters constituting by virtue of their physical relationship a unitary whole and normally flowing into a common terminus."[48] This term has gained wide international acceptance and incorporates connected groundwater.

43 Stephen C. McCaffrey, *The Law of International Watercourses*, 2nd ed (Oxford University Press, 2007) at 376.

44 Stephen McCaffrey, "The contribution of the UN Convention on the law of the non-navigational uses of international watercourses" (2001) 1:3/4 International Journal of Global Environmental Issues 250 at 257; *Convention on the Law of Non-Navigational Uses of International Watercourses*, 21 May 1997, 2999 UNTS 77, 36 ILM 700 (*UN Watercourses Convention*) (entered into force 17 August 2014).

45 Stephen McCaffrey, "The UN Convention on the law of the Non-Navigational Uses of International Watercourses: Prospects and Pitfalls" in Salman M.A. Salman and Laurence Boisson de Chazournes, eds, *International Watercourses: Enhancing Cooperation and Managing Conflict, Proceedings of a World Bank Seminar, World Bank Technical Paper No 414* (The World Bank, 1998) 17 at 18.

46 Salman M.A. Salman, *The World Bank Policy for Projects on International Waterways: An Historical and Legal Analysis* (World Bank, 2009).

47 United Nations General Assembly, *Progressive development and codification of the rules of international law relating to international watercourses* GA Res 2669 (XXV), UNGAOR, 25th Sess, Supp No 28, UN Doc A/8028 (1970), 127.

48 *Convention on the Law of Non-Navigational Uses of International Watercourses*, 21 May 1997, 2999 UNTS 77, 36 ILM 700 (*UN Watercourses Convention*) art 2 (entered into force 17 August 2014).

Regarding the substantive provisions, of particular importance are:

Article 5 – Equitable and reasonable utilization;[49]
Article 7 – The obligation to prevent "Significant Harm" to other riparian states;[50]
Part III – Planned measures on an international watercourse,[51] specifically *Article 12*: the duty to notify other riparian states of planned measures with possible adverse effects.[52]

These three duties can be viewed as the central substantive norms embodied in the *UN Watercourses Convention*.[53]

The dispute resolution provisions contained in the *UN Watercourses Convention* are contained in Article 33. These provisions have met with significantly less widespread acceptance as the three substantive provisions listed above. Rather the dispute resolution provisions of the *UN Watercourses Convention* proved to be quite contentious[54] amongst some States.[55] Particularly

49 *Ibid* at art 5.
50 *Ibid* at art 7.
51 *Ibid* at art III.
52 *Ibid* at art 12.
53 Stephen McCaffrey, "The UN Convention on the law of the Non-Navigational Uses of International Watercourses: Prospects and Pitfalls" in Salman M.A. Salman and Laurence Boisson de Chazournes, eds, *International Watercourses: Enhancing Cooperation and Managing Conflict, Proceedings of a World Bank Seminar, World Bank Technical Paper No 414* (The World Bank, 1998) 17 at 27.
54 Stephen C. McCaffrey, *The Law of International Watercourses*, 3rd ed (Oxford University Press, 2019) at 436–437; Attila Tanzi and Gian Maria Farnelli, "The Settlement of Disputes through Non-Judicial Means (Article 33(1)–33(9))" in Laurence Boisson de Chazournes et al, eds, *The UN Convention on the Law of the Non-Navigational Uses of International Watercourses: A Commentary* (Oxford University Press, 2018) 349 at 349; Laurence Boisson de Chazournes, "The Settlement of Disputes through Judicial Means (Article 33(10) and Annex on Arbitratin)" in Laurence Boisson de Chazournes et al, eds, *The UN Convention on the Law of the Non-Navigational Uses of International Watercourses: A Commentary* (Oxford University Press, 2018) 364 at 364; L. Caflisch, "La convention du 21 mai 1997 sur l'utilisation des cours d'eau internationaux à des fins autres que la navigation" (1997) 43 Annuaire français de droit international 793.
55 In the end China, Colombia, France, India and Turkey voted against article 33 while Algeria, Bolivia, Bulgaria, Ecuador, Egypt, Ethiopia, Iran, Isreal, Japan, Jordan, Lebanon, Lesotho, Liechenstein, Malawi, Mali, Pakistan, Rawanda, Slovakia, Sudan, Switzerland, Syria, Macedonia, Tanzania, Venezuela and Zimbabwe abstained. UNGA, 51st Sess, 62nd Mtg, UN Doc A/C.6/51/SR.62 (1997); UNGA, 51st Sess, 99th Plen Mtg, UN Doc A/51/PV.99 (1997).

the tension seems to have revolved around the role of the third-parties in inter-State dispute resolution.[56] Article 33 was adopted by the sixth Committee convening as the Working Group of the Whole by a vote of 33 votes in favour, 25 abstentions, and 5 votes against, with much of the criticism of the article centering around the compulsory nature of the fact-finding provisions of this article.[57]

Article 33
Settlement of disputes

1. In the event of a dispute between two or more Parties concerning the interpretation or application of the present Convention, the Parties concerned shall, in the absence of an applicable agreement between them, seek a settlement of the dispute by peaceful means in accordance with the following provisions.
2. If the Parties concerned cannot reach agreement by negotiation requested by one of them, they may jointly seek the good offices of, or request mediation or conciliation by, a third party, or make use, as appropriate, of any joint watercourse institutions that may have been established by them or agree to submit the dispute to arbitration or to the International Court of Justice.
3. Subject to the operation of paragraph 10, if after six months from the time of the request for negotiations referred to in paragraph 2, the Parties concerned have not been able to settle their dispute through negotiation or any other means referred to in paragraph 2, the dispute shall be submitted, at the request of any of the parties to

56 In particular there seems to have been considerable disagreement on the pertinence of compulsory third party dispute resolution mechanisms in the *UN Watercourses* Convention such as the compulsory fact-finding provisions. Stephen C. McCaffrey, *The Law of International Watercourses*, 3rd ed (Oxford University Press, 2019) at 436–437; Attila Tanzi and Gian Maria Farnelli, "The Settlement of Disputes through Non-Judicial Means (Article 33(1)–33(9))" in Laurence Boisson de Chazournes et al, eds, *The UN Convention on the Law of the Non-Navigational Uses of International Watercourses: A Commentary* (Oxford University Press, 2018) 349; Laurence Boisson de Chazournes, "The Settlement of Disputes through Judicial Means (Article 33(10) and Annex on Arbitratin)" in Laurence Boisson de Chazournes et al, eds, *The UN Convention on the Law of the Non-Navigational Uses of International Watercourses: A Commentary* (Oxford University Press, 2018) 364.

57 UNGA, 51st Sess, 62nd Mtg, UN Doc A/C.6/51/SR.62 (1997); UNGA, 51st Sess, 99th Plen Mtg, UN Doc A/51/PV.99 (1997).

the dispute, to impartial fact-finding in accordance with paragraphs 4 to 9, unless the Parties otherwise agree.

4. A Fact-finding Commission shall be established, composed of one member nominated by each Party concerned and in addition a member not having the nationality of any of the Parties concerned chosen by the nominated members who shall serve as Chairman.
5. If the members nominated by the Parties are unable to agree on a Chairman within three months of the request for the establishment of the Commission, any Party concerned may request the Secretary-General of the United Nations to appoint the Chairman who shall not have the nationality of any of the parties to the dispute or of any riparian State of the watercourse concerned. If one of the Parties fails to nominate a member within three months of the initial request pursuant to paragraph 3, any other Party concerned may request the Secretary-General of the United Nations to appoint a person who shall not have the nationality of any of the parties to the dispute or of any riparian State of the watercourse concerned. The person so appointed shall constitute a single-member Commission.
6. The Commission shall determine its own procedure.
7. The Parties concerned have the obligation to provide the Commission with such information as it may require and, on request, to permit the Commission to have access to their respective territory and to inspect any facilities, plant, equipment, construction or natural feature relevant for the purpose of its inquiry.
8. The Commission shall adopt its report by a majority vote, unless it is a single-member Commission, and shall submit that report to the Parties concerned setting forth its findings and the reasons therefor and such recommendations as it deems appropriate for an equitable solution of the dispute, which the Parties concerned shall consider in good faith.
9. The expenses of the Commission shall be borne equally by the Parties concerned.
10. When ratifying, accepting, approving or acceding to the present Convention, or at any time thereafter, a Party which is not a regional economic integration organization may declare in a written instrument submitted to the Depositary that, in respect of any dispute not resolved in accordance with paragraph 2, it recognizes as compulsory *ipso facto* and without special agreement in relation to any Party accepting the same obligation:

(a) Submission of the dispute to the International Court of Justice; and/or

(b) Arbitration by an arbitral tribunal established and operating, unless the parties to the dispute otherwise agreed, in accordance with the procedure laid down in the annex to the present Convention.

A Party which is a regional economic integration organization may make a declaration with like effect in relation to arbitration in accordance with subparagraph (b).[58]

The *UN Watercourses Convention* is a framework convention and as such it possesses fairly flexible provisions on dispute resolution leaving much up to the individual choices of the parties involved. As a multilateral framework convention, the *UN Watercourses Convention* by necessity needed to be relatively broad and flexible, to appeal to the broadest grouping of States and to be useful and adaptable to watercourses around the world. The only truly compulsory mechanism is the impartial fact-finding articulated in Article 33(3). Despite the objections, by some States, to the compulsory nature of the fact-finding provisions,[59] a plain reading of the text of article 33 makes it apparent that the findings of such a fact-finding commission would in fact not be binding on the parties to a dispute.

Despite being a flexible framework convention, the *UN Watercourses Convention* does seem to articulate a 'Stepped Approach' to disputes while providing a series of dispute resolution mechanisms for States to choose from. There is a clear set of 'Steps' that a dispute could travel through from negotiation in Article 33(2) to a selection or "menu"[60] of alternative mechanisms in that same article and, finally, impartial fact-finding in Article 33(3). The sequence of these 'Steps' is laid out but the ability of parties to choose amongst a suite of mechanisms in Article 33(2) makes charting a clear path through this sequence more elusive. There is also not a dedicated adjudicative 'Step' nor is the final mechanism in the progression ultimately binding on the parties.

58 *Convention on the Law of Non-Navigational Uses of International Watercourses*, 21 May 1997, 2999 UNTS 77, 36 ILM 700 (*Watercourses Convention*) at 136–138 art 33 (entered into force 17 August 2014).

59 UNGA, 51st Sess, 62nd Mtg, UN Doc A/C.6/51/SR.62 (1997); UNGA, 51st Sess, 99th Plen Mtg, UN Doc A/51/PV.99 (1997).

60 Laurence Boisson de Chazournes, "The Settlement of Disputes through Judicial Means (Article 33(10) and Annex on Arbitration)" in Laurence Boisson de Chazournes et al, eds, *The UN Convention on the Law of the Non-Navigational Uses of International Watercourses: A Commentary* (Oxford University Press, 2018) 364 at 364.

The *UN Watercourses Convention* integrates several types of mechanisms in its dispute resolution provisions: traditional judicial means, diplomatic means, as well as technical means. Article 33(2) indicates the first 'Step' to be taken in its approach to dispute resolution is a diplomatic one, negotiation. If negotiation fails to resolve the matter, then the parties may choose from a suite of mechanisms outlined in Article 33(2) including more diplomatic mechanisms such as mediation but also judicial means such as litigation or arbitration before international courts or tribunals. Article 33(3) of the *UN Watercourses Convention* offers a technical mechanism for dispute resolution in the form of compulsory fact-finding, a relatively unique dispute resolution mechanism,[61] "essentially an expert enquiry outside a judicial framework",[62] which can be triggered by any one of the parties and will occur six months after a request to negotiate by one of the parties. Integrating these various types of dispute resolution mechanics creates a dispute resolution framework that is more flexible, stronger and more effective than the sum of its parts. "In this sense, non-adjudicative dispute settlement mechanisms and adjudication are not only fully compatible with one another, but also mutually complementary [...]."[63]

Ultimately, however, many of the dispute resolution mechanisms under the *UN Watercourses Convention* are left to the discretion and consent of the State parties to a dispute, even the findings of the compulsory fact-finding commission, as already mentioned, are not binding on the parties unless accepted by them. This weakness can be seen to reflect the tensions during the negotiation of article 33.[64] Another potential weakness is the lack of mention in regard to the use of experts in the arbitral rules other than in Article 8 of the annex "This seems like a missed opportunity ... involvement of experts at the judicial stage would indeed be useful".[65]

---

61 *Ibid.*

62 Makane Moïse Mbengue and Rukmini Das, *Use of Experts in International Freshwater Disputes* (Brill Research Perspectives in International Water Law, 2019) at 7–8.

63 Attila Tanzi and Gian Maria Farnelli, "The Settlement of Disputes through Non-Judicial Means (Article 33(1)–33(9))" in Laurence Boisson de Chazournes et al, eds, *The UN Convention on the Law of the Non-Navigational Uses of International Watercourses: A Commentary* (Oxford University Press, 2018) 349 at 362.

64 Laurence Boisson de Chazournes, "The Settlement of Disputes through Judicial Means (Article 33(10) and Annex on Arbitratin)" in Laurence Boisson de Chazournes et al, eds, *The UN Convention on the Law of the Non-Navigational Uses of International Watercourses: A Commentary* (Oxford University Press, 2018) 364 at 377.

65 Makane Moïse Mbengue and Rukmini Das, *Use of Experts in International Freshwater Disputes* (Brill Research Perspectives in International Water Law, 2019) at 7–8.

Of the nine (9) criteria analysed as part of the review of treaties for this work, the *UN Watercourses Convention* satisfied seven (7), a majority of the criteria, only lacking a distinctly adjudicative 'Step' and binding final mechanism. It could be argued, however, that this Convention lacks a clearly defined progression through the 'Steps' due to the suite of options available to parties under article 33(2). Generally, the *UN Watercourses Convention* presents some innovative mechanisms, such as compulsory fact-finding, in a reasonably well articulated progressive 'Stepped Approach' to dispute resolution, which serve its function as a global framework agreement.

2.2.2 The UNECE Water Convention

The United Nations Economic Commission for Europe's *Convention on the Protection and Use of Transboundary Watercourses and International Lakes* (the "*UNECE Water Convention*")[66] is the other multilateral treaty of global scope that deals with the non-navigational uses of international watercourses in particular and is generally viewed as a complementary agreement to the *UN Watercourses Convention.*[67] Originally this convention was more limited in its scope as a regional agreement between the countries of the UNECE but the scope of the agreement has subsequently been expanded to allow States beyond the UNECE region to accede to it.[68]

The dispute resolution provisions of the *UNECE Water Convention* are found in Article 22 and are less structured than the *UN Watercourses Convention*'s dispute resolution provisions. Article 22 of the *UNECE Water Convention* essentially leaves the settlement of disputes to the discretion of the State parties to that dispute specifically mentioning "negotiation or by any other means of dispute settlement acceptable to the parties to the dispute."[69] Here, negotiation, as diplomatic mechanism is the only means of dispute resolution

66 *Convention on the Protection and Use of Transboundary Watercourses and International Lakes*, 17 March 1992, 1936 UNTS 269 (*UNECE Water Convention*).

67 Stephen C. McCaffrey, *The Law of International Watercourses*, 3rd ed (Oxford University Press, 2019) at 414–421; Attila Tanzi, *The Economic Commission for Europe Water Convention and the United Nations Watercourses Convention: An analysis of their harmonized contribution to international water law*, Water Series No 6 (UN, 2015).

68 *Amendments to Articles 25 and 26 of the Convention on the Protection and use of Transboundary Watercourses and International Lakes*, 28 November 2003, 2897 UNTS 92 (entered into force 6 February 2013).

69 *Convention on the Protection and Use of Transboundary Watercourses and International Lakes*, 17 March 1992, 1936 UNTS 269 (*UNECE Water Convention*) at 281 art 22(1).

specifically mentioned, no other 'Steps', hierarchy or timeline are provided for and no binding means of dispute resolution is required unless the parties agree to the jurisdiction of the ICJ or an arbitral tribunal as per article 22(2).

Article 22
SETTLEMENT OF DISPUTES

1. If a dispute arises between two or more Parties about the interpretation or application of this Convention, they shall seek a solution by negotiation or by any other means of dispute settlement acceptable to the parties to the dispute.
2. When signing, ratifying, accepting, approving or acceding to this Convention, or at any time thereafter, a Party may declare in writing to the Depositary that, for a dispute not resolved in accordance with paragraph 1 of this article, it accepts one or both of the following means of dispute settlement as compulsory in relation to any Party accepting the same obligation:
   (a) Submission of the dispute to the International Court of Justice;
   (b) Arbitration in accordance with the procedure set out in annex IV.
3. If the parties to the dispute have accepted both means of dispute settlement referred to in paragraph 2 of this article, the dispute may be submitted only to the International Court of Justice, unless the parties agree otherwise.[70]

Of the nine (9) criteria analysed as part of the review of treaties for this work, the *UNECE Water Convention* satisfied only one (1), a minority of the criteria, only possessing a distinct diplomatic 'Step' due to its reference to negotiation, but even this is debatable as States may elect any other means that they deem appropriate. Many of the other criteria measured could be reasonably satisfied by mechanisms outside of the dispute resolution provisions of Article 22 such as the compliance and governance mechanisms of the *UNECE Water Convention*.[71] While these other mechanisms serve important functions in

70 *Ibid* at 281 art 22.

71 "[T]he Meeting of the Parties provides an important forum for dispute prevention and 'management'. Moreover, States parties to the ECE Water Convention are required to establish joint bodies for bilateral and multilateral cooperation, whose tasks under articles 9 ff. cover a wide range of prevention and joint management measures that

preventing disputes they are beyond the scope of this work, which is focused on the use of such functions as part of a dispute resolution framework that integrates several procedural 'Steps' to address disputes at different levels.

3 Inter-State Dispute Resolution regarding the Non-navigational Uses of International Watercourses

As discussed above disputes over international watercourses may become increasingly frequent and take on even greater importance as competition for global freshwater resources becomes more acute.[72] It is important to have sufficient legal tools to deal with these disputes but an analysis of disputes over international water resources can be difficult due to the unique nature of each dispute, as stated by Stephen McCaffrey "[i]n fact, if one examines individual cases closely, one finds that each is *sui generis*; each has its own unique characteristics and falls into its own unique category."[73] Still the unique nature and challenges of international watercourse disputes in general necessitate specially tailored mechanisms to deal with them.[74]

have a direct impact on dispute avoidance." Attila Tanzi, *The Economic Commission for Europe Water Convention and the United Nations Watercourses Convention: An analysis of their harmonized contribution to international water law*, Water Series No 6 (UN, 2015) at 71. [footnotes omitted]; The UNECE Water Convention also has an Implementation Committee established in 2012 which is empowered to "facilitate, promote and safeguard the implementation and application of and compliance with the Convention on the Protection and use of Transboundary Watercourses and International Lakes." Economic Commission for Europe Meeting of the Parties to the Convention on the Protection and Use of Transboundary Watercourses and International Lakes, *Decision VI/1 Support to implementation and compliance*, UNECOSOCOR, 2012, ECE/MP.WAT/37/Add.2 (2013) 2.

72 Comment by Mr. Sreenivasa RAO, "2313th Meeting Friday, 29 June 1993, at 10.10 A.M." in *Yearbook of the International Law Commission 1993* vol 1 (1995) 104 at 110 para 40 (UN Doc A/CN.4/SER.A/1993).

73 Stephen C. McCaffrey, "Water Disputes Defined: Characteristics and Trends for Resolving Them" in The International Bureau of the Permanent Court of Arbitration, ed, *The Permanent Court of Arbitration/Peace Palace Papers Resolution of International Water Disputes* (Kluwer Law International, 2003) 49 at 52.

74 Comment by Mr. Yamada, "2312th Meeting Friday, 25 June 1993, at 10.05 A.M." in *Yearbook of the International Law Commission 1993* vol 1 (1995) 96 at 98 para 13 (UN Doc A/CN.4/SER.A/1993).

The then special rapporteur on the subject, Stephen Schwebel, observed in his third report to the ILC that the nature of international watercourse law required mechanisms to settle disputes due to the importance of the resource involved and the urgency with which disputes may need to be resolved. "The absence of such provisions may contribute to delay of important projects, suspension of expensive works under construction, postponement of critical pollution control programmes or inability to undertake measures to deal with very real hazards."[75] Dispute resolution mechanisms therefore have an important and urgent role to play in regard to international water resources. Indeed, Stephen McCaffrey, in looking at the subject, identified the presence of a functional treaty and/or joint mechanism between riparian States as a key contributing factor in decreasing the severity of water problems and disputes:

> First, perhaps the greatest single factor responsible for increasing the severity and intractability of water disputes, and sometimes even causing the disputes in the first instance, is political tension between the states concerned. This factor may exist regardless of whether there is a treaty or joint institution, but it is more likely to be present where there is neither an agreement nor an institution – these typically being features of a stable political relationship. Second, the presence of a functional treaty – that is, a treaty that remains relevant and appropriate in current circumstances – seems to decrease the severity of water problems (such as insufficient supply or pollution) and thus resulting disputes. This is even more true of joint institutions, which have in many cases helped to avoid disputes or have even been used by the parties to assist in resolving them.[76]

In the following section we will see some of the key features, mechanisms and practices available regarding international watercourse disputes and

75 Stephen M. Schwebel, "Third report on the law of the non-navigational uses of international watercourses" (UN Doc A/CN.4/348) in *Year Book of the International Law Commission 1982* vol 2 part 1 (1984) 65 at 181 (UN Doc A/CN.4/SER.A/1982/Add.1(Part 1)).

76 Stephen C. McCaffrey, "Water Disputes Defined: Characteristics and Trends for Resolving Them" in The International Bureau of the Permanent Court of Arbitration, ed, *The Permanent Court of Arbitration/Peace Palace Papers Resolution of International Water Disputes* (Kluwer Law International, 2003) 49 at 53.

endeavour to place the concept of a 'Stepped Approach' to the resolution of such disputes into the context of these component mechanisms and practices.

3.1 *'Dispute Resolution' in the Law of the Non-navigational Uses of International Watercourses*

To begin we must ask what is a 'dispute' in the context of the law of international watercourses. The court in the *Mavrommatis Case* defined a dispute as "a disagreement on a point of law or fact, a conflict of legal views or of interests between two persons."[77] How does this definition fit with the uniqueness of disputes on intranational watercourses? McCaffrey in his sixth report to the International Law Commission relied on a definition of "International water law dispute"[78] that we find convenient to rely on here as well.

> an international dispute between two or more than two international drainage basin states [...], with respect to
> (i) the conservation, use, sharing (including sharing of benefits), control, development or management of the water resource of an international drainage basin, [or]
> (ii) the interpretation of the terms of any agreement relating to the conservation, use, sharing (including sharing of benefits), control, development and management of such water resources or the implementation of such an agreement including all matters rising out of the implementation of such an agreement.[79]

In fact, many such disputes between basin States have arisen over the years and many of these have been resolved by formal proceedings or diplomatic

77 *Case of the Mavrommatis Palestine Concessions (Greece v Great Britain)*, (1924) PCIJ (Ser A) No 2 at 11.

78 Stephen C. McCaffrey, "Sixth report on the law of the non-navigational uses of international watercourses" (UN Doc A/CN.4/427 and Add.1) in *Yearbook of the International Law Commission 1990*, vol 2, part 1 (1993) 41 at 66 para 43, note 117 (UN Doc A/CN.4/SER.A/1990/Add.1 (Part 1)).

79 B.R. Chauhan, *Settlement of International Water Law Disputes in International Drainage Basins* (Erich Schmidt, 1981) at 96–97.

negations,[80] still many of these disputes have adversely affected the long-term relations between these States.[81]

The obligation to settle international disputes by pacific means is ubiquitous throughout international law, this is the same regarding disputes on international watercourses.[82] Article 33 of the Charter of the United Nations is the most well noted source of this obligation under international law where a dispute is likely to "endanger the maintenance of international peace and security."[83] Many disputes on international watercourses would fall outside the threshold of endangering the maintenance of international peace and security.[84] The law of international watercourses also contemplates dispute

80 See B.R. Chauhan, *Settlement of International Water Law Disputes in International Drainage Basins* (Erich Schmidt, 1981); Stephen C. McCaffrey, "Sixth report on the law of the non-navigational uses of international watercourses" (UN Doc A/CN.4/427 and Add.1) in *Yearbook of the International Law Commission 1990*, vol 2, part 1 (1993) 41 (UN Doc A/CN.4/SER.A/1990/Add.1 (Part 1)); Stephen M. Schwebel, "Third report on the law of the non-navigational uses of international watercourses" (UN Doc A/CN.4/348) in *Year Book of the International Law Commission 1982* vol 2 part 1 (*1984*) 65 note 776 (UN Doc A/CN.4/SER.A/1982/Add.1(Part 1)); Laurence Boisson de Chazournes, "The Settlement of Disputes through Judicial Means (Article 33(10) and Annex on Arbitratin)" in Laurence Boisson de Chazournes et al, eds, *The UN Convention on the Law of the Non-Navigational Uses of International Watercourses: A Commentary* (Oxford University Press, 2018) 364; The International Bureau of the Permanent Court of Arbitration, ed, *The Permanent Court of Arbitration/Peace Palace Papers Resolution of International Water Disputes* (Kluwer Law International, 2003); Sergei Vinogradov, Patricia Wouters and Patricia Jones, *Transforming Potential Conflict into Cooperation Potential: The Role of International Water Law* (UNESCO-IHP, PCCP, 2003); C.B. Bourne, "Mediation, Conciliation and Adjudication in the Settlement of International Drainage Basin Disputes" (1971) 9 Canadian Yearbook of International Law 114.

81 Stephen M. Schwebel, "Third report on the law of the non-navigational uses of international watercourses" (UN Doc A/CN.4/348) in *Year Book of the International Law Commission 1982* vol 2 part 1 (*1984*) 65 at 181 (UN Doc A/CN.4/SER.A/1982/Add.1(Part 1)) [footnotes omitted].

82 *Ibid* at 186 para; Stephen C. McCaffrey, "Sixth report on the law of the non-navigational uses of international watercourses" (UN Doc A/CN.4/427 and Add.1) in *Yearbook of the International Law Commission 1990*, vol 2, part 1 (1993) 41 at 67 para 47 (UN Doc A/CN.4/SER.A/1990/Add.1 (Part 1)); C.B. Bourne, "Mediation, Conciliation and Adjudication in the Settlement of International Drainage Basin Disputes" (1971) 9 Canadian Yearbook of International Law 114.

83 Charter of the United Nations art 33; C.B. Bourne, "Mediation, Conciliation and Adjudication in the Settlement of International Drainage Basin Disputes" (1971) 9 Canadian Yearbook of International Law 114, at 152, 157–158.

84 Professor M. Juraj Andrassy, "Utilisation des eaux internationales non maritimes (en dehors de la navigation) (Neuvième Commission) Rapport provisoire" in *Annuaire de L'Institut de Droit International*, vol 48:1 (1959) 131 at 199–200.

resolution even in situations where international peace and security are not "endangered".[85] Article 33 of the UN Charter would apply to disputes on international watercourses as State parties would be required to settle their disputes peacefully but there are also a range of circumstances on international watercourses that can produce disputes that would not necessarily "endanger" international peace and security. For instance, a particular "work or utilization cannot by itself be regarded as a breach of the peace. If it were then any act that might affect the economy of another country and which was strongly objected to by that country would constitute a breach of international peace and security."[86]

Unlike other areas of international law, such as the law of the sea ('UNCLOS'),[87] the law of international watercourses does not possess a "permanent standing mechanism to deal with water problems in a comprehensive manner."[88] Jens Evensen, in his first report as the special rapporteur to the International Law Commission (the "ILC"), commented on the suitability of compulsory settlement procedures in what became the United Nations Watercourses Convention, ultimately finding it inadvisable to include them in his draft due to its nature as a framework agreement, instead favouring compulsory mechanisms as part of basin specific agreements "such as commissions of inquiry, conciliation and, in more serious cases, resort to compulsory proceedings before international courts or arbitral tribunals."[89] The *UN Watercourses Convention* did ultimately include compulsory fact-finding, but the findings of this commission would not be binding unless agreed on by the parties, otherwise it does not possess compulsory third party dispute resolution provisions.

---

85 Stephen C. McCaffrey, "Sixth report on the law of the non-navigational uses of international watercourses" (UN Doc A/CN.4/427 and Add.1) in *Yearbook of the International Law Commission 1990*, vol 2, part 1 (1993) 41 at 67 para 47 (UN Doc A/CN.4/SER.A/1990/Add.1 (Part 1)).

86 C.B. Bourne, "Mediation, Conciliation and Adjudication in the Settlement of International Drainage Basin Disputes" (1971) 9 Canadian Yearbook of International Law 114, at 157.

87 *United Nations Convention on the Law of the Sea*, 10 December 1982, 1833 UNTS 397 part XV, XI.

88 S.P. Subedi, "Challenges for the 21st Century" in The International Bureau of the Permanent Court of Arbitration, ed, *Resolution of International Water Disputes* (The Permanent Court of Arbitration/Peace Palace Papers, 2003) 33 at 35; C.B. Bourne, "Mediation, Conciliation and Adjudication in the Settlement of International Drainage Basin Disputes" (1971) 9 Canadian Yearbook of International Law 114, at 126–128.

89 Jens Evensen, "First report on the law of the non-navigational uses of international watercourses" (UN Doc A/CN.4/367) in *Yearbook of the International Law Commission 1983*, vol 2, part 1 (1985) 155 at 189–190 (UN Doc A/CN.4/SER.A/1983/Add.1 (Part 1)).

Ultimately the same considerations that Evensen wrestled with exist today and are reflected in the final *UN Watercourses Convention*.

In his sixth report to the ILC, McCaffrey stressed the unique reasons why dispute resolution provisions were important in the context of the draft articles on the law of the non-navigational uses of international watercourses, which became the 1997 Watercourses Convention. "Chief among these reasons is the general and flexible nature of some of the most fundamental provisions of the draft articles (such as article 6, "Equitable and reasonable utilization and participation"). The very same generality and flexibility of these provisions that make them so well suited to a framework instrument on international watercourses may also make them difficult to apply with precision in some cases. Furthermore, the operation of many of the provisions of the draft articles depends upon certain key facts. To the extent that the watercourse States concerned do not know or agree upon these facts, their legal obligations will not be clear. Some means of objectively establishing the operative facts will therefore be necessary in such cases."[90]

Due to the importance of the resource and the need for flexible systems, the law of international watercourses allows a range of options to States with regard to disputes. There are a variety of mechanisms and procedures for States "wishing to clarify facts, to adjust their relations, or to avoid or settle disputes."[91] This can be reflected in agreements of global, regional, or basin specific application, with most agreements providing a "range of formal dispute settlement mechanisms: from negotiation to third-party involvement, including optional or mandatory arbitration and adjudication."[92]

90 Stephen C. McCaffrey, "Sixth report on the law of the non-navigational uses of international watercourses" (UN Doc A/CN.4/427 and Add.1) in *Yearbook of the International Law Commission 1990*, vol 2, part 1 (1993) 41 at 66 para 40 (UN Doc A/CN.4/SER.A/1990/Add.1 (Part 1)).

91 *Ibid* at 69 para 56.

92 Patricia Wouters, "Universal and Regional Approaches to Resolving International Water Disputes: What Lessons Learned from State Practice?" in The International Bureau of the Permanent Court of Arbitration, ed, *The Permanent Court of Arbitration/Peace Palace Papers Resolution of International Water Disputes* (Kluwer Law International, 2003) 111 at 152–153; see also Sergei Vinogradov, Patricia Wouters and Patricia Jones, *Transforming Potential Conflict into Cooperation Potential: The Role of International Water Law* (UNESCO-IHP, PCCP, 2003) at 65–66.

3.1.1 Diplomatic Mechanisms: Negotiation, Good Offices, and Mediation

Negotiation is a common diplomatic dispute resolution mechanism that is available to parties at all stages of a dispute or difference,[93] even after recourse to another mechanism of dispute resolution such as adjudication.[94] The court in the *Mavrommatis Case* had occasion to discuss negotiations and found that "before a dispute can be made the subject of an action at law, its subject matter should have been clearly defined by means of diplomatic negotiations."[95] This ability to help define the issues of a dispute through diplomatic means is an important function of this 'Step' in the dispute resolution process.

The special rapporteur to the ILC on the issue of the non-navigational uses of international watercourses, Jens Evensen, observed in his first report, as many others have, that "[t]he obvious starting-point for the peaceful settlement of disputes" regarding international watercourses was good-faith negotiations and consultations.[96] Indeed, an early decision in the field, the *Lac Lanoux* arbitration, found that turning to negotiation was a "normal" course of action by States.[97]

> [I]l appartient à chaque Etat d'apprécier, raisonnablement et de bonne foi, les situations et les règles qui le mettent en cause; son appréciation peut se trouver en contradiction avec celle d'un autre Etat; dans ce cas, apparaît un différend que les Parties cherchent normalement à résoudre par la négociation, ou bien en se soumettant à l'autorité d'un tiers.[98]

93 David Anderson, "Negotiation and Dispute Settlement" in Malcom Evans, ed, *Remedies in International Law: The Institutional Dilemma* (Hart Publishing, 1998) chapter 6 at 115; Marcelo G. Kohen, "Interaction between Diplomatic and Judicial Means at the Initiation of Proceedings" in Laurence Boisson de Chazournes et al, eds, *Diplomatic and Judicial Means of Dispute Settlement* (Martinus Nijhoff Publishers, 2013) 13 at 22–23.

94 Kari Hakapää, "Negotiation" (last updated 2013) at para 36, online: *Max Planck Encyclopedias of International Law* <https://opil.ouplaw.com/home/mpil>.

95 *Case of the Mavrommatis Palestine Concessions (Greece v Great Britain)*, (1924) PCIJ (Ser A) No 2 at 15.

96 Jens Evensen, "First report on the law of the non-navigational uses of international watercourses" (UN Doc A/CN.4/367) in *Yearbook of the International Law Commission 1983*, vol 2, part 1 (1985) 155 at 190 (UN Doc A/CN.4/SER.A/1983/Add.1 (Part 1)).

97 *Affaire du Lac Lanoux (France v Spain)* (1957), Judgment, 12 RIAA 281 at 310.

98 "It is for each State to evaluate in a reasonable manner and in good faith the situations and rules which will involve it in controversies; its evaluation may be in contradiction with that of other States; in that case, should a dispute arise the Parties normally seek to resolve it by negotiation or, alternatively, by submitting to the authority of a third party." *Affaire du Lac Lanoux (France v Spain)* (1957), Judgment, 12 RIAA 281 at 310.

Evensen observed that such negotiations must be constrained to a "reasonable period of time. When all reasonable attempts at negotiations in good faith have been exhausted, the parties shall resort to the other procedures for peaceful settlement [...]."[99]

More perhaps could be done in the sense of designing systems that bring the parties to a dispute together to encourage negotiations, especially in the nascent stages of a dispute. "[A] problem facing very many countries around the globe is the absence of a mechanism designed to facilitate negotiations to break stalemates or diffuse tensions between the riparian states of an international watercourse."[100]

Despite the finding of the court in the *Mavrommatis Case*[101] no mechanism of dispute resolution enjoys an inherent preference under general international law.[102] While many international agreements will include provisions allowing recourse to adjudication upon the exhaustion of non-binding diplomatic or technical mechanisms,[103] parties to a dispute are not obliged to attempt to negotiate a settlement prior to recourse to judicial settlement under general international law.[104]

Generally good offices and mediation are slightly more structured diplomatic mechanisms involving the participation of a third party and may serve as a useful corollary to negotiations.[105] The most noted example of this in international watercourse law is the work of the World Bank, over a period

99 Jens Evensen, "First report on the law of the non-navigational uses of international watercourses" (UN Doc A/CN.4/367) in *Yearbook of the International Law Commission 1983*, vol 2, part 1 (1985) 155 at 190 (UN Doc A/CN.4/SER.A/1983/Add.1 (Part 1)).

100 S.P. Subedi, "Challenges for the 21st Century" in The International Bureau of the Permanent Court of Arbitration, ed, *Resolution of International Water Disputes* (The Permanent Court of Arbitration/Peace Palace Papers, 2003) 33 at 35.

101 *Case of the Mavrommatis Palestine Concessions (Greece v Great Britain)*, (1924) PCIJ (Ser A) No 2 at 15.

102 Kari Hakapää, "Negotiation" (last updated 2013) at para 27, online: *Max Planck Encyclopedias of International Law* <https://opil.ouplaw.com/home/mpil>.

103 *Ibid* at para 29; Marcelo G. Kohen, "Interaction between Diplomatic and Judicial Means at the Initiation of Proceedings" in Laurence Boisson de Chazournes et al, eds, *Diplomatic and Judicial Means of Dispute Settlement* (Martinus Nijhoff Publishers, 2013) 13 at 21–22; *Case concerning the land and maritime boundary between Cameroon and Nigeria (Cameroon v Nigeria)*, [1998] ICJ Rep 275 at 303 para 56.

104 "Neither in the [UN] Charter nor otherwise in international law is any general rule to be found to the effect that the exhaustion of diplomatic negotiations constitutes a precondition for a matter to be referred to the Court." *Case concerning the land and maritime boundary between Cameroon and Nigeria (Cameroon v Nigeria)*, [1998] ICJ Rep 275 at 303 para 56.

105 Jens Evensen, "First report on the law of the non-navigational uses of international watercourses" (UN Doc A/CN.4/367) in *Yearbook of the International Law Commission 1983*, vol 2, part 1 (1985) 155 at 191 (UN Doc A/CN.4/SER.A/1983/Add.1 (Part 1)).

of nine years, in helping to bring Pakistan and India into agreement in regard to the Indus waters dispute and conclude *The Indus Waters Treaty 1960* (*with annexes*), 19 September 1960, 419 UNTS 125 (*Indus Waters Treaty*).[106]

These diplomatic mechanisms, like negation, good offices, and mediation form an essential underlying component of international dispute resolution. International law in general is based on the consent of States, under the principle of the independence of States, even compulsory adjudication is based on consent to the jurisdiction of a specific court or body by the State parties given at some point in time.[107]

> It is well established in international law that no State can, without its consent, be compelled to submit its disputes with other States either to mediation or to arbitration, or to any other kind of pacific settlement. Such consent can be given once and for all in the form of an obligation freely undertaken, but it can, on the contrary, also be given in a special case apart from any existing obligation.[108]

These diplomatic mechanisms therefore simply represent the rawest form of international dispute resolution based on state consent.

3.1.2 Technical Mechanisms: Inquiry, Fact-Finding and Conciliation

As discussed above the law of international watercourses can be very fact specific, especially in assessing the more substantive obligations under the law such as 'equitable and reasonable utilization' and the prohibition against 'significant harm'. Mechanisms that help to ascertain the facts and to provide a firm basis for States to move ahead in resolving their disputes are therefore of central importance to the law of international watercourses. Inquiry, fact-finding and conciliation are three examples of such mechanisms. River Basin Organizations (RBOs) and other joint mechanisms can also play an important institutional role in regard to technical mechanisms like these.[109]

---

106 B.R. Chauhan, *Settlement of International Water Law Disputes in International Drainage Basins* (Erich Schmidt, 1981) at 325.

107 Sir Robert Jennings, "Keynote Address" in The International Bureau of the Permanent Court of Arbitration, ed, *Resolution of International Water Disputes* (The Permanent Court of Arbitration/Peace Palace Papers, 2003) 23 at 30.

108 *Status of Eastern Carelia* (1923), Advisory Opinion, PCIJ (Ser B) No 5 at 27; see also the Case concerning the Aerial Incident of July 27th, 1955 (Israel v Bulgaria).

109 Joint organizations or RBOs are a fertile area of study and work which has produced diverse and interesting scholarship, for example see Anoulak Kittikhoun and Susanne Schmeier, eds, *River Basin Organizations in Water Diplomacy* (Routledge, 2021).

It is not surprising, given the importance of establishing a solid factual basis for dispute resolutions on international watercourses that the *UN Watercourses Convention* incorporates a compulsory fact-finding provision as a central component of its dispute resolution framework.[110] Providing adequate dispute resolution mechanisms in the draft articles, which would become the *UN Watercourses Convention*, was recognized during the ILC process and so was the "essential" role that fact-finding would play as an element of the dispute settlement framework of the Convention.[111] The fact-finding mechanism articulated in the *UN Watercourses Convention* was intended to deal with disputes before they posed a threat to 'international peace and security' and could have an important dispute avoidance role, by articulating the factual basis underlying a matter before a true dispute had even crystalized.[112]

These technical mechanisms can also provide a useful 'Step' between the diplomatic processes such as negotiation and mediation and the more adjudicative processes such as submitting a matter to an international court or arbitral tribunal. "The 1997 UN Watercourses Convention [...] endorses the compulsory fact-finding procedure, which bridges the gap between purely diplomatic means, entirely dependent upon the discretion of the parties to the dispute, and binding third-party dispute resolution."[113] These technical mechanisms can also help supplement the rest of the dispute resolution framework, like negotiation or mediation to help the parties reach a peaceful solution founded on a factual basis,[114] this seems to be the intention contemplated in the *UN Watercourses Convention*'s article 33 as the matter is not concluded

110 *Convention on the Law of Non-Navigational Uses of International Watercourses*, 21 May 1997, 2999 UNTS 77, 36 ILM 700 (*Watercourses Convention*) at 136–138 art 33 (entered into force 17 August 2014).

111 "The settlement of disputes was a uniquely important aspect of the topic of international watercourses and fact-finding was an essential element of the dispute-settlement machinery." "2188th meeting Friday, 6 July 1990, at 10.05 A.M." in *Yearbook of the International Law Commission 1990* vol 1 (1993) 287 at 293 para 77 (UN Doc A/CN.4/SER.A/1990).

112 "Fact-finding as envisaged in the draft articles [...] could come into play well before any threat to international peace and security arose, and indeed prior to the emergence of a 'dispute'." Stephen C. McCaffrey, "Sixth report on the law of the non-navigational uses of international watercourses" (UN Doc A/CN.4/427 and Add.1) in *Yearbook of the International Law Commission 1990*, vol 2, part 1 (1993) 41 at 68 para 51 (UN Doc A/CN.4/SER.A/1990/Add.1 (Part 1)).

113 Sergei Vinogradov, Patricia Wouters and Patricia Jones, *Transforming Potential Conflict into Cooperation Potential: The Role of International Water Law* (UNESCO-IHP, PCCP, 2003) at 66.

114 Jens Evensen, "First report on the law of the non-navigational uses of international watercourses" (UN Doc A/CN.4/367) in *Yearbook of the International Law Commission 1983*, vol 2, part 1 (1985) 155 at 191 (UN Doc A/CN.4/SER.A/1983/Add.1 (Part 1)).

by the fact-finding commission but rather parties are required to "consider in good faith" the report and recommendations of the commission.[115]

These types of mechanisms can be flexible in their procedure and are generally empowered, as is customary, to set their own rules of procedure.[116] They may also draw upon any technical expertise held by their appointed members, allowing these mechanisms to draw on broader and more situation specific technical experience than a traditional court.

> The establishment of conciliation commissions has in practice proved to be useful in the search for peaceful solutions to international disputes. The advantage of such commissions consists, *inter alia*, in that their procedures are less cumbersome than court or arbitration proceedings. They are also less time consuming and less expensive. The fact that the recommendations of conciliation commissions are not formally binding upon the parties may likewise make them politically more acceptable than court proceedings in certain cases. On the other hand, the fact that the recommendations of a conciliation commission are not binding on the parties may make the procedure less effective in the case of recalcitrant parties. Furthermore, in making its findings and recommendations, the conciliation commission, by its very nature, will not feel constrained to make its recommendations strictly within the confines of international law, which in practice may prove to be an advantage or a disadvantage.[117]

3.1.3 Adjudicative Mechanisms: Arbitration and Judicial Settlement

Adjudication will generally involve bringing a dispute before a third party for a decision with legally binding effect.[118] It is the finality of this means of dispute resolution that can prove attractive to some parties. "[T]his method is highly

115 *Convention on the Law of Non-Navigational Uses of International Watercourses*, 21 May 1997, 2999 UNTS 77, 36 ILM 700 (*Watercourses Convention*) at 136–138 art 33(8) (entered into force 17 August 2014).

116 Stephen C. McCaffrey, "Sixth report on the law of the non-navigational uses of international watercourses" (UN Doc A/CN.4/427 and Add.1) in *Yearbook of the International Law Commission 1990*, vol 2, part 1 (1993) 41 at 77 (UN Doc A/CN.4/SER.A/1990/Add.1 (Part 1)); Jens Evensen, "First report on the law of the non-navigational uses of international watercourses" (UN Doc A/CN.4/367) in *Yearbook of the International Law Commission 1983*, vol 2, part 1 (1985) 155 at 192 para 217 (UN Doc A/CN.4/SER.A/1983/Add.1 (Part 1)).

117 Jens Evensen, "First report on the law of the non-navigational uses of international watercourses" (UN Doc A/CN.4/367) in *Yearbook of the International Law Commission 1983*, vol 2, part 1 (1985) 155 at 191–192 (UN Doc A/CN.4/SER.A/1983/Add.1 (Part 1)).

118 Kari Hakapää, "Negotiation" (last updated 2013) at para 28, online: *Max Planck Encyclopedias of International Law* <https://opil.ouplaw.com/home/mpil>.

suitable for disputes of considerable political importance, and which have proved intractable in attempts at negotiated settlement [...] where the parties are in effect determined to dispose of the dispute finally, no doubt hopeful of victory, but also willing to take a risk in order to achieve some degree of finality."[119] Often adjudicative mechanisms are seen as a mechanism of 'last resort' for parties to a dispute, only being utilized after other avenues and mechanisms available have been exhausted.[120]

Adjudicative mechanisms serve an important role in dispute resolution on international watercourses, as evidenced by the increasing number of cases brought before international courts and tribunals in the field. "[O]ver the last twenty years international courts and tribunals have proved to be relatively successful at resolving disputes concerned with water. Moreover, the number of disputes about water being referred to international adjudication has increased, which would suggest that States have greater confidence in courts and tribunals, and recognize the role that they can play in this area."[121]

The importance of adjudicative mechanisms to the resolution of disputes on international watercourses can also be seen reflected through the various authorities in the field. The *Helsinki Rules*, a work of central importance to the progressive development of the law of international watercourses and a precursor to the *UN Watercourses Convention*, in Article XXXIV recommended that co-riparian States, unable to reach an agreement, should "submit their legal disputes to an *ad hoc* arbitral tribunal, to a permanent arbitral tribunal or to the International Court of Justice".[122] The Seventh International Conference of American States went further, in its declaration adopted at Montevideo in 1933, making adjudication of disputes mandatory.[123] The two major multilateral

119 Sir Robert Jennings, "Keynote Address" in The International Bureau of the Permanent Court of Arbitration, ed, *Resolution of International Water Disputes* (The Permanent Court of Arbitration/Peace Palace Papers, 2003) 23 at 30–31.

120 *Ibid* at 31.

121 Laurence Boisson de Chazournes, "The Settlement of Disputes through Judicial Means (Article 33(10) and Annex on Arbitratin)" in Laurence Boisson de Chazournes et al, eds, *The UN Convention on the Law of the Non-Navigational Uses of International Watercourses: A Commentary* (Oxford University Press, 2018) 364 at 378.

122 The International Law Association, "*Helsinki Rules on the Uses of the Waters of International Rivers*" ('*Helsinki Rules*') in *Report of the Fifty-Second Conference of the International Law Association Held at Helsinki, August 14–20, 1966*, vol 52 (1967) 484, art XXXIV at 529.

123 C.B. Bourne, "Mediation, Conciliation and Adjudication in the Settlement of International Drainage Basin Disputes" (1971) 9 Canadian Yearbook of International Law 114, at 126; "The parties shall have a month to state whether they accept the conciliatory award or not. In the latter case and at the request of the interested parties the disagreement shall then be submitted to arbitration, the respective tribunal being constituted by the

treaties in the field, the *UN Watercourses Convention*[124] and the *UNECE Water Convention*[125] both allow parties to additionally consent to the jurisdiction of the ICJ or to an international arbitral tribunal.

International arbitration, whether through an *ad hoc* process or through a standing arbitral tribunal like the Permanent Court of Arbitration in the Hague, is a versatile dispute resolution mechanism in international law. "*Arbitration* [...] involves the application of rules of international law to the facts of the case and leads to a binding settlement of a dispute."[126] The procedures and composition of arbitral tribunals are often quite flexible in comparison to international courts, allowing the tribunal to be tailored to the needs of the parties and to the particular nature of the dispute. Arbitration has been used in disputes on international watercourses, notably in the case of the *Lac Lanoux* arbitration[127] and the *Indus Waters Kishenganga Arbitration.*[128] Standing bodies such as the PCA in the Hague can provide registry and administrative services and draw on a breadth of institutional experience to support and conduct arbitrations.[129]

International courts can be an invaluable mechanism for dispute resolution. The ICJ, the 'principle judicial organ' of the United Nations, in particular has

procedure provided in the Second Hague Convention for the peaceful solution of international conflicts." *Declaration of Montevideo concerning the industrial and agricultural use of international rivers approved by the seventh international conference of American States*, 24 December 1933, 28 American Journal of International Law 59, art 10 at 60, Pan American Union, Seventh International Conference of American States, Plenary Sessions, Minutes and antecedents, 114 (*1933 Montevideo Declaration*).

124 *Convention on the Law of Non-Navigational Uses of International Watercourses*, 21 May 1997, 2999 UNTS 77, 36 ILM 700 (*UN Watercourses Convention*) art 33(2), (10) (entered into force 17 August 2014).

125 *Convention on the Protection and Use of Transboundary Watercourses and International Lakes*, 17 March 1992, 1936 UNTS 269 (*UNECE Water Convention*) at 281 art 22(2).

126 Stephen C. McCaffrey, "Sixth report on the law of the non-navigational uses of international watercourses" (UN Doc A/CN.4/427 and Add.1) in *Yearbook of the International Law Commission 1990*, vol 2, part 1 (1993) 41 at 69 para 54 (UN Doc A/CN.4/SER.A/1990/Add.1 (Part 1)); For example the 1966 Helsinki Rules in Article XXXVI stated that "recourse to arbitration implies the undertaking by the States concerned to consider the award to be given as final and to submit in good faith to its execution." The International Law Association, "*Helsinki Rules on the Uses of the Waters of International Rivers*" ('*Helsinki Rules*') in *Report of the Fifty-Second Conference of the International Law Association Held at Helsinki, August 14–20, 1966*, vol 52 (1967) 484, art XXXVI at 530.

127 *Affaire du Lac Lanoux (France v Spain)* (1957), Judgment, 12 RIAA 281 at 310.

128 *Indus Waters Kishenganga Arbitration (Pakistan v India)* (20 December 2013), Final Award, 31 RIAA 309, (Permanent Court of Arbitration).

129 Ruth Mackenzie et al, *The Manual on International Courts and Tribunals*, 2nd ed (Oxford University Press, 2010) at 121–122.

dealt with a significant number of disputes concerning international watercourses.[130] It has played an instrumental role in helping to interpret and clarify the law of the non-navigational uses of international watercourses. The increasing access to such varied dispute resolution mechanisms has meant that international courts and tribunals have developed greater awareness and sensitivity to each other, "broadening the sources of persuasive case law, this has led to decisions that include more diverse cross-references to other courts and tribunals, and has helped to strengthen the interpretation and application of law in water disputes."[131]

While the use of international courts and tribunals is increasing in the field of the non-navigational uses of international watercourses, C.B. Bourne's 1971 observations remain true today. In examining several statements of principles in the field he found that they "unanimously recommended recourse to judicial settlement of drainage basin disputes when the parties are unable to settle them by agreement. They do not, however, justify a conclusion that co-basin states are under a duty to submit their disputes to judicial settlement in the absence of an agreement to do so."[132] Still adjudication retains much to recommend it as a mechanism for dispute resolution. For example, Sir Robert Jennings observed that it is a mechanism that can insulate political leaders from negative outcomes.

> The great attraction of judicial decision to members of a government is that it is the judges who are, and often dramatically seen to be, directly responsible for the decision. The politicians involved are only responsible at least once removed – a circumstance that often makes even the very unpredictability of the process attractive in terms of domestic politics. [...] [T]his method is highly suitable for disputes of considerable

130 For example *Gabčíkovo-Nagymaros Project* (*Hungary v Slovakia*), Judgment of September 25 1997, [1997] ICJ Rep 7; *Case Concerning the Dispute Regarding Navigational and Related Rights* (*Costa Rica v Nicaragua*), Judgement of July 13 2009, [2009] ICJ Rep 213; *Case Concerning Pulp Mills on the River Uruguay* (*Argentina v Uruguay*), Judgment of April 20 2010, [2010] ICJ Rep 14; *Certain Activities Carried Out by Nicaragua in the Border Area* (*Costa Rica v Nicaragua*) *and Construction of a Road Along the San Juan River* (*Nicaragua v Costa Rica*), Judgment of 16 December 2015, [2015] ICJ Rep 665.

131 Laurence Boisson de Chazournes, "The Settlement of Disputes through Judicial Means (Article 33(10) and Annex on Arbitratin)" in Laurence Boisson de Chazournes et al, eds, *The UN Convention on the Law of the Non-Navigational Uses of International Watercourses: A Commentary* (Oxford University Press, 2018) 364 at 378 [footnote omitted].

132 C.B. Bourne, "Mediation, Conciliation and Adjudication in the Settlement of International Drainage Basin Disputes" (1971) 9 Canadian Yearbook of International Law 114 at 129.

> political importance, and which have proved intractable in attempts at negotiated settlement.[133]

Adjudicative means of dispute resolution with respect to international watercourses are not without their detractors.[134] Not all disputes or even all aspects of individual disputes on international watercourses will be justiciable before international courts and tribunals. "A distinction must be drawn between their legal and non-legal aspects, admittedly not an easy task in any particular case but one that is within the competence of a court."[135] It is certain that some parties will be reluctant to enter into binding third party dispute resolution, this does represent a limitation of international legal mechanisms that are based on State consent.[136] As a dispute resolution mechanism it can also be costly and time consuming,[137] which may pose an obstacle to its use by some parties or in certain cases.

Adjudication seems to have been accepted in many cases as a suitable mechanism for the resolution of disputes in the field as evidenced by the growing number of cases that have been submitted to international courts and tribunals for adjudication. Whether adjudication is the most suitable means of dispute resolution regarding a rather technical field, such as the law of international watercourses is a subject for further debate, but it certainly can make a significant contribution to dispute resolution in the field as part of a suite of options available to parties. Adjudication represents a compelling final 'Step' in a 'Stepped Approach' framework to dispute resolution on international watercourses. That is not to say that other mechanisms cannot operate in parallel to adjudication, for instance negotiation may continue to be undertaken by the parties to a dispute after the initiation of an adjudicative procedure. In fact, a negotiated settlement 'on the courthouse steps' with the threat of an uncertain and binding adjudicated settlement hanging over the heads of the parties, is a real possibility.

---

133 Sir Robert Jennings, "Keynote Address" in The International Bureau of the Permanent Court of Arbitration, ed, *The Permanent Court of Arbitration/Peace Palace Papers Resolution of International Water Disputes* (Kluwer Law International, 2003) 23 at 30.

134 For a further discussion on this see C.B. Bourne, "Mediation, Conciliation and Adjudication in the Settlement of International Drainage Basin Disputes" (1971) 9 Canadian Yearbook of International Law 114.

135 C.B. Bourne, "Mediation, Conciliation and Adjudication in the Settlement of International Drainage Basin Disputes" (1971) 9 Canadian Yearbook of International Law 114, at 138.

136 *Ibid* at 141, 158.

137 *Ibid* at 140.

3.2 *Dispute Resolution in the Law of the Non-navigational Uses of International Watercourses, in Practice*

Although there are multilateral agreements of global scope and binding customary international law in the field of the non-navigational uses of international watercourses, as discussed above, much of the law is governed by regional and basin specific agreements. Such was the intention of the drafters of the ILC's draft articles and the *UN Watercourses Convention* in creating a framework convention that could be adapted and modified by more specific agreements.[138] "[T]he conclusion of specific and specialized water treaties remains far and away the best solution".[139] If we look at dispute resolution mechanisms in the field broadly, incorporating multilateral, regional and watercourse specific agreements, we find a wide variety of dispute resolution mechanisms used across a broad cross section of international watercourse related agreements.[140]

The settlement of disputes on international watercourses comes down to the relations between the State parties, the very presence of an agreement or of a joint mechanism on an international watercourse can be a powerful factor in peacefully resolving disputes, as it generally means there is a functioning relationship between the States in question. In an analysis of fourteen (14) different international water disputes McCaffrey found that "there is only one case (the Indus) in which there is political tension [between the parties] but the dispute was resolved."[141] He also found a correlation between a failure to resolve disputes and the absence of a joint-mechanism, as well as a connection between the existence of a functional treaty and the likelihood of a dispute

---

138 Stephen McCaffrey, "The contribution of the UN Convention on the law of the non-navigational uses of international watercourses" (2001) 1:3/4 International Journal of Global Environmental Issues 250 at 257; *Convention on the Law of Non-Navigational Uses of International Watercourses*, 21 May 1997, 2999 UNTS 77, 36 ILM 700 (*UN Watercourses Convention*) (entered into force 17 August 2014).

139 Friedrich J. Berber, *Rivers in International Law* translated by R.K. Batstone (1959) at 270; as quoted in The International Law Association, "*Helsinki Rules on the Uses of the Waters of International Rivers*" ('*Helsinki Rules*') in *Report of the Fifty-Second Conference of the International Law Association Held at Helsinki, August 14–20, 1966*, vol 52 (1967) 484, Comment to art XXX at 524.

140 *See also* Laurence Boisson de Chazournes, *Fresh Water in International Law*, 2nd ed (Oxford University Press, 2021) at 337.

141 Stephen C. McCaffrey, "Water Disputes Defined: Characteristics and Trends for Resolving Them" in The International Bureau of the Permanent Court of Arbitration, ed, *The Permanent Court of Arbitration/Peace Palace Papers Resolution of International Water Disputes* (Kluwer Law International, 2003) 49 at 87.

TABLE 1 Number and percentage of treaties by region with each type of 'Step'[a]

Region/Continent	Total number of agreements with distinct dispute resolution provisions	Two or more 'Steps'	Graduated 'Steps' (Three or more)	Distinct diplomatic 'Step'	Distinct technical 'Step'	Distinct adjudicative 'Step'	A compulsory 'Step'	Ultimate 'Step' is Binding
S. America	19 (8%)	11 (7%)	5 (8%)	18 (9%)	5 (10%)	6 (5%)	17 (8%)	6 (5%)
N. America	13 (6%)	10 (6%)	4 (6%)	10 (5%)	6 (13%)	10 (8%)	13 (6%)	9 (7%)
General	2 (1%)	1 (1%)	1 (2%)	2 (1%)	1 (2%)	0	2 (1%)	0
Europe	88 (39%)	66 (42%)	26 (42%)	77 (39%)	21 (44%)	52 (40%)	84 (39%)	51 (41%)
Asia	45 (20%)	22 (14%)	9 (15%)	42 (21%)	7 (15%)	16 (12%)	43 (20%)	15 (12%)
Africa	58 (26%)	46 (29%)	17 (27%)	50 (25%)	8 (17%)	45 (35%)	55 (26%)	44 (35%)
Total	**225** (100%)	**156** (100%)	**62** (100%)	**199** (100%)	**48** (100%)	**129** (100%)	**214** (100%)	**125** (100%)

a In this work distinct 'Steps' were measured. Where a provision allowed for a suite of options such as in article 33(2) of the *UN Watercourses Convention*, these were not measured. This means that an agreement could provide for several mechanisms in a 'menu' for the parties that are not accounted for. This work also did not count general provisions that allowed parties to consent to the jurisdiction of the ICJ or another international court or tribunal as a distinct 'Step' as it was not a given that parties would elect to do so.

being resolved.[142] Of the six hundred and seven (607) treaties or international instruments that pertained to international water resources identified in the research for this work, two hundred and twenty-five (225) treaties were identified containing distinct dispute resolution provisions between State actors, from 1900. A review of the 'Steps' available in these agreements provides some insight into the practice in the field.

It is interesting to observe the regional distribution of agreements with dispute resolution provisions and the various types of 'Steps' or mechanisms employed. Of the two hundred and twenty-five (225) treaties identified with dispute resolution provisions a large proportion of them come from Europe, thirty-nine percent (39%), which is to be expected based on the historical basis of our current system of international law as a system of largely European origins. We do see a fairly strong representation from Africa, at roughly twenty-six

142 *Ibid.*

TABLE 2 Number and percentage of treaties overall with each type of 'Step'

Total number of agreements with distinct dispute resolution provisions	Two or more 'Steps'	Graduated 'Steps' (Three or more)	Distinct diplomatic 'Step'	Distinct technical 'Step'	Distinct adjudicative 'Step'	A compulsory 'Step'	Ultimate 'Step' is binding
225 (100%)	156 (69%)	62 (28%)	199 (88%)	48 (21%)	129 (57%)	214 (95%)	125 (56%)

percent (26%), and Asia, with approximately twenty percent (20%). North America has a relatively small percentage of treaties with dispute resolution provisions, around six percent (6%) but this may be accounted for by the relatively small number of riparian States in this region. Combined, the Americas represent roughly fourteen percent (14%).

The regional distribution of the various 'Steps' and criteria measured are relatively consistent with the distribution of agreements with dispute resolution provisions. Africa seems to have a disproportionately higher share of the agreements with a distinct adjudicative 'Step', and agreements with a final or ultimate 'Step' that is binding, while the North American region seems to have a disproportionately higher use of a distinct technical 'Step'. Asia seems to make less use of a distinct adjudicative 'Step' in agreements which may also account for the lower levels of a binding ultimate 'Step' in this region.

As one can see from the data of the two hundred and twenty-five (225) assessed international agreements, a diplomatic 'Step' is the most utilized, being found in roughly eighty-eight percent (88%) of these treaties. Adjudication as a 'Step' is also quite common being found in roughly fifty-seven percent (57%) of the agreements. A technical 'Step' is the least utilized, showing up as a distinct 'Step' in only approximately twenty-one percent (21%). It is not surprising to see a heavy emphasis on the traditional mechanisms of dispute resolution in international law, diplomatic means and adjudicative processes. The value of third party involvement in dispute resolution in the field has long been recognized.[143] Writing in 1961 Brice Clagett observed that "a very high proportion of the international (boundary and successive) watercourses of the world

143 C.B. Bourne, "Mediation, Conciliation and Adjudication in the Settlement of International Drainage Basin Disputes" (1971) 9 Canadian Yearbook of International Law 114, at 125.

are covered by formal agreements providing for compulsory adjudication of third-party determination."[144]

Ninety-five percent (95%) of the agreements had at least one compulsory 'Step' and fifty-six percent (56%), had an ultimate or final 'Step' that was binding in its decision. The high number of agreements that had at least one compulsory 'Step' is interesting and can in part be attributed to the operative language of 'will' or 'shall', or some variation on this, used in many diplomatic dispute resolution 'Steps'. The high number of treaties that created a binding final 'Step' can, in part, be attributed to the high number of treaties that had adjudicative 'Steps', fifty-seven percent (57%), which unless otherwise specified were treated as presumptively binding. The fact that there was such a high number that had a binding final 'Step' is also interesting given the reluctance shown by many States to such strident dispute resolution tools in the drafting of the *UN Watercourses Convention* and the absence of such binding provisions in either major multilateral treaty of global scope. This peculiarity can perhaps be explained by the nature of the *UN Watercourses Convention* and the *UNECE Water Convention* as framework agreements, meant to be supplemented by more specific agreements. In fact, the data seems to show that State parties are generally more open to committing to such binding and compulsory dispute resolution 'Steps' in more region or basin specific agreements than in multilateral agreements of a broader and more global scope.

There are also several practical considerations that arise in the resolution of disputes on international watercourses that are worth mentioning here, even briefly. The appropriateness of a particular mechanism for resolving a

144 Brice McAdoo Clagett, "Survey of Agreements Providing for Third-Party Resolution of International Waters Disputes" (1961) 55:3 The American Journal of International Law 645 at 646; see also C.B. Bourne, "Mediation, Conciliation and Adjudication in the Settlement of International Drainage Basin Disputes" (1971) 9 Canadian Yearbook of International Law 114, at 142–143; McCaffrey in his sixth report to the ILC on the subject of the non-navigational uses of international watercourses cites Chauhan as listing one hundred and sixteen (116) different agreements in which the parties expressly agreed to resolve their water-related disputes by recourse to arbitration and forty-six (46) which contain provisions for the judicial settlement of disputes. B.R. Chauhan, *Settlement of International Water Law Disputes in International Drainage Basins* (Erich Schmidt, 1981) at 344–355, 361–366; Stephen C. McCaffrey, "Sixth report on the law of the non-navigational uses of international watercourses" (UN Doc A/CN.4/427 and Add.1) in *Yearbook of the International Law Commission 1990*, vol 2, part 1 (1993) 41 at 69 para 55 (UN Doc A/CN.4/SER.A/1990/Add.1 (Part 1)); Laurence Boisson de Chazournes, "The Settlement of Disputes through Judicial Means (Article 33(10) and Annex on Arbitratin)" in Laurence Boisson de Chazournes et al, eds, *The UN Convention on the Law of the Non-Navigational Uses of International Watercourses: A Commentary* (Oxford University Press, 2018) 364 at 365.

watercourse dispute may be impacted by the practical considerations of the matter at hand. A framework that allows for the deployment of several different mechanisms or 'Steps' could be employed to flexibly address any shortcomings in a particular mechanism.

For example, there would be various expenses associated with different dispute resolution mechanisms, an important consideration. How costs and expenses are divided will be dealt with by the specific agreement and the nature of the dispute resolution mechanism; for instance, McCaffrey observes in his sixth report that fact-finding "will entail expenses. If it is undertaken by a competent joint organization, associated expenses would presumably be paid from the budget of that organization. If fact-finding is not conducted by such an existing organization, some provision would have to be made for the expenses of the *ad hoc* expert commission or the commission of inquiry."[145] It is certainly an important consideration when crafting an international agreement or joint body regarding an international watercourse, or in the selection of a dispute resolution mechanism. The consideration of expenses and costs is also somewhat beyond the scope of this present work, except in the most general sense. As has been stated, these matters will often be covered by basin specific agreements, it is hard therefore to draw bright-line rules regarding this issue in the context of international watercourse law as a whole, except to say that, in general, discretion is afforded to riparian State actors in crafting their own agreements and joint bodies.

The timeliness of a mechanism can also be of interest in selecting a resolution mechanism. As stated above, based on the importance of international water resources the resolution of disputes can take on a certain urgency. Some mechanisms such as international adjudication can take considerable time to reach a conclusion. "[I]nternational claims – whether before the Court or a tribunal – can take many years to resolve, during which time the project in question – whether dam, bridge, or large-scale land reclamation project – may have been completed with little prospect of reversal."[146] Some of the prejudice of such a mechanism can be addressed by interim measures but this can also risk delaying vital projects or uses for the other riparians.

145 Stephen C. McCaffrey, "Sixth report on the law of the non-navigational uses of international watercourses" (UN Doc A/CN.4/427 and Add.1) in *Yearbook of the International Law Commission 1990*, vol 2, part 1 (1993) 41 at 77 (UN Doc A/CN.4/SER.A/1990/Add.1 (Part 1)).

146 James Crawford, *Brownlie's Principles of Public International Law*, 9th ed (Oxford University Press, 2019) at 338 [footnotes omitted].

3.3 *Dispute Resolution and Avoidance in the Law of the Non-navigational Uses of International Watercourses, an Integrated Approach*

Tables 1 and 2 above also show some interesting numbers regarding the degree to which these international water resource agreements utilize or integrate more than one type of dispute resolution 'Steps'. We see that of the two hundred and twenty-five (225) treaties that were identified containing distinct dispute resolution provisions, one hundred and fifty-six (156), or sixty-nine percent (69%), utilized two or more 'Steps' and sixty-two (62), or approximately twenty-eight (28%) had three or more 'Steps'.[147] While a minority of agreements had three or more 'Steps' the number of agreements that incorporated two or more 'Steps' represented a majority. This seems to indicate broad support, in State practice, for integrating various dispute resolution mechanisms into international agreements dealing with transboundary water resources. The level of integration could in fact be higher as this research did not account for provisions which provided parties with a suite or 'menu' of mechanisms from which to choose.[148]

We also see a statistically high number of these agreements from Europe and Africa. Europe represented forty-two percent (42%) of agreements that incorporated two or more 'Steps' as well as agreements with three or more 'Steps'. Africa was the next most significant region with around twenty-nine percent (29%) of agreements with two or more 'Steps' and twenty-seven percent (27%) of those with three or more. Asia followed with fourteen percent (14%) with two or more and fifteen percent (15%) with three or more. South and North America had around seven percent (7%) and six percent (6%), respectively, of the agreements that had two or more 'Steps', they also had eight percent (8%) and six percent (6%) respectively, of the agreements with three or more 'Steps'. Asia, and South America saw an increase in the percentage representation from two 'Steps' to three, while Africa and North America saw a decrease. Europe stayed even at forty-two percent (42%) for both two 'Steps' and three.

---

147 For the purpose of this work three or more 'Steps' constituted the threshold for determining a graduated framework of 'Steps' as part of a 'Stepped Approach'.

148 In this work distinct 'Steps' were measured. Where a provision allowed for a suite of options, such as in article 33(2) of the *UN Watercourses Convention*, these were not measured. This means that an agreement could provide for several mechanisms in a 'menu' for the parties that are not accounted for. This work also did not count general provisions that allowed parties to consent to the jurisdiction of the ICJ or another international court or tribunal as a distinct 'Step' as it was not a given that parties would elect to do so.

Integrating diverse mechanisms to deal with disputes in international watercourse agreements is an effective approach for creating flexible and adaptable dispute resolution and avoidance frameworks that are not exposed to the weaknesses inherent in any one approach and take advantage of the different strengths of the varied dispute resolution mechanisms. The drafters of the *UN Watercourses* Convention, for example, deliberately constructed the dispute resolution provisions of that agreement to be a flexible and adaptable framework which enable parties to choose between a suite of options. This can also allow more diverse expertise to be employed in the resolution of disputes under such agreements. "Because of the complexity of the issues involved in resolving a dispute over water – a resource which is unique in character – and due to the desirability of involving professionals from other disciplines (such as geographers, engineers and social scientists) in settling such disputes, there is scope and a need for further development of both formal and informal fora for their resolution."[149] The operation of procedures that allow for the use of diverse mechanisms for dispute resolution can mean that some mechanisms, like adjudication, may be seldom used, this may not be a rejection of any particular mechanism but rather a sign of the success of the other processes available in resolving the matter.[150]

As discussed above, the spectre of an impending adjudicated decision on a matter may help precipitate fruitful negotiations and the resolution of a dispute, but negotiations can also supplement the adjudicative process by helping to clarify issues and articulate the positions of the parties. Such was the observation of the tribunal in the *Lac Lanoux* arbitration.[151] Similarly technical mechanisms can also aid in helping to provide clarification of issues and a factual basis for future negotiations or adjudication. For that matter, a similar argument can be made that adjudication can help facilitate future settlement

149 S.P. Subedi, "Challenges for the 21st Century" in The International Bureau of the Permanent Court of Arbitration, ed, *Resolution of International Water Disputes* (The Permanent Court of Arbitration/Peace Palace Papers, 2003) 33 at 34–35.

150 C.B. Bourne, "Mediation, Conciliation and Adjudication in the Settlement of International Drainage Basin Disputes" (1971) 9 Canadian Yearbook of International Law 114, at 144.

151 "Il est délicat d'apprécier s'il a été satisfait à une telle obligation. Mais, sans se substituer aux Parties, le juge est en mesure de procéder à cette apprécitaion sur la base des éléments fournis par les négociations." *Affaire du Lac Lanoux* (*France v Spain*) (1957), Judgment, 12 RIAA 281 at 315; "It is delicate to appreciate whether such an obligation has been satisfied. But, without taking the place of the Parties, the judge is in a position to carry out such an assessment on the basis of the elements provided by the negotiations." [translated by Author].

of a dispute simply by helping to define issues and the respective legal positions and rights of the parties.

The ability to utilize different dispute resolution mechanisms can assist parties in breaking deadlocks and avoid the risk of disputes becoming eternally locked in the stasis of a process that has met a roadblock and grown stale. Sometimes a fresh approach can allow parties to divorce themselves from certain problematic positions and allow a dispute to move forward. In an area as technical as the law of the non-navigational uses of international watercourses the ability to utilize diverse methods to address disputes, to clarify the issues at hand and to ascertain the relevant facts can be of great help in moving matters forward in a peaceful and constructive manner.

CHAPTER 2

Disputes at a 'Technical Level'

In this chapter we will explore the resolution of international watercourse disputes at a 'Technical Level' or 'Step'. As discussed above a technical 'Step' shows up as a distinct 'Step' in only approximately twenty-one percent (21%) or forty-eight (48) of the two hundred and twenty-five (225) international agreements reviewed for this work. One hundred and one (101) agreements, or roughly forty-five percent (45%) of this same two hundred and twenty-five (225) agreements, allow specific recourse to technical experts or decision makers, fifty-three (53) while not containing a distinct technical 'Step' in their respective dispute resolution mechanisms. 'Technical Level' dispute resolution on international watercourses allows for subsequent 'Steps' in a 'Stepped Approach' to function more efficiently, in part by helping to identify the issues at stake, divert matters away from other 'Steps' by resolving them at a 'Technical Level' and creating a factual basis for later 'Steps'. "Many disputes turn essentially on disagreements over facts and their evaluation, rather than on questions of law."[1] This 'Technical Level' is a particularly important 'Step' of the 'Stepped Approach' explored in this work, and so extra time will be given to the discussion of the resolution of disputes at a 'Technical Level'.

In this chapter we will first look at what a 'Technical Level' of dispute resolution is. We will then look at why a 'Technical Level' of dispute resolution might be considered important or useful in the context of international watercourse disputes. Then we will discuss when such a 'Technical Level' of dispute resolution is best employed in the overall architecture of dispute resolution mechanisms on international watercourses. Finally, we will look at 'Technical Level' dispute resolution mechanisms in the context of a 'Stepped Approach' to the resolution of international watercourse disputes.

In some cases, it can be difficult to draw a clear line between dispute resolution, dispute avoidance, compliance, or governance mechanisms.[2] In fact, these various mechanisms can often have overlapping functions in regard to

1 John Collier and Vaughan Lowe, *The Settlement of Disputes in International Law* (Oxford University Press, 1999) at 91.

2 Christina Leb, *Cooperation in the Law of Transboundary Water Resources* (Cambridge University Press, 2013) at 193; see also Salman Salman, "Evolution and Context of International Water Resources Law" in Laurence Boisson de Chazournes and Salman Salman, eds, Les resources en eau et le droit international – Water resources and International Law (Martinus Nijhoff Publishers, 2005) 45 at 89.

 | DOI:10.1163/9789004736771_005

dispute avoidance and settlement. As discussed above in this work the author has taken a rather broad interpretation of what qualifies as a "dispute" or "dispute resolution" often encapsulating what would often be termed as "dispute avoidance" or cooperative/preventative actions particularly in this chapter. Such is the nature of the proposed 'Stepped Approach' that it implicates various joint mechanisms that serve to prevent disputes. By taking this broader more holistic approach it is hoped that the discourse can be enriched, and a more useful and adaptable dispute resolution framework can be put forward, than if a more restrictive approach was taken.

1 A 'Technical Level'?

A 'Technical Level' of dispute resolution, for our purposes, is defined as a phase or 'Step' primarily concerned with factual and technical issues, systems or functions or dominated by technical experts such as scientists or engineers. It is defined by the expert nature of those assessing the matter but also what they are assessing, primarily technical, scientific and factual considerations. For a 'Technical Level' of dispute resolution to be effective it is important to keep in mind, as McCaffrey observed in commenting on his proposed draft articles to the ILC, "that fact finding 'should be comprehensive, objective and impartial'".[3] The value of the examination of matters through an objective and technical lens cannot be understated.[4]

Specialist 'Technical Level' dispute resolution can be found in other regimes of international law outside of the law of the non-navigational uses of international watercourses.[5] For instance, the UNCLOS permits non legal experts to be appointed under Annexes VII and VIII[6] and allows special tribunals to be utilized as fact-finding commissions to perform factual inquiries and make findings of facts that are conclusive between the parties.[7] The 1951 International

3 Stephen C. McCaffrey, "Sixth report on the law of the non-navigational uses of international watercourses" (UN Doc A/CN.4/427 and Add.1) in *Yearbook of the International Law Commission 1990*, vol 2, part 1 (1993) 41 at 68,76 (UN Doc A/CN.4/SER.A/1990/Add.1 (Part 1)).

4 C.B. Bourne, "Mediation, Conciliation and Adjudication in the Settlement of International Drainage Basin Disputes" (1971) 9 Canadian Yearbook of International Law 114, at 115.

5 Alan Boyle, "Environmental Dispute Settlement" (last updated 2009) at paras 11–12, online: *Max Planck Encyclopedias of International Law* <https://opil.ouplaw.com/home/mpil>.

6 *United Nations Convention on the Law of the Sea*, 10 December 1982, 1833 UNTS 397 annexes VII, VIII.

7 *Ibid* at annex VIII, art 5; see discussion in John Collier and Vaughan Lowe, *The Settlement of Disputes in International Law* (Oxford University Press, 1999) at 92.

Plant Protection Convention provides a useful example for our purposes.[8] This convention makes use of experts in the resolution of disputes regarding its interpretation and application.[9] Article IX of the convention contains interesting provisions regarding dispute settlement.[10] Here the Director-General of the FAO is empowered to empanel a committee of experts at the request of the governments involved in a dispute.[11] This committee of experts is required to submit a non-binding report[12] that shall form a "basis for renewed consideration by the contracting parties concerned"[13] on the dispute's "technical aspects."[14]

The Convention relating to the Development of Hydraulic Power Affecting More than One State of December 9th, 1923[15] provides a relatively early example of the recognition of the importance of involving experts in international dispute resolution on international watercourses in a multilateral agreement.[16] The Convention allows for disputes between State parties to be submitted "for an advisory opinion to the body established by the League of Nations as the advisory and technical organisation of the Members of the League in matters of communications and transit".[17] Here parties are not required to submit a dispute to this 'Technical Level' of dispute resolution but they are empowered to submit matters where other options for the peaceful settlement of disputes have not borne a satisfactory resolution of the matter. The IDI/IIL's 1961 *Salzburg Resolution* finds, in regard to watercourse States, that it is "desirable that the States in disagreement should have recourse to technical experts and,

8 Stephen C. McCaffrey, "Sixth report on the law of the non-navigational uses of international watercourses" (UN Doc A/CN.4/427 and Add.1) in *Yearbook of the International Law Commission 1990*, vol 2, part 1 (1993) 41 at 66 note 116 (UN Doc A/CN.4/SER.A/1990/Add.1 (Part 1)).

9 *International Plant Protection Convention (new revised text)*, 17 November 1997, 2367 UNTS 223 art XIII (2) (entered into force 2 October 2005).

10 *Ibid* at art XIII (entered into force 2 October 2005).

11 *Ibid* at art XIII (2)–(3).

12 *Ibid* at art XIII (3)–(4).

13 *Ibid* at art XIII (4).

14 *Ibid* at art XIII (3).

15 *Convention Relating to the Development of Hydraulic Power Affecting More than One State*, 9 December 1923, 36 LNTS 76.

16 Stephen C. McCaffrey, "Sixth report on the law of the non-navigational uses of international watercourses" (UN Doc A/CN.4/427 and Add.1) in *Yearbook of the International Law Commission 1990*, vol 2, part 1 (1993) 41 at 73 para 76 (UN Doc A/CN.4/SER.A/1990/Add.1 (Part 1)).

17 *Convention Relating to the Development of Hydraulic Power Affecting More than One State*, 9 December 1923, 36 LNTS 76, art 12.

should occasion arise, to commissions and appropriate agencies in order to arrive at solutions assuring the greatest advantage to all concerned."[18]

1.1 *Form of 'Technical Level' Dispute Resolution and Avoidance Mechanisms on International Watercourses*

1.1.1 Composition of 'Technical Level' Mechanisms and Engagement of Riparian States

'Technical Level' dispute resolution mechanisms on international watercourses will often engage the participation of the riparian States involved in the specific 'Technical Level' dispute resolution mechanism. Ordinarily the State parties will appoint the members of a 'Technical Level' dispute resolution mechanism, whether to serve in a private capacity or as a representative of the State parties.[19] In this way such a mechanism is usually representative of the States involved.[20] Such is the case with the "consultative committee" created by the 1966 *Agreement with Final Protocol Regulating the Withdrawal of Water from Lake Constance*, which states that "[t]he consultative committee shall be composed of one representative of each of the riparian States."[21] The *Helsinki Rules* recommended that non-basin States which enjoy the right to use the waters of an international drainage basin by treaty be invited to associate themselves with the work of the joint agency or appear before the agency.[22]

18 L'Institut de Droit International/Institute of International Law, "*Utilization of Non-Maritime International Waters (Except for Navigation)*" ('*Salzburg Resolution*') in *Annuaire de L'Institut de Droit International*, vol 40 (1961) 381, art 6 at 383.

19 In some cases neutral members will be appointed, such as the "Fact-finding Commission" of the *UN Watercourses Convention* where a "Chairman" from a neutral nation will also be appointed. *Convention on the Law of Non-Navigational Uses of International Watercourses, 21 May 1997, 2999 UNTS 77, 36 ILM 700* (*Watercourses Convention*) at 137 art 33(4) (*entered into force 17 August 2014*).

20 For some examples see; *Treaty on the Lesotho Highlands Water Project between the Government of the Kingdom of Lesotho and the Government of the Republic of South Africa*, 24 October 1986, https://www.fao.org/faolex/results/details/en/c/LEX-FAOC015909/, art 9 (1)–(2) (*Treaty on the Lesotho Highlands Water Project*); *The Indus Waters Treaty 1960 (with annexes)*, 19 September 1960, 419 UNTS 125, art VIII (1) (*Indus Waters Treaty*); *Treaty Relating to Boundary Waters, and Questions Arising Between the United States and Canada, Great Britain and United States*, 11 January 1909, UKTS 1910 No 23, art VII (*Boundary Waters Treaty*).

21 *Agreement with Final Protocol Regulating the Withdrawal of Water from Lake Constance*, 30 April 1966, 620 UNTS 191, art 8(2).

22 The International Law Association, "*Helsinki Rules on the Uses of the Waters of International Rivers*" ('*Helsinki Rules*') in *Report of the Fifty-Second Conference of the International Law Association Held at Helsinki, August 14–20, 1966*, vol 52 (1967) 484, art XXXI(3) at 524.

Often such appointed representatives will be required to possess a certain technical background or expertise as a prerequisite to their appointment, this requirement often being articulated in the specific constituting agreement. "The highly intricate and specialized nature of disputes concerning international rivers makes it desirable that the membership of the joint agency includes engineers, hydrographers and other technical experts, as well as diplomats and lawyers."[23] The technical background of these experts can have important implications for how decisions are made and how disputes are avoided or resolved. For example, arbitral tribunals established under Annex VII of the Law of the Sea Convention are able, it seems, to utilize experts whose expertise does not necessarily lie in the law of the sea but in a relevant technical field. "This may, indeed, open the door for arbitral decisions based less upon the law than upon compromises based on an interpretation of a 'reasonable' response to the factual circumstances of the dispute."[24]

'Technical Level' mechanisms frequently have the ability to also rely on additional expert advisers to supplement the expertise of the mechanism. The International Joint Commission under the 1909 Boundary Waters Treaty (the 'IJC') "may employ engineers and clerical assistants from time to time as it may deem advisable."[25] These same provisions apply under the various subsidiary agreements between Canada and the United States of America that implicate the IJC, such as the treaties and protocols concerning the Columbia River.[26] The *Treaty on the Lesotho Highlands Water Project between the Government of the Kingdom of Lesotho and the Government of the Republic of South Africa* (*Treaty on the Lesotho Highlands Water Project*) creates a "The Joint Permanent Technical Commission", and allows this "Commission" to "appoint technical experts and consultants to provide expert opinion and advice whenever this appears to be necessary."[27] The *Agreement with Final Protocol Regulating the*

23 *Ibid.*

24 John Collier and Vaughan Lowe, *The Settlement of Disputes in International Law* (Oxford University Press, 1999) at 90–91.

25 *Treaty Relating to Boundary Waters, and Questions Arising Between the United States and Canada, Great Britain and United States*, 11 January 1909, UKTS 1910 No 23 (*Boundary Waters Treaty*), art XII.

26 *Treaty between Canada and the United States of America relating to co-operative development of the water resources of the Columbia River Basin*, 17 January 1961, 542 UNTS 246, art XVI; *Exchange of Notes (with attachments) constituting an agreement authorizing the Canadian Entitlement Purchase Agreement provided for under the Treaty relating to co-operative development of the water resources of the Columbia River Basin*, Canada and the United States of America, 16 September 1964, 542 UNTS 244, Can TS 1964 No 2, art 14.

27 *Treaty on the Lesotho Highlands Water Project between the Government of the Kingdom of Lesotho and the Government of the Republic of South Africa*, 24 October 1986,

Withdrawal of Water from Lake Constance allows the State representatives comprising the "consultative committee" to be "accompanied by advisers".[28] The "Mixed Technical Commission" created by the 1946 *Agreement concerning the utilization of the rapids of the Uruguay River in the Salto Grande area* between Argentina and Uruguay has the power to "employ such permanent or temporary technical and administrative staff as it needs. For this purpose it shall, except in special circumstances, employ an equal number of nationals of each of the High Contracting Parties."[29]

The fact that these 'Technical Level' dispute resolution mechanisms are often comprised of representatives of the riparian States themselves seems to indicate that there is a natural implication that these mechanisms, to function, foster a degree of exchange and even cooperation between the States in question. Such mechanisms often require unanimous agreement, as is the case in *Indus Waters Treaty*[30] and the *Treaty on the Lesotho Highlands Water Project*,[31] which can force the parties to engage with each other through these 'Technical Level' mechanisms. The *Agreement with Final Protocol Regulating the Withdrawal of Water from Lake Constance* limits the voting on some certain fact specific matters, here on matters "relating exclusively to the Lower Lake", to only some of the riparians.[32] Other mechanisms can require different decision-making arrangements, for instance, the *UN Watercourses Agreement*,[33] the *Agreement concerning the utilization of the rapids of the Uruguay River in the Salto Grande area* between Argentina and Uruguay[34] and

https://www.fao.org/faolex/results/details/en/c/LEX-FAOC015909/, art 9(23) (*Treaty on the Lesotho Highlands Water Project*).

28 *Agreement with Final Protocol Regulating the Withdrawal of Water from Lake Constance*, 30 April 1966, 620 UNTS 191, art 8(2).

29 *Agreement concerning the utilization of the rapids of the Uruguay River in the Salto Grande area*, Argentina and Uruguay, 30 December 1946, 671 UNTS 17, art 3(d).

30 *The Indus Waters Treaty 1960 (with annexes)*, 19 September 1960, 419 UNTS 125, art IX (1),(2) (*Indus Waters Treaty*).

31 "All decisions of the Joint Permanent Technical Commission shall require the agreement of both delegations." *Treaty on the Lesotho Highlands Water Project between the Government of the Kingdom of Lesotho and the Government of the Republic of South Africa*, 24 October 1986, https://www.fao.org/faolex/results/details/en/c/LEX-FAOC015909/, art 9 (3) (*Treaty on the Lesotho Highlands Water Project*).

32 *Agreement with Final Protocol Regulating the Withdrawal of Water from Lake Constance*, 30 April 1966, 620 UNTS 191, art 8(3).

33 *Convention on the Law of Non-Navigational Uses of International Watercourses, 21 May 1997, 2999 UNTS 77, 36 ILM 700* (*Watercourses Convention*) at 137 art 33(8) (*entered into force 17 August 2014*).

34 *Agreement concerning the utilization of the rapids of the Uruguay River in the Salto Grande area*, Argentina and Uruguay, 30 December 1946, 671 UNTS 17, art 3(b).

the *Boundary Waters Treaty* between Canada and the United States[35] require a majority vote in their respective mechanisms. These mechanisms can still prove to be important forums for dialogue and provide powerful incentives for cooperation and the resolution of disputes.

1.1.2 Joint Organizations

'Technical Level' dispute resolution on international watercourses can take a myriad of forms. Perhaps the most common is the use of joint organizations to address technical questions or disputes.[36] "[W]here such joint commissions have been established they are often in the best position to engage in fact-finding and to resolve any questions that may arise with regard to the respective obligations of the watercourse States concerned."[37] The use of joint organizations in the resolution of technical matters on international watercourses has been a well observed practice for some time in agreements between States.[38] "The

35 *Treaty Relating to Boundary Waters, and Questions Arising Between the United States and Canada, Great Britain and United States*, 11 January 1909, UKTS 1910 No 23, arts VIII,IX,X (*Boundary Waters Treaty*).

36 Stephen C. McCaffrey, "Sixth report on the law of the non-navigational uses of international watercourses" (UN Doc A/CN.4/427 and Add.1) in *Yearbook of the International Law Commission 1990*, vol 2, part 1 (1993) 41 at 78 (UN Doc A/CN.4/SER.A/1990/Add.1 (Part 1)); a similar passage appears in Stephen C. McCaffrey, *The Law of International Watercourses*, 3rd ed (Oxford University Press, 2019) at 575.

37 Stephen C. McCaffrey, "Sixth report on the law of the non-navigational uses of international watercourses" (UN Doc A/CN.4/427 and Add.1) in *Yearbook of the International Law Commission 1990*, vol 2, part 1 (1993) 41 at 66 para 41 (UN Doc A/CN.4/SER.A/1990/Add.1 (Part 1)).

38 Some examples include: *The Indus Waters Treaty 1960 (with annexes)*, 19 September 1960, 419 UNTS 125, (*Indus Waters Treaty*); *Agreement Concerning the Frontier Between Germany and Belgium*, Belgium and Germany, 7 November 1929, 121 LNTS 329; *Convention to regulate the hydroelectric development of the international sections of the river Douro and its tributaries (with additional protocol), Spain and Portugal, 16 July 1964, 1288 UNTS 191*; *Treaty Concerning the Integrated Development of the Mahakali River including Sarada Barrage, Tanakpur Barrage and Pancheshwar Project*, India and Nepal, 12 February 1996, 36 ILM 531; *Treaty between the Kingdom of the Netherlands and the Federal Republic of Germany concerning the course of the common frontier, the boundary waters, real property situated near the frontier, traffic crossing the frontier on land and via inland waters, and other frontier questions*, 8 April 1960, 508 UNTS 148 (*Frontier Treaty*); *Treaty on the Lesotho Highlands Water Project between the Government of the Kingdom of Lesotho and the Government of the Republic of South Africa*, 24 October 1986, https://www.fao.org/faolex/results/details/en/c/LEX-FAOC015909/, (*Treaty on the Lesotho Highlands Water Project*); *Agreement with Final Protocol Regulating the Withdrawal of Water from Lake Constance*, 30 April 1966, 620 UNTS 191; *Agreement concerning the utilization of the rapids of the Uruguay River in the Salto Grande area*, Argentina and Uruguay, 30 December 1946, 671 UNTS 17; *Treaty Relating to Boundary Waters, and Questions Arising Between the United States and Canada, Great Britain and United States*, 11 January 1909, UKTS 1910 No 23, (*Boundary Waters Treaty*).

present tendency is an increased reliance on various institutional bodies, such as joint river commissions, as a main forum where potential conflicts over water can be considered and 'disarmed' without being elevated to a formal diplomatic level."[39] The Special Rapporteur to the Institut de Droit International (IDI)/Institute of International Law (IIL) ('IDI/IIL'), L. von Bar, observed in 1911 that it was a common practice of States to utilize joint commissions for technical issues.[40] In fact, L. von Bar recommended the use of joint organisations to help parties reach decisions in regard to international watercourses,[41] a recommendation that was echoed in the IDI/IIL's 1961 *Salzburg Resolution*. "It is recommended that States interested in particular hydrographic basins investigate the desirability of creating common organs for establishing plans of utilization designed to facilitate their economic development as well as to prevent and settle disputes which might arise."[42] The ILA in their seminal *Helsinki Rules* embraced the utility of joint bodies in preparing technical studies and the

---

39 Sergei Vinogradov, Patricia Wouters and Patricia Jones, *Transforming Potential Conflict into Cooperation Potential: The Role of International Water Law* (UNESCO-IHP, PCCP, 2003) at 73.

40 "Or comme actuellement l'usage des commissions communes dans les questions de technique n'est pas rare, comme il y a un très grand nombre de traités d'arbitrage et que la question de l'exploitation d'un cours d'eau n'implique pas, en général, une question d'honneur ou d'intérêts vitaux." L. von Bar, "Deuxième rapport de M. L. von Bar, rapporteur, et contre-propositions de Mr Kaufmann" in *Annuaire de L'Institut de Droit International 1911*, vol 24 (1911) 168 at 172.

41 "Mais, comme il semble impossible de circonscrire avec plus de détails les droits et les devoirs des Etats intéressés, les règles proposées n'étant que des indications pouvant conduire à une décision juste et équitable sur les cas qui se produisent en fait, j'ai, dans le numéro 4, recommandé aux Etats d'instituer de commun accord des Commissions permanentes qui, dans chaque cas éventuel, prononceraient leur décision ou tout au moins exprimeraient leur avis, ainsi que le stipule un traité conclu récemment entre les Etats-Unis de l'Amérique et le Canada, traité qui pourtant ne vise que des cours d'eau *séparant* les deux territoires. Naturellement, en l'absence d'accord, la question devrait être tranchée par voie d'arbitrage." L. von Bar, "Deuxième rapport de M. L. von Bar, rapporteur, et contre-propositions de Mr Kaufmann" in *Annuaire de L'Institut de Droit International 1911*, vol 24 (1911) 168 at 170; "But, as it seems impossible to circumscribe in more detail the rights and duties of the States concerned, the proposed rules being only indications which can lead to a just and equitable decision on the cases which occur in fact, I have, in number 4, recommended to the States to set up by mutual agreement Permanent Commissions which, in each possible case, would pronounce their decision or at least express their opinion, as stipulated in a treaty recently concluded between the United States of America and Canada, a treaty which however only covers watercourses separating the two territories. Naturally, in the absence of an agreement, the matter would have to/should be decided by arbitration." [translated by Author].

42 L'Institut de Droit International/Institute of International Law, "*Utilization of Non-Maritime International Waters (Except for Navigation)*" ('*Salzburg Resolution*') in *Annuaire de L'Institut de Droit International*, vol 40 (1961) 381, art 9 at 384.

provision of recommendations on the uses of an international watercourses.[43] The *UN Watercourses Convention*, discussed above,[44] uses a joint fact-finding mechanism for 'Technical Level' resolution of disputes on international watercourses.[45] The UN Handbook on the Peaceful Settlement of Disputes observes that "[i]t should be noted that disputes relating to international waterways are often dealt with in the framework of standing joint commissions established by treaties."[46] Joint commissions "may obviously possess expertise, knowledge or a more detached and impartial approach to the dispute and thus be able to assist the parties in many respects."[47]

One famous example of a joint organization which serves a 'Technical Level' dispute resolution function on an international watercourse can be found in Article VIII of the *Indus Waters Treaty* of 1960 between India and Pakistan[48] which calls for the two countries to establish a "Permanent Indus Commission",[49] which will meet "regularly at least once a year"[50] and make yearly reports to the two governments on the work of the Commission.[51] Under the treaty the "Permanent Indus Commission" is comprised of two commissioners[52] whose qualifications reflect the technical expertise of the

43 "In international practice highly successful use has been made of joint bodies in connection with the preparation of technical studies and recommendations on the exploitation of a river or river system." The International Law Association, "*Helsinki Rules on the Uses of the Waters of International Rivers*" ('*Helsinki Rules*') in *Report of the Fifty-Second Conference of the International Law Association Held at Helsinki, August 14–20, 1966*, vol 52 (1967) 484, comment (a) to art XXXI at 524.

44 *Convention on the Law of Non-Navigational Uses of International Watercourses*, 21 May 1997, 2999 UNTS 77, 36 ILM 700 (*Watercourses Convention*) at 136–138 art 33 (entered into force 17 August 2014).

45 Stephen C. McCaffrey, "Sixth report on the law of the non-navigational uses of international watercourses" (UN Doc A/CN.4/427 and Add.1) in *Yearbook of the International Law Commission 1990*, vol 2, part 1 (1993) 41 at 68 para 51 (UN Doc A/CN.4/SER.A/1990/Add.1 (Part 1)).

46 United Nations, *Handbook on the Peaceful Settlement of Disputes* (UN, 1992) at 13 [footnote omitted].

47 Jens Evensen, "First report on the law of the non-navigational uses of international watercourses" (UN Doc A/CN.4/367) in *Yearbook of the International Law Commission 1983*, vol 2, part 1 (1985) 155 at 190 (UN Doc A/CN.4/SER.A/1983/Add.1 (Part 1)).

48 The International Bank for Reconstruction and Development is also a named party to the treaty. *The Indus Waters Treaty 1960 (with annexes)*, 19 September 1960, 419 UNTS 125, (*Indus Waters Treaty*).

49 *The Indus Waters Treaty 1960 (with annexes)*, 19 September 1960, 419 UNTS 125, art VIII (*Indus Waters Treaty*).

50 *Ibid* art VIII (5) (*Indus Waters Treaty*).

51 *Ibid* art VIII (8) (*Indus Waters Treaty*).

52 *Ibid* art VIII (3) (*Indus Waters Treaty*).

"Permanent Indus Commission". Article VIII states that Commissioners should ordinarily be "high-ranking engineer[s] competent in the field of hydrology and water-use."[53] India and Pakistan will each appoint a commissioner who will "be the representative of his Government for all matters arising out of this Treaty, and will serve as the regular channel of communication on all matters relating to the implementation of the Treaty [...]."[54] We can see precursors to this use of technical experts in the domestic legislation of India, under the *Government of India Act*, 1935, the Governor-General was empowered to "appoint a Commission consisting of such persons having special knowledge and experience in irrigation, engineering, administration, finance or law, as he thinks fit, and request that Commission to investigate in accordance with such instructions as he may give to them [...]"[55] regarding complaints of interference with water supplies from natural sources from other provinces or Federated States of India.[56] Under this act a "Commission so appointed shall investigate the matters referred to them and present to the Governor-General a report setting out the facts as found by them and making such recommendations as they think proper."[57]

McCaffrey in his Sixth report to the ILC cites the IJC between Canada and the United States of America, established under the 1909 *Boundary Waters Treaty*, as a particularly successful example demonstrating the usefulness of joint institutions to assist watercourse States in resolving questions regarding international watercourses.[58] As a particular example he cites the proposed coal mine at Cabin Creek by Sage Creek Coal Limited in the Canadian Province of British Columbia,[59] which the IJC was asked to examine in regard to the water quality and quantity implications for the transboundary Flathead

---

53 *Ibid* art VIII (1) (*Indus Waters Treaty*).

54 *Ibid.*

55 *Government of India Act*, 1935 (UK), 26 Geo V, c 2, s 131(1).

56 *Ibid* at s 130.

57 *Ibid* s at 131(2).

58 Stephen C. McCaffrey, "Sixth report on the law of the non-navigational uses of international watercourses" (UN Doc A/CN.4/427 and Add.1) in *Yearbook of the International Law Commission 1990*, vol 2, part 1 (1993) 41 at 70 para 59 (UN Doc A/CN.4/SER.A/1990/Add.1 (Part 1)); See also Patricia K. Wouters, "Allocation of the Non-Navigational Uses of International Watercourses: Efforts at Codification and the Experience of Canada and the United States" (1992) 30 Canadian Yearbook of International Law/Annuaire Canadien de Droit International 43 at 76–78.

59 Stephen C. McCaffrey, "Sixth report on the law of the non-navigational uses of international watercourses" (UN Doc A/CN.4/427 and Add.1) in *Yearbook of the International Law Commission 1990*, vol 2, part 1 (1993) 41 at 70 para 60 (UN Doc A/CN.4/SER.A/1990/Add.1 (Part 1)).

River.[60] The IJC established the Flathead River International Study Board, which comprised various experts, to undertake a technical assessment of the proposed mine at Cabin Creek.[61] The reports and recommendations produced by this Study Board[62] formed an important basis for the deliberations of the IJC on this matter.[63] These reports provided a technical foundation for the IJC's ultimate recommendations,[64] among which was the recommendation to not approve the project as presented.[65] Despite its widespread acceptance as an example of a successful application of a facts-based resolution of a potential international watercourse dispute by a competent joint body, it is important to note that "[t]he relationship between British Columbia and the IJC has been contentious since the [Cabin] Creek Coal Reference."[66]

One interesting example of a joint organization which could, at its discretion, form additional "sub-commissions for individual boundary waters if the need therefore arises"[67] can be found in the Commission created under

60 International Joint Commission, *Impacts of a Proposed Coal Mine in the Flathead River Basin*, (December 1988) Appendix A at 13–16, online: <https://www.ijc.org/en/impacts-proposed-coal-mine-flathead-river-basin> (accessed 8 May 2025).

61 *Ibid* at Appendix B at 19.

62 "The Cabin Creek Case is rather unusual [...], the report is more than a compilation of non-biased facts: it also recommends actions that the governments may wish to take." Keith W. Muckleston, *International Management in the Columbia River System* (UNESCO-IHP, PCCP Series, 2003) at 27; *The report of the Flathead River International Study Board Summary and Conclusions can be found at* International Joint Commission, *Impacts of a Proposed Coal Mine in the Flathead River Basin*, (December 1988) Appendix B at 17–26, online: <https://www.ijc.org/en/impacts-proposed-coal-mine-flathead-river-basin> (accessed 8 May 2025).

63 International Joint Commission, *Impacts of a Proposed Coal Mine in the Flathead River Basin*, (December 1988) at 3–4, online: <https://www.ijc.org/en/impacts-proposed-coal-mine-flathead-river-basin> (accessed 8 May 2025); "The Sage Creek Coal Reference process was a creative, science-based process in which one layer of data was used to build the next layer of information until all potential impacts could be assessed." Richard Moy and Jonathan O'Riordan, "The International Joint Commission's Unique and Colourful Role in Three Projects in the Pacific Northwest" in Daniel Macfarlane and Murray Clemen, eds, *The First Century of the International Joint Commission* (University of Calgary Press, 2020) 239 at 274.

64 International Joint Commission, *Impacts of a Proposed Coal Mine in the Flathead River Basin*, (December 1988) at 5,6, online: <https://www.ijc.org/en/impacts-proposed-coal-mine-flathead-river-basin> (accessed 8 May 2025).

65 *Ibid* at 11.

66 Richard Moy and Jonathan O'Riordan, "The International Joint Commission's Unique and Colourful Role in Three Projects in the Pacific Northwest" in Daniel Macfarlane and Murray Clemen, eds, *The First Century of the International Joint Commission* (University of Calgary Press, 2020) 239 at 274.

67 *Treaty between the Kingdom of the Netherlands and the Federal Republic of Germany concerning the course of the common frontier, the boundary waters, real property situated near*

the *Treaty between the Kingdom of the Netherlands and the Federal Republic of Germany concerning the course of the common frontier, the boundary waters, real property situated near the frontier, traffic crossing the frontier on land and via inland waters, and other frontier questions* (*Frontier Treaty*). The membership of these "sub-commissions" are to be appointed on equal basis between the riparian States and "shall include representatives of local authorities and corporations."[68]

1.1.3 Permanent or Ad Hoc

'Technical Level' mechanisms can be *ad hoc* or permanent. For instance, the *Pact of Bogotà* contains provisions for the formation of an *Ad Hoc* Commission of Investigation and Conciliation[69] to "clarify the points in dispute between the parties and to endeavor to bring about an agreement between them upon mutually acceptable terms. The Commission shall institute such investigations of the facts involved in the controversy as it may deem necessary for the purpose of proposing acceptable bases of settlement."[70] In the Kasikili/Sedudu Island dispute between Namibia and Botswana the two governments empowered an *Ad Hoc* body consisting of technical experts to settle a boundary dispute along an international watercourse. In articulating the terms of reference for this "Joint Team of Technical Experts" (the "JTTE") the two countries issued a "Memorandum of Understanding". Judge Oda, in his separate opinion to the ICJ decision, stated

> The 'Memorandum of Understanding' states in its Preamble that a dispute exists relative to the *boundary* between Botswana and Namibia, and also refers to the desire of both countries to 'settl[e] such *dispute* by peaceful means in accordance with the principles of both the Charter of the United Nations and the Charter of the Organisation of African Unity' (emphasis added). The 'Memorandum of Understanding' sets up a JTTE, consisting of three *technical experts* from each country 'to determine the *boundary* between Botswana and Namibia around Kasikili/ Sedudu Island in accordance with the [1890] Anglo-German Treaty' (emphasis

---

the frontier, traffic crossing the frontier on land and via inland waters, and other frontier questions, 8 April 1960, 508 UNTS 148 arts 68(1) (*Frontier Treaty*).

68 *Ibid* at arts 68(2).

69 *American Treaty* on Pacific Settlement, 30 April 1948, 30 UNTS 55, art XV–XVII, XIX at 88,90 (*Pact of Bogotá*).

70 *Ibid* at art XXII at 92.

> added); in other words to find whether the northern or the southern channel should be regarded as the 'main channel'.[71]

The 1950 Treaty between Austria and Bavaria Concerning the Österreichisch-Bayerische Kraftwerke AG (Austrian Bavarian Hydroelectric Company) article 10 allows for the governments to "call upon an internationally recognized expert to act as a mediator" upon the failure of negotiation to settle a difference between them[72] in regard to the governance of a company established to jointly develop and utilize hydropower on the frontier rivers between them.[73] McCaffrey in his sixth report proposed a series of draft articles which included provisions for the creation of a commission of inquiry if requested by any of the watercourse States concerned. Such a commission was to be created only if there was no other "competent joint organization and the parties are unable to agree upon the establishment of an *ad hoc* expert commission within six months of the initial request for fact-finding."[74]

Some treaty regimes allow for recourse to both permanent and *ad hoc* mechanisms. For example, the "Permanent Indus Commission" under the *Indus Waters Treaty* mentioned above is a permanent body but matters may also be referred to an *ad hoc* "Neutral Expert"[75] for certain prescribed questions.[76]

71 *Case Concerning Kasikili/Sedudu Island* (*Botswana v Namibia*), Separate Opinion of Judge Oda of December 13 1999, [1999] ICJ Rep 1116 at para 15.

72 *Agreement Between the Federal Government of the Republic of Austria and the Free State of Bavaria Concerning the Osterreichisch-Bayerische Kraftwerke AG* (*Austrian Bavarian Hydroelectric Company*), Republic of Austria and Free State of Bavaria, 16 October 1950 in United Nations Legislative Series, *Legislative Texts and Treaty Provisions Concerning the Utilization of International Rivers for Other Purposes than Navigation* (UN Doc No ST/Leg/SER.B/12, 1963) 470 at 472 art 10.

73 *Agreement Between the Federal Government of the Republic of Austria and the Free State of Bavaria Concerning the Osterreichisch-Bayerische Kraftwerke AG* (*Austrian Bavarian Hydroelectric Company*), Republic of Austria and Free State of Bavaria, 16 October 1950 in United Nations Legislative Series, *Legislative Texts and Treaty Provisions Concerning the Utilization of International Rivers for Other Purposes than Navigation* (UN Doc No ST/Leg/SER.B/12, 1963) 470.

74 Stephen C. McCaffrey, "Sixth report on the law of the non-navigational uses of international watercourses" (UN Doc A/CN.4/427 and Add.1) in *Yearbook of the International Law Commission 1990*, vol 2, part 1 (1993) 41 at 77 (UN Doc A/CN.4/SER.A/1990/Add.1 (Part 1)).

75 *The Indus Waters Treaty 1960* (*with annexes*), 19 September 1960, 419 UNTS 125, art IX (2)(a) (*Indus Waters Treaty*).

76 *Ibid* at Annexure F, Part 1 (*Indus Waters Treaty*); The Indus Waters Treaty also allows a "Neutral Expert" to decide themselves if a matter falls within their purview, in the circumstance that the Commission is "unable to agree that any particular difference falls within Part 1 of [Annexure F] [...]." *The Indus Waters Treaty 1960* (*with annexes*), 19 September 1960, 419 UNTS 125, Annexure F, Part 2, 7 (*Indus Waters Treaty*).

The Treaty states that a "Neutral Expert shall be a highly qualified engineer"[77] and shall have the power to issue "final and binding" decisions "on all matters within his competence".[78] Despite frequent meetings of the Permanent Indus Commission, the Baglihar Dam dispute was not settled by the joint-body but rather by a neutral expert under Article IX of the *Indus Waters Treaty*.[79] The *Pact of Bogotá*, while allowing for the formation of an *ad hoc* Commission of Investigation and Conciliation,[80] also allows the parties to use a permanent panel of "American Conciliators" formed under the aegis of the Pan American Union.[81] It has also been suggested that a third party, such as a UN organization or another neutral organization or individual, rather than a standing commission, might appoint a group of experts to resolve disputes in the context of international watercourses.[82]

While *ad hoc* bodies can be quite effective and adaptable to the needs of a particular dispute, standing or permanent bodies possess certain advantages.

> The particular value of standing, rather than *ad hoc*, expert bodies should not be lost sight of, however. Permanent joint commissions can form working relationships over time, build trust, establish effective lines of communication and acquire more perspective and a more detailed knowledge of the characteristics and circumstances of the international watercourse system concerned than is possible in the case of an *ad hoc* body.[83]

Article II, paragraph 7, of the 1911 *Madrid Declaration* recommends the creation of permanent commissions by co-riparian states.[84] Smith observed that

---

77 *The Indus Waters Treaty 1960 (with annexes)*, 19 September 1960, 419 UNTS 125, Annexure F, Part 2, 4 (*Indus Waters Treaty*).

78 *Ibid* at Annexure F, Part 2, 11.

79 *Ibid* art IX (1); Christina Leb, *Cooperation in the Law of Transboundary Water Resources* (Cambridge University Press, 2013) at 193–194.

80 *American Treaty on Pacific Settlement*, 30 April 1948, 30 UNTS 55, art XV–XVII, XIX at 88,90 (*Pact of Bogotá*).

81 *Ibid* at art XVIII at 90.

82 Stephen C. McCaffrey, "Sixth report on the law of the non-navigational uses of international watercourses" (UN Doc A/CN.4/427 and Add.1) in *Yearbook of the International Law Commission 1990*, vol 2, part 1 (1993) 41 at 71 para 68 (UN Doc A/CN.4/SER.A/1990/Add.1 (Part 1)).

83 *Ibid* at 73 para 79.

84 "Il est recommandé d'instituer des Commissions communes et permanentes des États intéressés qui prendront des décisions, ou tout au moins donneront leur avis, lorsqu'il se fera de nouveaux établissements ou des modifications aux établissements existants

where an international watercourse may have frequent questions regarding its proper use, a permanent international commission is desirable.[85] Permanent and Semi-Permanent Bodies can help provide consistency and reliability in dispute resolutions. For instance, although outside the realm of international watercourse law, under the current World Trade Organization (the 'WTO') regime decisions are binding only in relation to the "particular case between the parties to that dispute, nonetheless the Appellate Body has recognized that consistency of jurisprudence is relevant to enhancing the security and predictability to which the dispute settlement system should contribute."[86]

1.2 *Functions of 'Technical Level' Dispute Resolution and Avoidance Mechanisms on International Watercourses*

1.2.1 Scope of Functions

The technical nature of 'Technical Level' dispute resolution mechanisms can also be found in the functions that these mechanisms fulfill. Often these mechanisms are empowered to conduct fact-finding or inquiry and often to make non-binding findings or recommendations. This contrasts with the binding final decisions that many adjudicative mechanisms are empowered to give. Article IX of the *Boundary Waters Treaty* allows "any other questions or matters of difference arising between [the parties] involving the rights, obligations or interests of either in relation to the other [...] shall be referred from time to

---

et qu'il pourrait en résulter quelque conséquence importante pour la partie du cours d'eau située sur le territoire de l'autre État." L'Institut de Droit International/Institute of International Law, "Texte des Résolutions adoptées en ce qui concerne la Règlementation internationale de l'usage des cours d'eau internationaux" in *Annuaire de L'Institut de Droit International 1911*, vol 24 (1911) 365, art II(7) at 367.; "It is recommended that the interested States appoint permanent joint commissions, which shall render decisions, or at least shall give their opinion, when, from the building of new establishments or the making of alterations in existing establishments, serious consequences might result in that part of the stream situated in the territory of the other State." *reprinted in English in* Secretary-General of the UN, "Long-Term Programme of Work, Including: Consideration of Recommendation Concerning Commencing the Work on the Law of Non-Navigational Uses of International Watercourses" (UN Doc A/5409) in *Year Book of the International Law Commission 1974* vol 2 part 2 (1974) 33 at 200 (UN Doc A/CN.4/SER.A/1974/Add.1(Part 2)).

85 H.A. Smith, *The Economic Uses of International Rivers* (P.K. King and Son, 1931). See principles no. 6 and 7.

86 Ruth Mackenzie et al, *The Manual on International Courts and Tribunals*, 2nd ed (Oxford University Press, 2010) at 78. [footnote omitted]; *United States – Final Anti-Dumping Measures on Stainless Steel from Mexico (Complaint by Mexico)*, WTO Doc WT/DS344/AB/R, at paras 160–161 (Appellate Body Report), online: WTO <http://docsonline.wto.org>.

time to the International Joint Commission for examination and report".[87] The Treaty allows for matters to be forwarded to the IJC for "examination and report, whenever either the Government of the United States or the Government of the Dominion of Canada shall request that such questions or matters of difference be so referred."[88] Despite requiring only one party to forward a matter to the IJC for an examination or report, in practice matters are referred by both parties. The technical nature of the "Permanent Indus Commission" can also be seen reflected in its mandate. Amongst its other "purpose[s] and functions" the "Permanent Indus Commission" is charged under the treaty:

> (a) to study and report to the two Governments on any problem relating to the development of the waters of the Rivers which may be jointly referred to the Commission by the two Governments: in the event that a reference is made by one government alone, the Commissioner of the other Government shall obtain the authorization of his Government before he proceeds to act on the reference; (b) to make every effort to settle promptly, in accordance with the provisions of Article IX (1), any questions arising thereunder.[89]

The *Treaty on the Lesotho Highlands Water Project* is another example of 'Technical Level' dispute resolution functions. The "Joint Permanent Technical Commission" is empowered to "conduct an investigation and to present a written report containing its recommendations to both parties"[90] upon request by either party or the entities formed in each State responsible for management under the treaty.[91] The generally non-binding nature of these broad 'Technical Level' functions should, in theory, prove less problematic for States[92] trou-

87 *Treaty Relating to Boundary Waters, and Questions Arising Between the United States and Canada, Great Britain and United States*, 11 January 1909, UKTS 1910 No 23, art IX (*Boundary Waters Treaty*).

88 *Ibid.*

89 *The Indus Waters Treaty 1960 (with annexes)*, 19 September 1960, 419 UNTS 125, art VIII (4) (*Indus Waters Treaty*).

90 *Treaty on the Lesotho Highlands Water Project between the Government of the Kingdom of Lesotho and the Government of the Republic of South Africa*, 24 October 1986, https://www.fao.org/faolex/results/details/en/c/LEX-FAOC015909/, art 16(4) (*Treaty on the Lesotho Highlands Water Project*).

91 *Ibid.*

92 For example: "The [UN Watercourses] Convention's provisions on fact finding should be non-threatening to states [...]. The report of the fact-finding commission envisaged in Article 33 is not binding on the states concerned, but may be of assistance to them in resolving their dispute. As a technical report, it is not likely to be seen as being judgmental,

bled by the loss of sovereign autonomy through compulsory dispute resolution provisions, as discussed above, although this has not always been the case regarding the compulsory fact-finding provisions of the *UN Watercourses Convention*.[93]

Agreements can also limit 'Technical Level' mechanisms to very specific functions. For instance, the *Convention between the Federal Republic of Germany, the French Republic, and the Grand-Duchy of Luxembourg on the subject of Moselle canalization* of 1956[94] had a very limited scope in regard to recourse to 'Technical Level' dispute resolution. Here matters were limited by the nature of the treaty to disputes occurring during the construction of the canal providing for recourse to third party arbitration by a neutral expert if a dispute could not be settled within one month and if the parties agreed.[95]

1.2.2 Power and Autonomy to Fulfill Functions

'Technical Level' dispute resolution mechanisms are often given a considerable degree of autonomy to allow them to pursue their functions. These mechanisms are often empowered with the freedom to flexibly set their own procedure. Representatives are often given diplomatic powers and protections to allow them to fulfill their duties without fear of reprisals by the State parties.[96] This

and could point to solutions not foreseen by the parties, or that they, for domestic political or other reasons, would otherwise have difficulty adopting on their own initiative." Stephen C. McCaffrey, *The Law of International Watercourses*, 3rd ed (Oxford University Press, 2019) at 579.

93 UNGA, 51st Sess, 62nd Mtg, UN Doc A/C.6/51/SR.62 (1997); UNGA, 51st Sess, 99th Plen Mtg, UN Doc A/51/PV.99 (1997).

94 *Convention between the Federal Republic of Germany, the French Republic, and the Grand-Duchy of Luxembourg on the subject of Moselle canalization*, 27 October 1956, 2375 UNTS 3.

95 "If, during the construction of the canal, a dispute cannot be settled within one month and if the parties to the dispute agree to have recourse to an emergency procedure, the dispute shall be submitted to the arbitration of a single expert from a third country, chosen by mutual agreement between the parties. If no expert has been appointed within one month after one of the parties has made known its intention of invoking the emergency procedure, each party may request the President of the International Court of Justice to appoint an expert." *Ibid* at art 60.

96 For some examples see: *Treaty on the Lesotho Highlands Water Project between the Government of the Kingdom of Lesotho and the Government of the Republic of South Africa*, 24 October 1986, https://www.fao.org/faolex/results/details/en/c/LEX-FAOC015909/, art 9 (27) (*Treaty on the Lesotho Highlands Water Project*); *The Indus Waters Treaty 1960 (with annexes)*, 19 September 1960, 419 UNTS 125, art VIII (6) (*Indus Waters Treaty*).

can extend to *ad hoc* experts or bodies such as in the *Indus Waters* Treaty.[97] To further allow these 'Technical Level' mechanisms to perform the functions with which they have been entrusted, these mechanisms or their representatives are often given access to data held by the State parties and are given freedom of access to collect data and to inspect facilities within the territory of the State parties. For example, under the *Treaty on the Lesotho Highlands Water Project* the "Members of the Joint Permanent Technical Commission shall have all the necessary access rights required in the course of the implementation, operation and maintenance of the Project."[98] Another example is found under the *UN Watercourses Convention* Article 33, where the concerned State parties "have the obligation to provide the [Fact-finding] Commission with such information as it may require and, on request, to permit the Commission to have access to their respective territory and to inspect any facilities, plant, equipment, construction or natural feature relevant for the purpose of its inquiry."[99] The Commission created under the *Frontier Treaty* of 1960 between the Netherlands and Germany was authorized to "inspect boundary waters. It shall, through the intermediary of its chairmen, receive from the authorities of both Contracting Parties such information as it may require in the exercise of its powers and the discharge of its functions."[100] These powers and protections allow these 'Technical Level' mechanisms to, in theory, perform their duties with a high degree of autonomy and flexibility, safeguarding to some degree the credibility and reliability of the findings and recommendations of such mechanisms.

97 "Each Government agrees to extend to the Neutral Expert such facilities as he may require for the discharge of his functions." *The Indus Waters Treaty 1960 (with annexes)*, 19 September 1960, 419 UNTS 125, Annexure F, Part 2, 8 (*Indus Waters Treaty*).

98 *Treaty on the Lesotho Highlands Water Project between the Government of the Kingdom of Lesotho and the Government of the Republic of South Africa*, 24 October 1986, https://www.fao.org/faolex/results/details/en/c/LEX-FAOC015909/, art 9 (22) (*Treaty on the Lesotho Highlands Water Project*).

99 *Convention on the Law of Non-Navigational Uses of International Watercourses, 21 May 1997, 2999 UNTS 77, 36 ILM 700* (*Watercourses Convention*) at 137 art 33(7) (*entered into force 17 August 2014*).

100 *Treaty between the Kingdom of the Netherlands and the Federal Republic of Germany concerning the course of the common frontier, the boundary waters, real property situated near the frontier, traffic crossing the frontier on land and via inland waters, and other frontier questions*, 8 April 1960, 508 UNTS 148 arts 66(6) (*Frontier Treaty*).

1.2.3 Management Functions

In some ways it is hard to distinguish between 'Technical Level' management of shared international watercourses and dispute resolution functions. In practice mechanisms can often serve both functions. For example, the "Joint Permanent Technical Commission" created under the *Treaty on the Lesotho Highlands Water Project* has clear dispute resolution functions discussed above.[101] The "Joint Permanent Technical Commission" also has clear managerial functions shown in its supervisory role[102] over the entities empowered to implement the treaty in the territories of the respective States, the "Lesotho Highlands Development Authority" and the "Trans-Caledon Tunnel Authority".[103] Much can be done to resolve or avoid disputes at a 'Technical Level' through the simple operation of joint organizations and in the regular course of shared management of shared international watercourses.[104] The preference for the joint management of a shared basin over adjudication was advocated by the ILA in the *Helsinki Rules* "[t]he great number of variables involved, the possibility of future changes in the condition of the waterway, the necessity of providing for affirmative conduct by the basin States, and the enormous complexity of a river basin make co-operative management of the basin greatly preferable to adjudication of each source of friction between the basin States."[105] Due to the inherent constraints of this work the research has focused on dispute resolution mechanisms in international watercourse agreements rather than management mechanisms. Such management mechanisms have been looked at only insofar as they are expressly implicated by the dispute resolution mechanisms. Regardless, it is clear from this limited viewpoint that there are many areas of crossover between management and dispute resolution functions in international watercourse agreements.

---

101 *Treaty on the Lesotho Highlands Water Project between the Government of the Kingdom of Lesotho and the Government of the Republic of South Africa*, 24 October 1986, https://www.fao.org/faolex/results/details/en/c/LEX-FAOC015909/, art 16(4) (*Treaty on the Lesotho Highlands Water Project*).

102 *Ibid* at art 9.

103 *Ibid* at art 6.

104 Anoulak Kittikhoun and Susanne Schmeier, "Do river basin organizations make a difference in water diplomacy and conflict management" in Anoulak Kittikhoun and Susanne Schmeier, eds, *River Basin Organizations in Water Diplomacy* (Routledge, 2021) 1.

105 The International Law Association, "*Helsinki Rules on the Uses of the Waters of International Rivers*" ('*Helsinki Rules*') in *Report of the Fifty-Second Conference of the International Law Association Held at Helsinki, August 14–20, 1966*, vol 52 (1967) 484, Comment to art XXX at 522–523. The United States Supreme Court has also expressed reservations regarding the use of adjudication to resolve transboundary water disputes between US States in their federal system in *Colorado v Kansas*, 320 US 383, 392 (1943).

The *Agreement to Regulate the Level of the Lake of the Woods* signed between the United States of America and Canada in 1925[106] creates an "International Lake of the Woods Control Board, composed of two engineers, one appointed by the Government of Canada and one by the Government of the United States".[107] This Board, along with a similar "Canadian Lake of the Woods Control Board",[108] are entrusted with the control and management of the Lake of the Woods and are expected to cooperate in an integrated way.[109] If the water level in the lake rises above or below a specified level then "the rate of total discharge of water from the lake shall be subject to the approval of [the International Lake of the Woods Control Board]."[110] Here we see the clear management functions of the "International Lake of the Woods Control Board" but the very structure of this binational joint organization allows the parties to make 'Technical Level' decisions in real time in a cooperative framework, which can help to resolve nascent matters that could form the basis for a dispute between the riparians, thus helping to avoid disputes. In this way this "Board's" managerial and dispute prevention/resolution functions are somewhat blurred. Nevertheless, the *Agreement to Regulate the Level of the Lake of the Woods* provides for disputes among the members of the "International Lake of the Woods Control Board" to be forwarded for final resolution to the IJC between the two countries for a final decision.[111]

1.2.4 Not Dedicated Technical Mechanisms

Some mechanisms while not dedicated watercourse specific technical bodies, can fulfil 'Technical Level' dispute resolution functions. Although not clearly an exclusively technical body, the IJC has a clear technical mandate and is able, through its powers, to essentially conduct fact finding to "examine into and report upon the facts and circumstances of the particular questions and matters referred, together with such conclusions and recommendations as may be

106 *Agreement to Regulate the Level of the Lake of the Woods and Protocol relating thereto*, United States and Canada, 24 February 1925, 43 LNTS 251.

107 *Ibid* at art 3.

108 *Ibid.*

109 *Agreement to Regulate the Level of the Lake of the Woods and Protocol relating thereto*, United States and Canada, 24 February 1925, 43 LNTS 251, Protocol accompanying Convention to Regulate the Level of the Lake of the Woods (4) at 260.

110 *Agreement to Regulate the Level of the Lake of the Woods and Protocol relating thereto*, United States and Canada, 24 February 1925, 43 LNTS 251, art 3.

111 *Ibid* at art 6.

appropriate […]",[112] effectively constituting a technical mechanism in its dispute resolution machinery as part of its advisory powers under Article IX of the *Boundary Waters Treaty*.

The *Agreement between the government of the French Republic and the Spanish government relating to Lake Lanoux* charges the parties to resolve disputes through the procedures in the *Arbitration Treaty* between the two countries of July the 10th, 1929.[113] The *Arbitration Treaty* of July the 10th, 1929 created a "Permanent Conciliation Commission" which serves as a 'Technical Level' dispute resolution mechanism for our purposes.

> The task of the Permanent Conciliation Commission shall be to elucidate questions in dispute, to collect with that object all necessary information by means of enquiry or otherwise, and to endeavour to bring the Parties to an agreement. It may, after the case has been examined, inform the Parties of the terms of settlement which seem suitable to it, and lay down a period within which they are to make known their decision.
>
> At the close of its proceedings the Commission shall draw up a report stating, as the case may be, either that the Parties have come to an agreement and, if necessary, the terms of the agreement, or that it has been impossible to effect a settlement.[114]

This "[Permanent Conciliation Commission], on its side, shall be entitled to request oral explanations from the agents, counsel and experts of the two Parties, as well as from all persons it may think useful to summon with the consent of their Government."[115] This power to question, particularly regarding experts, allows this body to compensate, to some degree, for any inherent lack of technical expertise on its part, allowing this body to perform its functions as a 'Technical Level' dispute resolution mechanism, despite not being a dedicated watercourse technical body.

1.2.5 Technical rather than Political

By focusing on objective scientific and technical criteria a 'Technical Level' of dispute resolution is inherently less politicized. Such a technical, rather than

112 *Treaty Relating to Boundary Waters, and Questions Arising Between the United States and Canada, Great Britain and United States*, 11 January 1909, UKTS 1910 No 23 (*Boundary Waters Treaty*), art IX.

113 *Agreement between the government of the French Republic and the Spanish government relating to Lake Lanoux*, 12 July 1958, 796 UNTS 217, art 7.

114 *Arbitration Treaty*, Spain and France, 10 July 1929, CXLVIII LNTS 369, art 9.

115 *Ibid* at art 13.

political, approach to matters pertaining to international watercourses can allow State parties to take a rational and fact-based approach to the sharing and governance of internationally shared freshwater resources. "The most satisfactory settlement of disputes of this kind is by agreement, the parties adopting the same technical solution of each problem, as if they were a single unified community undivided by political or administrative frontiers [...]"[116] The experience of Canada and the United States can provide examples of State practice regarding the technical rather than political management of matters on international watercourses. "Incidentally, the history of the Columbia River dispute suggests that one of the valuable aspects of a joint commission is that it provides a forum where co-basin states may dispute each other[']s claims vigorously without involving their governments at a high level."[117] McCaffrey observed the value of referring matters initially to such depoliticized fora of experts for "fact-finding, consensus-building, and reporting on technical matters", citing the Flathead River case between Canada and the US as an example that "a consensus as to such questions may be reached more readily by experts than would have been the case had the same questions been taken up initially on the diplomatic level. The report of the expert group may then form the basis of an agreed resolution of the question between the watercourse States involved."[118] McCaffrey also speculated that similar considerations "may also have inspired the framers of the Indus Waters Treaty 1960, which establishes institutions and procedures akin to those provided for in the 1909 [*Boundary Waters Treaty*]."[119]

116 Indus (Rau) Commission, *Report of the Indus (Rau) Commission and Printed Proceedings* 10 (1950) as quoted in The International Law Association, "*Helsinki Rules on the Uses of the Waters of International Rivers*" ('*Helsinki Rules*') in *Report of the Fifty-Second Conference of the International Law Association Held at Helsinki, August 14–20, 1966*, vol 52 (1967) 484, Comment to art XXX at 523.

117 C.B. Bourne, "Mediation, Conciliation and Adjudication in the Settlement of International Drainage Basin Disputes" (1971) 9 Canadian Yearbook of International Law 114, at 122 (footnotes omitted).

118 Stephen C. McCaffrey, "Sixth report on the law of the non-navigational uses of international watercourses" (UN Doc A/CN.4/427 and Add.1) in *Yearbook of the International Law Commission 1990*, vol 2, part 1 (1993) 41 at 70–71 para 62 (UN Doc A/CN.4/SER.A/1990/Add.1 (Part 1)); *A similar passage can be found in* Stephen C. McCaffrey, *The Law of International Watercourses*, 3rd ed (Oxford University Press, 2019) at 577.

119 Stephen C. McCaffrey, "Sixth report on the law of the non-navigational uses of international watercourses" (UN Doc A/CN.4/427 and Add.1) in *Yearbook of the International Law Commission 1990*, vol 2, part 1 (1993) 41 at 70–71 para 62 (UN Doc A/CN.4/SER.A/1990/Add.1 (Part 1)); *A similar passage can be found in* Stephen C. McCaffrey, *The Law of International Watercourses*, 3rd ed (Oxford University Press, 2019) at 577.

1.2.6 Overlapping Functions

As already discussed, dispute resolution mechanisms often will overlap in their functions. It is possible to have dispute resolution mechanisms that integrate 'Technical Level' dispute resolution with adjudicative or diplomatic 'Levels' or functions. For example, under a 1929 treaty concerning their mutual frontier Germany and Belgium created a "Joint Administrative Commission composed of four members, each country appointing one representative from the Ministry of Foreign affairs and one representative from the competent Department"[120] thus combining both diplomatic and technical capacities in a single joint body.[121] Under the *Convention to regulate the hydroelectric development of the international sections of the river Douro and its tributaries*, signed in 1964 between Spain and Portugal,[122] the "Commission", while not exclusively a technical body, is entrusted to "monitor the exercise of the rights recognized bilaterally and to solve the judicial or technical problems to which such rights may give rise.".[123] The IJC between Canada and the United States is also an example of these overlapping functions as the "Contracting Parties vested a joint (technical) mechanism with quasi-judicial functions."[124] Some procedures for the resolution of disputes on international watercourses "such as fact-finding also concern implementation of the articles [...] and avoidance of disputes."[125] It is therefore important to remember that many of the procedures discussed in this work may have other dimensions and applications outside dispute resolution, "It is only when questions have not been resolved in earlier stages of the process that the proposed procedures for the settlement of disputes become applicable."[126]

120 *Agreement Concerning the Frontier Between Germany and Belgium*, Belgium and Germany, 7 November 1929, 121 LNTS 329 at 379 art 94.

121 Stephen M. Schwebel, "Third report on the law of the non-navigational uses of international watercourses" (UN Doc A/CN.4/348) in *Year Book of the International Law Commission 1982 vol 2 part 1 (1984)* 65 at 183 para 479 (UN Doc A/CN.4/SER.A/1982/Add.1(Part 1)).

122 *Convention to regulate the hydroelectric development of the international sections of the river Douro and its tributaries (with additional protocol), Spain and Portugal, 16 July 1964, 1288 UNTS 191.*

123 *Ibid* at art 14.

124 Christina Leb, *Cooperation in the Law of Transboundary Water Resources* (Cambridge University Press, 2013) at 195 [footnotes omitted].

125 Stephen C. McCaffrey, "Sixth report on the law of the non-navigational uses of international watercourses" (UN Doc A/CN.4/427 and Add.1) in *Yearbook of the International Law Commission 1990*, vol 2, part 1 (1993) 41 at 71 para 67 (UN Doc A/CN.4/SER.A/1990/Add.1 (Part 1)).

126 *Ibid* at 66 para 43.

2 Why Are 'Technical Level' Mechanisms Important or Useful in the Law of the Non-navigational Uses of International Watercourses?

2.1 *Increasing Technical Nature of International Watercourse Disputes*

Disputes on international watercourses are of a rather technical nature and this reality is becoming more pronounced. "[T]he nature of disputes over water is changing and, in particular, they tend to have a more complex scientific character."[127] 'Technical Steps' that empower experts to articulate the factual basis of a dispute and potentially resolve such disputes should become increasingly important aspects of the dispute resolution process on international watercourses. The importance of technical expertise is being embraced at other 'Steps' as well. Laurence Boisson de Chazournes states that, due to the increasingly technical nature of disputes on international watercourses, adjudicative procedures will have to respond to this increased complexity. "For example, in the assessment of environmental harm or the calculation of damages, the need to resort to experts may become more compelling."[128] Scientific and technical issues are closely linked to the outcome of adjudication of disputes on international watercourses.[129] Philippe Sands provides useful guidance on the important role of experts, especially those familiar with the particular water body, in the context of international litigation.

> [I]t is important for a party to retain a team of experts that is balanced, involving locals and outsiders, nationals and non-nationals, with a view to establishing credibility and authority with the judges. You need expertise from individuals who are familiar with the particular body of water, and utilizing 'outsiders' alone risks missing the possibility of local expertise being brought to bear. Ideally, the expert team would comprise those who have first-hand knowledge of hydrography and biodiversity and the myriad of other issues that arise, and to supplement this with external expertise that can fill gaps and provide a broader comparative context. With the ICJ's new approach, indicating the increased questioning of

---

127 Laurence Boisson de Chazournes, "The Settlement of Disputes through Judicial Means (Article 33(10) and Annex on Arbitratin)" in Laurence Boisson de Chazournes et al, eds, *The UN Convention on the Law of the Non-Navigational Uses of International Watercourses: A Commentary* (Oxford University Press, 2018) 364 at 378.

128 *Ibid.*

129 Philippe Sands Q.C., "Water and international law: science and evidence in international litigation" (2010) 22 Environmental Law & Management 151, at 161.

experts by way of examination and cross-examination, the choice of experts will become all the more important.[130]

2.2 *Technical Complexity Can Pose Problems at Other 'Steps'*

The role of technical expertise in international watercourse disputes is being increasingly understood, although, at the same time the scientific and technical complexity of these disputes are posing unique challenges to adjudicative bodies attempting to resolve them.[131] Often international courts or tribunals are composed of legal experts with backgrounds in different legal and cultural traditions who may treat litigation in general and technical and scientific expert evidence in particular in very different ways.[132] These adjudicative bodies are often not technically specialized bodies tailored to technical and scientific matters but rather bodies comprised primarily of legal or diplomatic experts. These international judges may need to assess often conflicting scientific or expert evidence in a rather short period of time, despite not having particular training in the area themselves.[133] "[E]rrors in the appreciation or determination of facts can substantially undermine the credibility of the Court, and discourage parties to disputes involving scientific and technological issues from turning to the Court."[134] International courts were generally designed to deal with questions of law not necessarily complex technical or scientific factual determinations. "As a result, in contrast with many domestic legal systems, complex rules relating to the production and use of evidence were not foreseen. The rules on evidence before the ICJ have been broadly drafted…."[135]

International adjudicative bodies do have some tools to address such technical issues. Some of the tools available under UNCLOS have been discussed

---

130 *Ibid.*

131 *Ibid* at 151–152; Alan Boyle, "Environmental Dispute Settlement" (last updated 2009) at paras 9–10, online: *Max Planck Encyclopedias of International Law* <https://opil.ouplaw.com/home/mpil>.

132 Philippe Sands Q.C., "Water and international law: science and evidence in international litigation" (2010) 22 Environmental Law & Management 151, at 151–152; Alan Boyle, "Environmental Dispute Settlement" (last updated 2009) at para 9, online: *Max Planck Encyclopedias of International Law* <https://opil.ouplaw.com/home/mpil>.

133 Philippe Sands Q.C., "Water and international law: science and evidence in international litigation" (2010) 22 Environmental Law & Management 151, at 161.

134 *Case Concerning Pulp Mills on the River Uruguay* (*Argentina v Uruguay*), Declaration of Judge Yusef of April 20 2010, [2010] ICJ Rep 216 at para 13.

135 Philippe Sands Q.C., "Water and international law: science and evidence in international litigation" (2010) 22 Environmental Law & Management 151, at 153.

above, such as the use of specialized arbitral tribunals[136] and experts[137] to deal with specific technical matters. The ICJ, for instance, may make use of technical experts to provide assistance to the court in certain circumstances, and while these tools[138] have not been widely used they provide a promising avenue for addressing matters of technical and scientific complexity.[139] "The rationale behind the provisions on enquiry and the seeking of an expert opinion in the Statute and in the Rules of Court is to allow the Court to obtain the necessary assistance and support in acquiring such full knowledge of the facts."[140] In fact the ICJ has previously invoked its power to utilize independent experts pursuant to Article 50 of its Statute[141] in the *Corfu Channel* case[142] and the *Delimitation of the Maritime Boundary in the Gulf of Maine Area* case.[143] Some of the judges in the *Pulp Mills* case felt that the Court should have called its

---

136 *United Nations Convention on the Law of the Sea*, 10 December 1982, 1833 UNTS 397 annex VIII, art 1, 5.

137 *Ibid* at art 289, annexes VII, VIII.

138 For the options of the Court under its own Statute (Article 50) and Rules (Article 62, 64(b), 65, 67) see the discussion of Judges Al-Khasawneh and Simma. *Case Concerning Pulp Mills on the River Uruguay* (*Argentina v Uruguay*), Joint Dissenting Opinion of Judges Al-Khasawneh and Simma of April 20 2010, [2010] ICJ Rep 108 at paras 7–10; "The Court is therefore endowed with considerable discretion, and two well-defined procedures under its Statute and Rules, to have recourse to outside sources of expertise in handling complex scientific or technical disputes." *Case Concerning Pulp Mills on the River Uruguay* (*Argentina v Uruguay*), Joint Dissenting Opinion of Judges Al-Khasawneh and Simma of April 20 2010, [2010] ICJ Rep 108 at para 8; For a further discussion of the powers available to the ICJ to deal with the production and examination of evidence which is applicable to the Court's treatment of evidence of a technical nature see Philippe Sands Q.C., "Water and international law: science and evidence in international litigation" (2010) 22 Environmental Law & Management 151, at 153.

139 "[T]he point we wish to make is simply that the Court, when handling a dispute with complex scientific or technical aspects (which will become all the more common as the world will be faced with more environmental or other challenges), should more readily avail itself of the tools available to it under its constitutive instrument in order properly to assess the evidence placed before it." *Case Concerning Pulp Mills on the River Uruguay* (*Argentina v Uruguay*), Joint Dissenting Opinion of Judges Al-Khasawneh and Simma of April 20 2010, [2010] ICJ Rep 108 at para 9.

140 *Case Concerning Pulp Mills on the River Uruguay* (*Argentina v Uruguay*), Declaration of Judge Yusef of April 20 2010, [2010] ICJ Rep 216 at para 5.

141 *Case Concerning Pulp Mills on the River Uruguay* (*Argentina v Uruguay*), Joint Dissenting Opinion of Judges Al-Khasawneh and Simma of April 20 2010, [2010] ICJ Rep 108 at para 10.

142 *Corfu Channel case* (*United Kingdom v Albania*), Order of December 17 1948, [1948] ICJ Rep 124.

143 *Delimitation of the Maritime Boundary in the Gulf of Maine Area* (*Canada v United States of America*), Appointment of Expert, Order of March 30 1984, [1984] ICJ Rep 165.

own independent witnesses under Article 50 of the Court's Statute.[144] Despite these tools the limitations of adjudicative bodies in both time and technical expertise[145] mean that technical and scientific material and evidence is often best presented to adjudicative bodies in a concise and focused manner as there "is a limit to how much technical material can be digested at one sitting."[146]

In this author's experience courts often chart a middle ground between the positions of the parties. Philippe Sands seems to have shared this experience on the *Gabčíkovo-Nagymaros Project* (*Hungary v Slovakia*) case before the ICJ: "The Court seems to have side-stepped the scientific and environmental complexities … In the end, the Court cut the cake down the middle … the case seemed to indicate that the international legal system as currently structured through its courts may not be ideally equipped to adjudicate between two sets of well-put but competing scientific arguments."[147] The ICJ's decision in the *Gabčíkovo-Nagymaros Project* case could seem conspicuous for "the apparent lack of impact of the huge volume of scientific evidence put forward by both parties. After four years of arguments, thousands of pages of written pleadings, at least 20 scientists on both sides and countless hours preparing scientific arguments, what did the ICJ have to say on the subject of the scientific evidence? Rather little."[148] In that case the Court stated it was not "necessary" to assess the scientific merits of the arguments made by the parties.[149]

144 *Case Concerning Pulp Mills on the River Uruguay* (*Argentina v Uruguay*), Joint Dissenting Opinion of Judges Al-Khasawneh and Simma of April 20 2010, [2010] ICJ Rep 108 at para 10;rg *Case Concerning Pulp Mills on the River Uruguay* (*Argentina v Uruguay*), Declaration of Judge Yusef of April 20 2010, [2010] ICJ Rep 216; *Case Concerning Pulp Mills on the River Uruguay* (*Argentina v Uruguay*), Dissenting Opinion of Judge *ad hoc* Vinuesa of April 20 2010, [2010] ICJ Rep 266 at para 95.

145 Some adjudicative bodies, such as specialized arbitral tribunals can utilize a high degree of technical expertise in constituting a tribunal on a specific matter. For example, see the tribunal in the *Indus Waters Kishenganga Arbitration* (*Pakistan v India*) (20 December 2013), Final Award, 31 RIAA 309, (Permanent Court of Arbitration).

146 Philippe Sands Q.C., "Water and international law: science and evidence in international litigation" (2010) 22 Environmental Law & Management 151, at 161.

147 *Ibid* at 155. Philippe Sands Q.C. is reflecting here on the Court's decision in *Gabčíkovo-Nagymaros Project* (*Hungary v Slovakia*), Judgment of September 25 1997, [1997] ICJ Rep 7.

148 Philippe Sands Q.C., "Water and international law: science and evidence in international litigation" (2010) 22 Environmental Law & Management 151, at 155.

149 "Both Parties have placed on record an impressive amount of scientific material aimed at reinforcing their respective arguments. The Court has given most careful attention to this material, in which the Parties have developed their opposing views as to the ecological consequences of the Project. It concludes, however, that […] it is not necessary in order to respond to the questions put to it in the Special Agreement for it to determine which of those points of view is scientifically better founded." *Gabčíkovo-Nagymaros Project* (*Hungary v Slovakia*), Judgment of September 25 1997, [1997] ICJ Rep 7 at para 54.

In their joint dissenting opinion of April 20th 2010, appended to the judgment of the *Pulp Mills on the River Uruguay* case, judges Al-Khasawneh and Simma expressed reservations regarding the ICJ's handling of expert evidence in such a technical matter. "The exceptionally fact-intensive case before us is unlike most cases submitted to the Court and raises serious questions as to the role that scientific evidence can play in an international judicial institution. The traditional methods of evaluating evidence are deficient in assessing the relevance of such complex, technical and scientific facts".[150] This failure to adapt to the more technical scientific nature of this dispute comes in what judges Al-Khasawneh and Simma call a "case on international environmental law of an exemplary nature – a 'textbook example', so to speak, of alleged trans-frontier pollution – yet, the Court has approached it in a way that will increase doubts in the international legal community whether it, as an institution, is well-placed to tackle complex scientific questions [...]".[151] In fact these judges found that it was not the place for a court of justice to "give scientific assessment of what happened, but to evaluate the claims of parties before it and whether such claims are sufficiently well-founded so as to constitute evidence of a breach of a legal obligation."[152]

Although a 'Diplomatic Level' may be less structured than adjudication, including in the use of technical experts or in the timeline of the procedure, diplomatic dispute resolution mechanisms could also be disadvantaged in dealing with disputes on international watercourses of technical and scientific complexity. Decision makers in a 'Diplomatic Level' may generally be of a more diplomatic background and may lack the technical expertise to assess the factual and technical or scientific matters at hand. These decision makers may also be more committed to entrenched political positions and agendas that may drive these dispute resolution procedures, rather than reaching decisions on a factual and technical basis.

2.3 *Help Establish the Substantive Rights of the Parties*

The factual and technical basis for disputes on international watercourses is of great importance in trying to assess the substantive rights and obligations of State parties to a dispute vis-à-vis each other.[153] The 1966 *Helsinki Rules*

150 *Case Concerning Pulp Mills on the River Uruguay* (*Argentina v Uruguay*), Joint Dissenting Opinion of Judges Al-Khasawneh and Simma of April 20 2010, [2010] ICJ Rep 108 at para 3.

151 *Ibid.*

152 *Ibid* at para 4.

153 Stephen C. McCaffrey, "Sixth report on the law of the non-navigational uses of international watercourses" (UN Doc A/CN.4/427 and Add.1) in *Yearbook of the International Law*

embraced the beneficial impact of technical experts in aiding State parties to a dispute on an international watercourse.[154] Mechanisms that allow parties to objectively ascertain and clarify factual and technical elements of a dispute are significant to the successful resolution of disputes on international watercourses. "[A]s the number and range of international disputes over natural resources – and water in particular – increases, it becomes ever more important to refine clear standards and practises for the presentation, testing and assessment of matters of scientific and technical expertise."[155] Often disputes can simply be resolved at this 'Technical Level', diverting matters away from becoming entrenched diplomatic, political or legal disputes. "If a disagreement is of a purely technical nature, technical experts are better placed to find a pragmatic solution than legal experts, politicians, or public opinion."[156]

2.4 *Establish a Factual Basis for a Resolution*

Ignoring the factual reality of a watercourse dispute is an imprudent approach. McCaffrey, while acting as the Special Rapporteur to the International Law Commission (the 'ILC') on the subject of the law of the non-navigational uses of international watercourses, remarked that the resolution of disputes on international watercourses "often depend on the establishment of facts and the application of science and technology, and these processes can usually be carried out most effectively by experts."[157] If dispute resolution decisions on international watercourses are not adequality based on the factual and technical realities of the basin they risk creating further problems amongst the riparians and proving to be resolutions of poor durability. It is therefore

Commission 1990, vol 2, part 1 (1993) 41 at 66 para 40 (UN Doc A/CN.4/SER.A/1990/Add.1 (Part 1)).

154 "Consultation on a technical level or diplomatic negotiations conducted with the aid of technical personnel, such as hydrographers, economists and engineers, can often have beneficial effects when the rights and interests of States in rivers are at stake." The International Law Association, "*Helsinki Rules on the Uses of the Waters of International Rivers*" ('*Helsinki Rules*') in *Report of the Fifty-Second Conference of the International Law Association Held at Helsinki, August 14–20, 1966*, vol 52 (1967) 484, Comment to art XXX at 522.

155 Philippe Sands Q.C., "Water and international law: science and evidence in international litigation" (2010) 22 Environmental Law & Management 151, at 161.

156 Christina Leb, *Cooperation in the Law of Transboundary Water Resources* (Cambridge University Press, 2013) at 194 [footnotes omitted].

157 Stephen C. McCaffrey, "Sixth report on the law of the non-navigational uses of international watercourses" (UN Doc A/CN.4/427 and Add.1) in *Yearbook of the International Law Commission 1990*, vol 2, part 1 (1993) 41 at 73 para 80 (UN Doc A/CN.4/SER.A/1990/Add.1 (Part 1)).

important to have mechanisms that can help to establish and clarify this factual basis. 'Technical Level' dispute resolution can provide these mechanisms. For instance, the consultative committee under the *Agreement with final Protocol Regulating the Withdrawal of Water from Lake Constance* was tasked with "consideration at the technical level with a view to preparing the way for an agreement."[158] If a dispute cannot be resolved at the 'Technical Level' then at least the factual and technical findings established at this 'Step' can prove useful in providing a basis to resolve the dispute whether through diplomatic or adjudicative means. As Judge Yusef, in the *Pulp Mills* case, discusses the court's use of experts: "experts may assist the Court to develop a finer grasp of the scientific and technical details of factual issues arising in the case, it always remains the ultimate responsibility of the judge to decide on the relevance and significance of those facts to the adjudication of the dispute."[159] In a further example, we can look to the work of the "Engineering Board" established under the auspices of the IJC to research the factual basis for the development of the Columbia River between Canada and the United States. "It was not until the report of the [Engineering] Board was received in March 1959 that it had the essential factual basis for rational discussion of the development of the Columbia River."[160]

2.5 *Less Politicized*

A 'Technical Level' of dispute resolution can benefit from being less politicized by finding clear technical solutions to problems on international watercourses less encumbered by political considerations.[161] This process can lead to better resolutions of disputes, allowing factual certainty while still allowing room for legal disagreements.

> [B]ecause professionally qualified and experienced officers who are dealing on a day-to-day basis with international water resources problems and with their professional counterparts are in the best position to marshal and evaluate the extensive and complex factual data and to weigh the scientific, engineering and management considerations [...]

158 *Agreement with Final Protocol Regulating the Withdrawal of Water from Lake Constance*, 30 April 1966, 620 UNTS 191, art 8(1).

159 *Case Concerning Pulp Mills on the River Uruguay* (*Argentina v Uruguay*), Declaration of Judge Yusef of April 20 2010, [2010] ICJ Rep 216 at para 10, 12.

160 C.B. Bourne, "Mediation, Conciliation and Adjudication in the Settlement of International Drainage Basin Disputes" (1971) 9 Canadian Yearbook of International Law 114, at 121.

161 Stephen C. McCaffrey, *The Law of International Watercourses*, 3rd ed (Oxford University Press, 2019) at 574.

> Moreover, the influence of extraneous considerations, including political considerations where these are unrelated to the problem at hand, can be minimized when substantial decision-making authority is delegated at least in the first instance to the experts directly involved. The need for review of contested technical-level decisions and for ultimate resolution at the higher level should not be overlooked, but every effort should be made to promote the resolution of differences by the provision of competent accommodation machinery at the operating level. In this way, work on international water resources projects or programmes is least likely to be delayed or disrupted and the merits of the matter least likely to be distorted or misconstrued.[162]

Political considerations can nonetheless complicate matters even at a 'Technical Level'. An illustrative example is the Helmand River Delta Commission between Afghanistan and Iran.[163] The Commission was created by agreement between the two governments on September 7, 1950[164] and was charged to provide a recommendation to the two countries on "an engineering basis for mutual accord regarding the apportionment of the waters of the Helmand River".[165] Ultimately this commission's report was not accepted by the parties. This failure may have its roots in a few sources, as Bourne suggests, the long-standing nature of this historical dispute[166] with both parties occupying

162 Report of the Panel of Experts on the Legal and Institutional Aspects of International Water Resources Development, *Management of International Water Resources: Institutional and Legal Aspects, Natural Resources/Water* Series No 1 (UN, 1975) at 144–145 para 457.

163 C.B. Bourne, "Mediation, Conciliation and Adjudication in the Settlement of International Drainage Basin Disputes" (1971) 9 Canadian Yearbook of International Law 114, at 122.

164 Terms of Reference of the Helmand River Delta Commission and an Interpretative Statement Relative Thereto, Afghanistan and Iran, 7 September 1950 in United Nations Legislative Series, *Legislative Texts and Treaty Provisions Concerning the Utilization of International Rivers for Other Purposes than Navigation* (UN Doc No ST/Leg/SER.B/12, 1963) 270 at 270–273.

165 *Ibid* at 270.

166 The dispute had previously been subject to two previously frustrated arbitral awards by Colonel MacMahon (April 10, 1905) and General Goldsmid (August 19, 1872). For the text of these awards see Secretary-General of the UN, "Long-Term Programme of Work, Including: Consideration of Recommendation Concerning Commencing the Work on the Law of Non-Navigational Uses of International Watercourses" (UN Doc A/5409) in *Year Book of the International Law Commission 1974* vol 2 part 2 (1974) 33 at 188–190 (UN Doc A/CN.4/SER.A/1974/Add.1(Part 2)).

embittered positions[167] may have been a significant factor, but also the composition of the Commission itself may have been problematic, "three engineers from three disinterested countries, expert in the management of water resources in arid regions [...] shall serve as individual professional men".[168] This case may "suggest that a permanent joint commission composed of nationals of the co-basin states concerned may be a more effective instrument in reconciling differences."[169] Despite the Commission's undoubted competence from an engineering viewpoint Bourne questions its qualifications to deal with "deepseated political difference".[170]

3 When Should 'Technical Level' Be Applied?

According to State practice and the work of experts in the field[171] "wherever possible, it is advisable to attempt resolution of any differences at the technical level before proceeding to invoke more formal dispute-resolution procedures."[172] In his third report to the International Law Commission (the 'ILC'), Stephen Schwebel, the then Special Rapporteur on the subject of the law of the non-navigational uses of international watercourses, observed that a "review of differences that arise between system States may first be made by experts fully familiar with the situation at issue. Beginning the consideration at the technical level has been recommended".[173] McCaffrey, during his tenure as the special rapporteur on the subject, advanced a similar argument.

> The report of the Panel of Experts on the Legal and Institutional Aspects of International Water Resources Development recommends that differences be resolved at a technical level, whenever possible [...] This same

167 C.B. Bourne, "Mediation, Conciliation and Adjudication in the Settlement of International Drainage Basin Disputes" (1971) 9 Canadian Yearbook of International Law 114, at 122.

168 *Ibid.*

169 *Ibid.*

170 *Ibid* at 122.

171 Stephen C. McCaffrey, "Sixth report on the law of the non-navigational uses of international watercourses" (UN Doc A/CN.4/427 and Add.1) in *Yearbook of the International Law Commission 1990*, vol 2, part 1 (1993) 41 at 66 note 116 (UN Doc A/CN.4/SER.A/1990/Add.1 (Part 1)).

172 *Ibid* at 66 para 41 [footnote omitted]; Stephen C. McCaffrey, *The Law of International Watercourses*, 3rd ed (Oxford University Press, 2019) at 575.

173 Stephen M. Schwebel, "Third report on the law of the non-navigational uses of international watercourses" (UN Doc A/CN.4/348) in *Year Book of the International Law Commission 1982 vol 2 part 1 (1984)* 65 at 182 para 476 (UN Doc A/CN.4/SER.A/1982/Add.1(Part 1)).

> theme – that procedures should be made available for the resolution of disputes at lower levels before they referred to higher governmental authorities – has inspired the Special Rapporteur's recommendations.[174]

The *Treaty Concerning the Integrated Development of the Mahakali River including Sarada Barrage*[175] between Nepal and India creates a "Mahakali River Commission"[176] which is entrusted with technical expert functions[177] such as "provid[ing] expert evaluation of projects and recommendations thereto."[178] This Commission is also empowered to "examine any differences arising between the Parties concerning the interpretation and application of this Treaty."[179] If the recommendations of the Commission are rejected by one of the parties or if the Commission fails to issue recommendations within three months then a dispute will be deemed to have come into existence between the parties and the matter is submitted to arbitration.[180] In the example of the Mahakali River Commission we see that the matter in question will not even be designated as a "dispute" until the 'Technical Level' recommendations of the Commission have been rejected by one of the parties.

A similar feature can be observed in the 1960 Indus Waters Treaty.[181] Article IX is the section of the treaty dealing with the settlement of "differences and disputes" and Article IX (1) states that "[a]ny question which arises between the Parties concerning the interpretation or application of this Treaty shall first be examined by the Commission, which will endeavour to resolve the question by agreement."[182] If this 'Technical Level' joint body cannot reach an agreement on a "question" then "a difference will be deemed to have arisen".[183] If a "difference" falls outside the prescribed requirements laid down

174 Stephen C. McCaffrey, "Sixth report on the law of the non-navigational uses of international watercourses" (UN Doc A/CN.4/427 and Add.1) in *Yearbook of the International Law Commission 1990*, vol 2, part 1 (1993) 41 at 74–75 para 85 (UN Doc A/CN.4/SER.A/1990/Add.1 (Part 1)) [footnotes omitted].

175 *Treaty Concerning the Integrated Development of the Mahakali River including Sarada Barrage, Tanakpur Barrage and Pancheshwar Project*, India and Nepal, 12 February 1996, 36 ILM 531.

176 *Ibid* at art 9.

177 *Ibid* at art 9(3)(a)–(d).

178 *Ibid* at art 9(3)(c).

179 *Ibid* at art 9(3)(e).

180 *Ibid* at art 11.

181 *The Indus Waters Treaty 1960 (with annexes)*, 19 September 1960, 419 UNTS 125 (*Indus Waters Treaty*).

182 *Ibid* at art IX (1).

183 *Ibid* at art IX (2).

in Part I of Annexure F,[184] if a neutral expert appointed to deal with the "difference"[185] deems that the matter should instead be treated as a "dispute", or, if the "Commission" deems a particular matter to be a "dispute",[186] then a "dispute will be deemed to have arisen".[187] In this example we can see the importance of these 'Technical Level' mechanisms in working as gatekeepers to manage matters early in the process as "questions" or "differences". A matter must pass through these "Technical Level" mechanisms before progressing to a "dispute".

3.1 *Form the Factual Basis for Later 'Steps'*

The use of technical and scientific experts early in a dispute on an international watercourse can often prove beneficial. It is of great importance to the resolution of such complex technical and scientific disputes that a strong grasp of the factual and technical realities of the dispute be ascertained early in the process so that the subsequent proceedings can flow from this basis. As Philippe Sands observed in relation to international adjudication: "it is vital to get to grips with the scientific and technical issues at a very early stage in the proceedings and, if at all possible, before the litigation is initiated."[188]

"Professor Myers McDougal has [ ] spoken critically of using courts in this field, saying that they do not have the expertise or the staff to work out the best solutions."[189] It is true that international courts in particular are generally of a decidedly legal expertise and may lack some of the technical expertise appropriate for the matter at hand on an international watercourse. This concern should be lessened in the context of arbitration where a tribunal can be empaneled that possess the relevant technical expertise. Both international arbitral tribunals and courts can avail themselves of technical experts[190] who should be able to address such concerns but it is useful if matters can first pass through a technical 'Step' of dispute resolution where technical matters

184 *Ibid* at art IX (2)(a).

185 *Ibid* at art IX (2)(a).

186 *Ibid* at art IX (2)(b).

187 *Ibid* at art IX (2)(b).

188 Philippe Sands Q.C., "Water and international law: science and evidence in international litigation" (2010) 22 Environmental Law & Management 151, at 161.

189 C.B. Bourne, "Mediation, Conciliation and Adjudication in the Settlement of International Drainage Basin Disputes" (1971) 9 Canadian Yearbook of International Law 114, at 131; citing The International Law Association, "Uses of the Waters of International Rivers" in *Report of the Forty-Eighth Conference of the International Law Association Held at New York, September 1–7, 1958*, vol 48 (1958) 28, at 41–42.

190 Philippe Sands Q.C., "Water and international law: science and evidence in international litigation" (2010) 22 Environmental Law & Management 151.

could be addressed or, at least, identified and clarified for latter assessment by non-specialist adjudicative bodies.

3.2 *Dispute Avoidance and Diversion*

The referral of such disputes to technical experts may often be the most effective manner to resolve such a dispute or to avoid it crystalizing to begin with.[191] "Successful accommodation or early settlement avoids work stoppages, strained relations and, most important, the hardening of the national position that inevitably occurs once a difference emerges as a full-fledged dispute."[192] The use of experts in dispute avoidance is "often a more important objective than settling them."[193] The resolution in the first instance at a 'Technical Level' can be seen reflected in State practice.[194]

In commenting on his proposed draft articles to the ILC, McCaffrey observed that "it is envisaged that the availability to watercourse States of fact-finding machinery will often prevent disputes from arising by eliminating any questions as to the nature of the relevant facts."[195] Bourne described a "hardening of differences into international disputes" as an undesirable outcome.[196] In the draft articles on the non-navigational uses of international watercourses submitted by the ILC to the UN General Assembly, the commentary to the provision on fact-finding states that

> [t]he purpose [...] is to facilitate the resolution of the dispute through the objective knowledge of the facts. The information gathered is intended to permit the States concerned to resolve the dispute in an amicable and expeditious manner and to prevent the dispute from escalating. (Indeed,

191 Stephen C. McCaffrey, "Sixth report on the law of the non-navigational uses of international watercourses" (UN Doc A/CN.4/427 and Add.1) in *Yearbook of the International Law Commission 1990*, vol 2, part 1 (1993) 41 at 69 para 57 (UN Doc A/CN.4/SER.A/1990/Add.1 (Part 1)).

192 Report of the Panel of Experts on the Legal and Institutional Aspects of International Water Resources Development, *Management of International Water Resources: Institutional and Legal Aspects, Natural Resources/Water* Series No 1 (UN, 1975) at 144 para 455.

193 "2188th meeting Friday, 6 July 1990, at 10.05 A.M." in *Yearbook of the International Law Commission 1990 vol 1 (1993)* 287 at 293 para 78 (UN Doc A/CN.4/SER.A/1990).

194 Stephen C. McCaffrey, *The Law of International Watercourses*, 3rd ed (Oxford University Press, 2019) at 575.

195 Stephen C. McCaffrey, "Sixth report on the law of the non-navigational uses of international watercourses" (UN Doc A/CN.4/427 and Add.1) in *Yearbook of the International Law Commission 1990*, vol 2, part 1 (1993) 41 at 76 (UN Doc A/CN.4/SER.A/1990/Add.1 (Part 1)).

196 Stephen M. Schwebel, "Third report on the law of the non-navigational uses of international watercourses" (UN Doc A/CN.4/348) in *Year Book of the International Law Commission 1982 vol 2 part 1 (1984)* 65 at 186 para 498 (UN Doc A/CN.4/SER.A/1982/Add.1(Part 1)).

> it is envisaged that the availability to watercourse States of fact-finding machinery will often prevent disputes from arising by eliminating any questions as to the nature of the relevant facts.)[197]

Stephen M. Schwebel in his third report to the ILC as the special rapporteur on the subject of the non-navigational uses of international watercourses observed that the use of technical level dispute resolution mechanisms early in a process can operate to "forstall the matter's hardening into a formal dispute between the parties ... such a separate forum could be designated to function prior to the traditional 'referral to the Governments', which may mean that the matter will then become a formal dispute."[198]

3.3 *Avoid the Politicization of Disputes*

The politicization of disputes can prove an obstacle to their resolution as the parties may become too entrenched in their respective positions to easily resolve a matter, even where there is a straightforward technical solution. Addressing the matter early on at a 'Technical Level' can help to deal with the matter before it becomes overly politicized.[199]

> The question of the peaceful settlement of disputes was particularly important in the context of the uses of international watercourses. As the needs of populations increased and water resources became ever scarcer, disputes were bound to arise if the issues were not tackled at the technical and professional level. Any attempt to politicize disputes was bound to be counterproductive. Accordingly, the appointment at an early stage in the dispute of joint technical commissions with a mandate to give priority to the optimal management of the watercourse should be encouraged.[200]

---

197 "Report of the Commission to the General Assembly on the work of its forty-sixth session" (UN Doc A/49/10) in *Yearbook of the International Law Commission 1994* vol 2 part 2 (1997) 1 at 134 (UN Doc A/CN.4/SER.A/1994/Add.1 (Part 2)).

198 Stephen M. Schwebel, "Third report on the law of the non-navigational uses of international watercourses" (UN Doc A/CN.4/348) in *Year Book of the International Law Commission 1982 vol 2 part 1 (1984)* 65 at 182–183 para 479 (UN Doc A/CN.4/SER.A/1982/Add.1(Part 1)) [footnotes omitted].

199 Stephen C. McCaffrey, *The Law of International Watercourses*, 3rd ed (Oxford University Press, 2019) at 574.

200 Comment by Mr. Sreenivasa RAO, "2313th Meeting Friday, 29 June 1993, at 10.10 A.M." in *Yearbook of the International Law Commission 1993* vol 1 (1995) 104 at 110 para 40 (UN Doc A/CN.4/SER.A/1993).

Stephen McCaffrey cites the Flathead River case between Canada and the United States as an example of the merits of referring a matter to experts for fact-finding initially, stating that "a consensus as to such questions may be reached more readily by experts than would have been the case had the same questions been taken up initially on the diplomatic level."[201]

As discussed above disputes on international watercourses can be particularly time sensitive and costly given the importance of these vital resources and the cost inputs associated with infrastructure on international watercourses. By resolving matters at a 'Technical Level' early in the process certain preventative actions can be taken to minimize damages and notify the State parties to correct the situation early in the process.[202]

4 Technical 'Step' in a 'Stepped Approach' to Disputes in the Law of the Non-navigational Uses of International Watercourses in Practice

Whether as permanent joint organizations or operating in an *ad hoc* capacity, 'Technical Level' dispute resolution mechanisms are of great value to the peaceful settlement of disputes on international watercourses. They should rightly be viewed as a key element in a 'Stepped Approach'. 'Steps' occurring at a 'Diplomatic Level' or an 'Adjudicative Level' may find the increasingly technical nature of international watercourses disputes difficult to deal with without 'Technical Level' support. In utilizing 'Technical Level' mechanisms in conjunction with 'Diplomatic Level' and or 'Adjudicative Level' mechanisms in a 'Stepped Approach' dispute resolution machinery can better address the technical aspect of disputes on international watercourses.

Particularly where 'Technical Level' mechanisms are utilized as an early 'Step' in a 'Stepped Approach' the work of this technical mechanism can help to alleviate pressure on the later 'Steps' by diverting and settling disputes on a technical basis early on, by avoiding the politicization and hardening of disputes, by helping to establish the substantive rights of the parties, and by

---

201 Stephen C. McCaffrey, "Sixth report on the law of the non-navigational uses of international watercourses" (UN Doc A/CN.4/427 and Add.1) in *Yearbook of the International Law Commission 1990*, vol 2, part 1 (1993) 41 at 70–71 para 62 (UN Doc A/CN.4/SER.A/1990/Add.1 (Part 1)); *A similar passage can be found in* Stephen C. McCaffrey, *The Law of International Watercourses*, 3rd ed (Oxford University Press, 2019) at 577.

202 Stephen C. McCaffrey, *The Law of International Watercourses*, 3rd ed (Oxford University Press, 2019) at 575.

establishing a factual basis that may form an important foundation for the resolution of international watercourse disputes at subsequent 'Steps'.

While 'Technical Level' mechanisms were the least utilized in the survey of international agreements conducted for this work their importance cannot be overstated. The increasing technical nature of international watercourse disputes will mean that 'Technical Level' mechanisms will occupy an increasingly important role in the settlement of such disputes. As part of a 'Stepped Approach' 'Technical Level' mechanisms serve an in integral role in supplementing and complementing the functions of more traditional 'Diplomatic Level' and 'Adjudicative Level' mechanisms. In the next section we will explore in greater detail a 'Stepped Approach' to the settlement of international watercourse disputes.

CHAPTER 3

A 'Stepped Approach' to Disputes regarding the Non-navigational Uses of International Watercourses

McCaffrey in his sixth report to the ILC as the special rapporteur on the subject of the non-navigational uses of international watercourses proposed a dispute avoidance and resolution framework that was comprised of "stages", these recommendations can be instructive for our purposes.

> [T]he Special Rapporteur proposes [...] a process for the avoidance and settlement of watercourse disputes that consists of a graduated series of stages. The proposals are based on several propositions: first, that it will often be necessary in this field to rely heavily on technical expertise; secondly, that a non-binding expert report, possibly accompanied with a recommended course of action, will frequently result in resolution of an actual or potential dispute without the need to have recourse to a procedure that results in a binding settlement; and thirdly, that procedures of the latter kind should be resorted to only after attempts to settle differences at the technical level have failed.[1]

We have discussed the resolution of disputes at a 'Technical Level' above and how these mechanisms may be most efficiently utilized in a 'Stepped Approach' early in the process, so that later 'Steps' may be avoided or may rely on the factual and technical foundation laid down by 'Technical Level' mechanisms. In this chapter we will explore what McCaffrey termed a "graduated series of stages"[2] and which we have called a 'Stepped Approach' to disputes on international watercourses. First, we will attempt to articulate and define what is meant by a 'Stepped Approach' by discussing some of its key features. Second, we discuss some of the findings from our broad survey of treaty practice regarding dispute resolution provisions in the law of the non-navigational uses

1 Stephen C. McCaffrey, "Sixth report on the law of the non-navigational uses of international watercourses" (UN Doc A/CN.4/427 and Add.1) in *Yearbook of the International Law Commission 1990*, vol 2, part 1 (1993) 41 at 66 para 42 (UN Doc A/CN.4/SER.A/1990/Add.1 (Part 1)).

2 *Ibid.*

 | DOI:10.1163/9789004736771_006

of international watercourses. Third, we will attempt to show the importance of a 'Stepped Approach' to disputes in regard to the law of the non-navigational uses of international watercourses.

1 What Is a 'Stepped Approach' to Disputes in the Law of the Non-navigational Uses of International Watercourses?

What in fact is meant by a 'Stepped Approach' to the settlement of disputes on international watercourses? The term 'Stepped Approach' has been chosen after a considerable degree of reflection. Other terms have been used, such as: a "stepwise dispute-resolution system",[3] a "staged procedure for the avoidance and resolution of disputes",[4] a "series of stages, or echelons",[5] a "graded dispute resolution mechanism",[6] a "multi-tier dispute resolution system"[7] and, a "phased approach".[8] While these terms generally seem self-explanatory the relatively brief discussions of such dispute resolution procedures in the field of international water law have not clearly defined them.

For our purposes a 'Stepped Approach' to disputes on international watercourses encompasses a dispute resolution system dealing with an international watercourse and composed of a set of graduated, discrete 'Steps', phases, or echelons of limited scope or duration with a relatively clear progression from one 'Step' to another. For the purpose of this work, three or more 'Steps' constituted the threshold for determining a graduated framework of 'Steps' as part of a 'Stepped Approach' and we looked for a distinct technical 'Step', diplomatic

---

3 Stephen C. McCaffrey, *The Law of International Watercourses*, 3rd ed (Oxford University Press, 2019) at 577; the PCA in the *Indus Waters Treaty Arbitration* (*Pakistan v India*) (6 July 2023), Award on the Competence of the Court, PCA Case No. 2023-01 at para 199, (Permanent Court of Arbitration), online: <https://pca-cpa.org/en/cases/284/>. Refers to a "stepwise procedure".

4 Stephen C. McCaffrey, *The Law of International Watercourses*, 3rd ed (Oxford University Press, 2019) at 578–579.

5 Stephen C. McCaffrey, "Sixth report on the law of the non-navigational uses of international watercourses" (UN Doc A/CN.4/427 and Add.1) in *Yearbook of the International Law Commission 1990*, vol 2, part 1 (1993) 41 at 72 para 75 (UN Doc A/CN.4/SER.A/1990/Add.1 (Part 1)).

6 The *Indus Waters Treaty Arbitration* (*Pakistan v India*) (6 July 2023), Award on the Competence of the Court, PCA Case No. 2023-01 at paras 156, 199, 277, (Permanent Court of Arbitration), online: <https://pca-cpa.org/en/cases/284/>. The PCA referring to India's arguments.

7 Makane Moïse Mbengue and Rukmini Das, *Use of Experts in International Freshwater Disputes* (Brill Research Perspectives in International Water Law, 2019) at 9.

8 Sergei Vinogradov, Patricia Wouters and Patricia Jones, *Transforming Potential Conflict into Cooperation Potential: The Role of International Water Law* (UNESCO-IHP, PCCP, 2003) at 63.

'Step', and adjudicative 'Step'. We also looked for at least one compulsory 'Step' and for a binding ultimate 'Step'. In this section we will investigate this system of graduated 'Steps'.

1.1 *A Progressive Series of 'Steps'*

A dispute resolution and avoidance framework consisting of a progressive series of 'Steps', or a 'Stepped Approach' to disputes, is not a new idea to international law. The UN General Assembly has adopted several resolutions that contemplate alternative courses of dispute resolution in circumstances where negotiations fail to produce a settlement.[9] The review of disputes at escalating levels on international watercourses is reflected in State practice as was observed by special rapporteur Stephen Schwebel in his third and final report to the ILC on the subject of the non-navigational uses of international watercourses.[10]

> If a dispute or a disagreement arises, most international watercourse legal regimes tend to gradually elevate it from one level of dispute settlement procedure to another: from using technical experts within a joint institution to diplomatic negotiations and, eventually, to binding resolution by the impartial third party. This approach is consistent with general international practice and was mirrored in the work of the ILA, which in its 1966 Helsinki Rules identified the most appropriate mechanisms and procedures to be employed in resolving disputes over shared water resources.[11]

McCaffrey observes that the *UN Watercourses Convention* articulates a "staged procedure for the avoidance and resolution of disputes"[12] or, as Vinogradov

---

9 United Nations, *Handbook on the Peaceful Settlement of Disputes* (UN, 1992) at 23.

10 "When accommodation is not achieved at the operating level, a review at a higher level must take place. This review can still be by water resources professionals, such as members, or deputies, of the system States' international watercourse commission. Such arrangements are not uncommon in system State practice." Stephen M. Schwebel, "Third report on the law of the non-navigational uses of international watercourses" (UN Doc A/CN.4/348) in *Year Book of the International Law Commission 1982 vol 2 part 1 (1984)* 65 at 182 para 478 (UN Doc A/CN.4/SER.A/1982/Add.1(Part 1)) [footnote omitted].

11 Sergei Vinogradov, Patricia Wouters and Patricia Jones, *Transforming Potential Conflict into Cooperation Potential: The Role of International Water Law* (UNESCO-IHP, PCCP, 2003) at 62–63.

12 Stephen C. McCaffrey, *The Law of International Watercourses*, 3rd ed (Oxford University Press, 2019) at 578–579.

et al termed, a "phased approach".[13] Negotiation between the parties being the initial stage, followed by non-binding third party settlement or an applicable joint body, otherwise the parties may elect to submit their matter to binding arbitration or adjudication by the ICJ. Ultimately, if negotiation or any of the other optional mechanisms prove unable to resolve the matter, the parties are required to submit the matter, at the request of any of the parties, to compulsory but non-binding fact-finding.[14]

The *Indus Waters Treaty* is an excellent example of a 'Stepped Approach' to disputes on international watercourses. As observed by McCaffrey: "Article 9 of the [*Indus Waters Treaty*] is entitled 'Settlement of differences and disputes.' It establishes a stepwise dispute-resolution system, beginning with the lowest level of dispute, questions, and moving through differences, to disputes, the highest level of contention. Each level has its own resolution mechanism."[15] Under the treaty review undertaken as part of this work the *Indus Waters Treaty* satisfied all nine (9) criteria laid out for evaluating a 'Stepped Approach'. The framework of the *Indus Waters Treaty* provided an early model of a 'Stepped Approach' for this work.

The *Boundary Waters Treaty* of 1909 has also been identified as possessing dispute resolution procedures consisting of a series of "stages" or a "multi-tiered approach to conflict resolution".[16] The *Boundary Waters Treaty* creates innovative dispute resolution mechanics for its time by empowering a shared joint body, the IJC, through four (4) distinct forms of jurisdiction "(1) compulsory jurisdiction, (2) advisory jurisdiction, (3) administrative jurisdiction, and (4) arbitral jurisdiction".[17] The IJC's jurisdiction includes its very important advisory functions under its reference powers contained in Article IX of

---

13 Sergei Vinogradov, Patricia Wouters and Patricia Jones, *Transforming Potential Conflict into Cooperation Potential: The Role of International Water Law* (UNESCO-IHP, PCCP, 2003) at 63.

14 *Convention on the Law of Non-Navigational Uses of International Watercourses*, 21 May 1997, 2999 UNTS 77, 36 ILM 700 (*Watercourses Convention*) at 136–138 art 33 (entered into force 17 August 2014).

15 Stephen C. McCaffrey, *The Law of International Watercourses*, 3rd ed (Oxford University Press, 2019) at 577.

16 Sergei Vinogradov, Patricia Wouters and Patricia Jones, *Transforming Potential Conflict into Cooperation Potential: The Role of International Water Law* (UNESCO-IHP, PCCP, 2003) at 64.

17 Nigel Bankes and Barbara Cosens, *Protocols for Adaptive Water Governance: The Future of the Columbia River Treaty* (Munk School of Global Affairs University of Toronto, October 2014) at 37.

the *Boundary Waters Treaty*.[18] These reference powers in many senses may be viewed as an equivalent to the functions that fact-finding inquiries serve under other regimes such as the *UN Watercourses Convention*. By creating four (4) separate jurisdictions for the IJC, disputes can be channelled into different mechanisms based on the needs of the particular dispute and the desires of the parties. Despite these progressive elements and the fact that there are clear dispute resolution mechanisms that may be viewed as 'Steps', the *Boundary Waters Treaty* was found to satisfy only five (5) of the nine (9) criteria laid out for evaluating a 'Stepped Approach' in the treaty review undertaken as part of this work. It was not found that the *Boundary Waters Treaty* had three (3) clear graduated 'Steps', that it had 'Steps' that were limited in their scope or duration, that there was a clear progression through the 'Steps' that it did have, or that it possessed a clear diplomatic 'Step'.

In this section we will look at the various 'Steps' in this 'Stepped Approach' and the importance of their interaction with each other. In this work we looked for a clear progression of graduated 'Steps' that possessed some limits in scope and or duration. We also looked for three distinct 'Steps': diplomatic, technical, and adjudicative, 'Steps' that fulfill distinct functions and utilize diverse mechanisms. The 'Stepped Approach' discussed here is a dispute resolution framework and, as such, we looked for at least one compulsory 'Step' and a binding ultimate 'Step'.

1.2 *Graduated 'Steps'*

- **The presence of three (3) or more 'Steps'** – three (3) or more distinct 'Steps' were looked for in the specific provision(s) dealing with the resolution of disputes between State parties to an agreement during the implementation of the treaty.

It seems common sense that for a 'Stepped Approach' to disputes to exist there must be a series of progressive levels or set of graduated 'Steps'. Generally speaking, we will see a progression of 'Steps' from more flexible 'Diplomatic Steps' and 'Technical Steps' to less flexible and more process heavy 'Adjudicative Steps' later in the progression.

From the survey of international agreements conducted as part of this work we see a broad utilization of some degree of a 'Stepped Approach' across State practice. We see that of the two hundred and twenty-five (225) treaties that were identified as containing distinct dispute resolution provisions, one

18 *Treaty Relating to Boundary Waters, and Questions Arising Between the United States and Canada, Great Britain and United States*, 11 January 1909, UKTS 1910 No 23 (*Boundary Waters Treaty*) art IX.

hundred and fifty-six, or sixty-nine percent (69%), utilized two or more 'Steps' and sixty-two, or approximately twenty-eight percent (28%) had three or more 'Steps'.[19] The presence of distinct 'Steps' in a majority of international agreements dealing with international watercourses illustrates the importance of this approach to dispute resolution in the law of international watercourses.

These 'Steps' must be distinct from other mechanisms of the dispute resolution framework, as we see in the *UN Watercourses Convention* Article 33(2)[20] which groups various mechanisms together in one 'Step' as a suite of options for State parties to choose from. For our purposes this cannot be seen as separate and distinct 'Steps' but rather as one catch-all 'Step'. A rather succinct example of distinct 'Steps' can be found in the *Agreement concerning the utilization of the rapids of the Uruguay River in the Salto Grande area* between Argentina and Uruguay:

> (b) The Mixed Technical Commission shall take its decisions by the votes of a majority of its members. In the event of equally divided votes, the delegations shall report separately to their Governments. The High Contracting Parties shall strive to reach agreement and the terms of any agreement so reached shall be registered and communicated to the Mixed Technical Commission, which shall take the necessary action to implement it. If no agreement is reached, the High Contracting Parties shall resolve their disputes by diplomatic procedures and if no settlement is reached by this means, the disputes shall be submitted to arbitration.[21]

In this one provision we can see three distinct 'Steps' which a dispute progresses through if a matter cannot be resolved at a previous 'Step'. These distinct 'Steps' should not function concurrently with each other, rather parties should move from one 'Step' to the next in succession. For the purposes of this work we have looked for the presence of three (3) or more distinct 'Steps' in the specific provision(s) dealing with the resolution of disputes between State parties to an agreement during the implementation of the treaty.

In the 1961 *Salzburg resolution*, a 'Stepped Approach' is seemingly contemplated in regard to disputes over proposed works.

---

19 For the purpose of this work, three or more 'Steps' constituted the threshold for determining a graduated framework of 'Steps' as part of a 'Stepped Approach'.

20 *Convention on the Law of Non-Navigational Uses of International Watercourses*, 21 May 1997, 2999 UNTS 77, 36 ILM 700 (*Watercourses Convention*) at 136 art 32 (entered into force 17 August 2014).

21 *Agreement concerning the utilization of the rapids of the Uruguay River in the Salto Grande area*, Argentina and Uruguay, 30 December 1946, 671 UNTS 17, art 3(b).

Article 6

In case objection is made, the States will enter into negotiations with a view to reaching an agreement within a reasonable time.

For this purpose, it is desirable that the States in disagreement should have recourse to technical experts and, should occasion arise, to commissions and appropriate agencies in order to arrive at solutions assuring the greatest advantage to all concerned.

Article 7

During the negotiations, every State must, in conformity with the principle of good faith, refrain from undertaking the works or utilizations which are the object of the dispute or from taking any other measures which might aggravate the dispute or render agreement more difficult.

Article 8

If the interested States fail to reach agreement within a reasonable time, it is recommended that they submit to judicial settlement or arbitration the question whether the project is contrary to the above rules.

If the State objecting to the works or utilizations projected refuses to submit to judicial settlement or arbitration, the other State is free, subject to its responsibility, to go ahead while remaining bound by its obligations arising from the provisions of articles 2 to 4.

Article 9

It is recommended that States interested in particular hydrographic basins investigate the desirability of creating common organs for the establishing plans of utilization designed to facilitate their economic development as well as to prevent and settle disputes which might arise.[22]

It is possible to clearly delineate the distinct 'Steps' here. Disputes move from negotiation, a diplomatic 'Step' with recourse to technical expertise and

22 L'Institut de Droit International/Institute of International Law, "*Utilization of Non-Maritime International Waters (Except for Navigation)*" ('*Salzburg Resolution*') in *Annuaire de L'Institut de Droit International*, vol 40 (1961) 381, arts 6–9 at 383–384.

decision makers, to "judicial settlement or arbitration",[23] a clear adjudicative 'Step'. It is worth noting that here we do not have three (3) distinct 'Steps' but rather two (2). It should not be viewed as fatal to a treaty possessing a 'Stepped Approach' to have only two (2) 'Steps'. For the purposes of this study three (3) 'Steps' were chosen to clearly demonstrate a set of graduated 'Steps'. It is also worthy, as an aside, to note the emphasis that is placed on the creation of joint bodies and organizations to help formalize the dispute resolution machinery.

In article XXVII of the *Helsinki Rules* the ILA lays out a 'Stepped Approach' to disputes "recommend[ing]" that States "resort progressively to the means of prevention and settlement of disputes stipulated in articles XXIX to XXXIV of this Chapter."[24] In fact the provisions of the *Helsinki Rules* are meant not to replace other international agreements but rather as an effort to codify existing international law and provide recommendations, to supplement more specific watercourse agreements.[25] Meaning that, with regard to dispute resolution, the *Helsinki Rules* contemplate that State parties to a dispute will have already "unsuccessfully resorted to certain of the modes of settlement (*e.g.* conciliation, mediation) stipulated by treaty"[26] before turning to the mechanisms outlined in the *Helsinki Rules* as a next 'Step' or progression. The *Helsinki Rules* echo other international instruments in recommending negotiation between State parties to a dispute as a first 'Step'. Although the *Helsinki Rules* approach dispute resolution provisions less, it seems, as a clear progressive series of graduated 'Steps' and more as a suite of options that may be "undertaken progressively."[27] McCaffrey, in his sixth report, observes that the ILA's *Helsinki Rules* "establish a graduated series of means of dispute resolution that are recommended to the parties."[28]

Examples of these graduated 'Steps' can be found in treaties outside of the law of international watercourses, for instance, the 1977 *Agreement between the Government of Canada and the Government of the United States of America*

---

23 L'Institut de Droit International/Institute of International Law, "*Utilization of Non-Maritime International Waters (Except for Navigation)*" ('*Salzburg Resolution*') in *Annuaire de L'Institut de Droit International*, vol 40 (1961) 381, arts 8 at 383–384.

24 The International Law Association, "*Helsinki Rules on the Uses of the Waters of International Rivers*" ('*Helsinki Rules*') in *Report of the Fifty-Second Conference of the International Law Association Held at Helsinki, August 14–20, 1966*, vol 52 (1967) 484, art XXVII at 517.

25 *Ibid* at Comment to art XXVIII at 518.

26 *Ibid.*

27 *Ibid* at Comment to art XXVII at 517.

28 Stephen C. McCaffrey, "Sixth report on the law of the non-navigational uses of international watercourses" (UN Doc A/CN.4/427 and Add.1) in *Yearbook of the International Law Commission 1990*, vol 2, part 1 (1993) 41 at 74 para 84 (UN Doc A/CN.4/SER.A/1990/Add.1 (Part 1)).

Concerning Transit Pipelines,[29] dealing with the transit of hydrocarbons by pipeline, states in its section on dispute resolution that "any such dispute which [are] not settled by negotiation shall be submitted to arbitration at the request of either Party. Unless the Parties agree on a different procedure [...]".[30] We can see an escalating scale of dispute resolution mechanisms, from negotiation to arbitration. We can also see here the parties being allowed flexibility to deviate from this relatively simple two-'Step' process, to use other mechanisms by agreement.

1.3 *'Steps' of Limited Scope and Duration*

- **Steps of limited scope or duration** – agreements were assessed for either subject-matter or time-period limitations in the provision(s) dealing with the resolution of disputes between State parties to an agreement.

It is important that 'Steps' in a 'Stepped Approach' are limited in scope and or duration to preserve the integrity of such a system as a progressive process through various 'Steps'. If parties are able to effectively park their dispute at one 'Step' it undermines the effectiveness of such a 'Stepped Approach' to address a dispute by moving a matter through its framework of 'Steps'. To promote the movement of matters from one 'Step' to another we see provisions that are drafted to limit the scope of a particular 'Step' by either limiting the types of decisions that can be made at a specific 'Step' or the authority of that 'Step' to explore only some aspects of a dispute. We also see provisions that limit the duration that a specific 'Step' can be employed.

Where we see the duration of specific 'Steps' limited to a "reasonable period"[31] and while for our purposes this constituted a limitation of duration for a

---

29 *Agreement between the Government of Canada and the Government of the United States of America Concerning Transit Pipelines*, 8 January 1977, Can TS 1977 No 29.

30 *Ibid* at art IX(2).

31 I.e. *Treaty on the Lesotho Highlands Water Project between the Government of the Kingdom of Lesotho and the Government of the Republic of South Africa*, 24 October 1986, https://www.fao.org/faolex/results/details/en/c/LEX-FAOC015909/, art 16 (5); Jens Evensen, "First report on the law of the non-navigational uses of international watercourses" (UN Doc A/CN.4/367) in *Yearbook of the International Law Commission 1983*, vol 2, part 1 (1985) 155 at 190 (UN Doc A/CN.4/SER.A/1983/Add.1 (Part 1)); L'Institut de Droit International/Institute of International Law, "*Utilization of Non-Maritime International Waters (Except for Navigation)*" ('*Salzburg Resolution*') in *Annuaire de L'Institut de Droit International*, vol 40 (1961) 381, arts 6, 8 at 383–384; Stephen M. Schwebel, "Third report on the law of the non-navigational uses of international watercourses" (UN Doc A/CN.4/348) in *Year Book of the International Law Commission 1982 vol 2 part 1 (1984)* 65 at 186–187 para 498 art 16 (UN Doc A/CN.4/SER.A/1982/Add.1(Part 1)).

'Step' such general language can carry risks of the process stalling. As observed by the then special rapporteur Stephen McCaffrey:

> While in some cases six months may be too short a period for consultations and negotiations in the context of dispute settlement, the Special Rapporteur believes that a fixed period is necessary to make any subsequent requirement of recourse to compulsory procedures [...] meaningful. Otherwise, resort to such procedures could be delayed, even after it had become clear that consultations and negotiations would not be fruitful, on the ground that a 'reasonable' period of time had not elapsed.[32]

In this sense limitations of a fixed duration, as we see reflected in the several international agreements,[33] is certainly more precise and helps to create a more predictable dispute resolution framework that cannot be stalled as easily. For example, "The parties shall have a month to state whether they accept the conciliatory award or not. In the latter case and at the request of the interested parties the disagreement shall then be submitted to arbitration, the respective tribunal being constituted by the procedure provided in the Second Hague Convention for the peaceful solution of international conflicts."[34]

In particular we see 'Technical Steps' being more confined in their scope. Such 'Steps' are often being empowered to only make findings of fact or are constrained to reporting and recommendations in their powers. In contrast other 'Steps' such as 'Diplomatic Steps' and 'Adjudicative Steps' often have

---

32 Stephen C. McCaffrey, "Sixth report on the law of the non-navigational uses of international watercourses" (UN Doc A/CN.4/427 and Add.1) in *Yearbook of the International Law Commission 1990*, vol 2, part 1 (1993) 41 at 78 (UN Doc A/CN.4/SER.A/1990/Add.1 (Part 1)).

33 I.e. *Declaration of Montevideo concerning the industrial and agricultural use of international rivers approved by the seventh international conference of American States*, 24 December 1933, 28 American Journal of International Law 59, art 8 at 60, Pan American Union, Seventh International Conference of American States, Plenary Sessions, Minutes and antecedents, 114 (*1933 Montevideo Declaration*); *The Indus Waters Treaty 1960 (with annexes)*, 19 September 1960, 419 UNTS 125, art IX (5) (*Indus Waters Treaty*); *Statute of the river Uruguay, signed at Salto*, Argentina and Uruguay, 26 February 1975, 1295 UNTS 339, art 59 (*Statute of the river Uruguay*); *Convention on the Law of Non-Navigational Uses of International Watercourses*, 21 May 1997, 2999 UNTS 77, 36 ILM 700, art 33 (3) (*UN Watercourses Convention*) (entered into force 17 August 2014).

34 *Declaration of Montevideo concerning the industrial and agricultural use of international rivers approved by the seventh international conference of American States*, 24 December 1933, 28 American Journal of International Law 59, art 10 at 60, Pan American Union, Seventh International Conference of American States, Plenary Sessions, Minutes and antecedents, 114 (*1933 Montevideo Declaration*).

broader powers and are asked to deal with a broader scope of issues such as legal, factual and diplomatic.

The question of what qualifies as a "dispute" can be an important factor in limiting specific dispute resolution provisions. The *Indus Waters Treaty* divides matters into three distinct categories.[35] "Question[s]", "Difference[s]" and "Dispute[s]". This gatekeeper function helps facilitate a 'Stepped Approach' by limiting the scope of issues dealt with at each progressive 'Step'. In some cases, we can see a more expansive definition of "dispute" so as to bring more matters within the scope of a specific provision. The *Helsinki Rules* of the ILA, for instance, take a broader approach to defining a dispute. Stating in the *Comment* to Article XXVII that "[t]he term 'dispute' is not to be construed restrictively. It would embrace both a 'difference' and a 'dispute' within the meaning of Article IX of the [*Indus Waters Treaty*] between India and Pakistan".[36]

The 1966 agreement and final protocol relating to withdrawals of water from Lake Constance[37] limits the scope of submission to the consultative committee for consideration of objections at the technical level by limiting such submissions to matters under articles 4, 5 and 7 where objections are raised.[38] Article 4 deals with water withdrawals that require reparation under international law resulting from unforeseen damage.[39] Article 5 deals with the combined effects of a number of water withdrawals requiring compensatory measures, the payment of an indemnity or reparations under articles 3 and 4.[40] Article 7 allows riparian States the opportunity to express their views if certain criteria are met by the withdrawals.[41]

Some international agreements allow State parties themselves to place certain limitations on the scope of dispute resolution provisions. Though outside

35 *The Indus Waters Treaty 1960 (with annexes)*, 19 September 1960, 419 UNTS 125, art IX (*Indus Waters Treaty*).

36 The International Law Association, "*Helsinki Rules on the Uses of the Waters of International Rivers*" ('*Helsinki Rules*') in *Report of the Fifty-Second Conference of the International Law Association Held at Helsinki, August 14–20, 1966*, vol 52 (1967) 484 at 518.

37 *Agreement with Final Protocol Regulating the Withdrawal of Water from Lake Constance*, 30 April 1966, 620 UNTS 191.

38 *Ibid* at art 8(1).

39 *Ibid at* art 4.

40 *Ibid at* art 5.

41 "In the following cases, the riparian States shall, before authorizing withdrawals of water, afford one another in good time an opportunity to express their views:
(a) When the water is to be used outside the hydrological catchment area of Lake Constance and is to be withdrawn at a rate exceeding 750 l/sec.;
(b) When the water is to be used within the hydrological catchment area of Lake Constance and is to be withdrawn at a rate exceeding 1,500 l/sec." *Ibid at* art 7.

the realm of the law of the non-navigational uses of international watercourses the 1982 Convention on the Law of the Sea[42] provides us with an example where State parties may "impose other limitations, thereby opting out of the compulsory dispute settlement procedures in respect of certain defined categories of dispute."[43] Such an exclusion functions reciprocally,[44] where a State party to the 1982 Convention on the Law of the Sea has opted to exclude specific categories of disputes from the compulsory dispute settlement provisions they also cannot initiate such compulsory dispute settlement procedures in regard to those specific categories of disputes.[45] The 1982 Convention on the Law of the Sea allows State parties to limit the scope of dispute resolution mechanisms and tailor them to specific categories of disputes by allowing them to choose the forum of dispute resolution. Practice in respect of the choice of tribunal is in fact quite varied.[46] "States need not choose the same forum for every purpose (…)."[47] While the example of the 1982 Convention on the Law of the Sea would not necessarily lead to a clear universal 'Stepped Approach' for every party under a particular agreement it does illustrate some of the tools available within a treaty regime to allow the limitation in scope of specific dispute resolution mechanisms.

By controlling the scope and duration of specific 'Steps' an international agreement can build in a degree of flexibility for the parties concerned, allowing them to move through the process and utilize the 'Steps' that best suit the needs of their specific dispute. Utilizing limitations of scope in this manner, a dispute resolution framework can help State parties avoid being trapped by a particular dispute resolution procedure, preventing the process itself from becoming static and facilitating a movement through the 'Steps'.

1.4 *A Clear Progression through the 'Steps'*

- **A clear progression through the 'Steps'** – this criterion assessed whether there was an obvious and clearly articulated progression through the various 'Steps' dealing with the resolution of disputes between State parties to

42 *United Nations Convention on the Law of the Sea*, 10 December 1982, 1833 UNTS 397, art 298.

43 John Collier and Vaughan Lowe, *The Settlement of Disputes in International Law* (Oxford University Press, 1999) at 92–93.

44 *United Nations Convention on the Law of the Sea*, 10 December 1982, 1833 UNTS 397, art 298(3).

45 John Collier and Vaughan Lowe, *The Settlement of Disputes in International Law* (Oxford University Press, 1999) at 93.

46 *Ibid* at 94.

47 *Ibid* at 94 (footnote omitted).

an agreement. For example, provisions which provided parties to a dispute with a series of choices were regarded as a single 'Step'.

This work involved identifying both discernible 'Steps' and specific 'Steps' of limited scope and/or duration, while also establishing a clear roadmap for progression through these 'Steps'. For a consistent and predictable 'Stepped Approach' dispute resolution framework to exist the State parties will need to be able to anticipate and chart their path through the process. Part of this is a having a clear hierarchy of 'Steps' that are triggered by the completion of earlier 'Steps' allowing a clear path through the dispute resolution framework.

In contrast to a structured framework of graduated 'Steps' with a clear progression discussed in this section we can see agreements structured to provide a suite of choices to State parties with no discernable hierarchy or progression. For instance, the *Pact of Bogotá* Article III articulates a flexible order for dispute settlement procedures: "The order of the pacific procedures established in the present Treaty does not signify that the parties may not have recourse to the procedure which they consider most appropriate in each case, or that they should use all these procedures, or that any of them have preference over others except as expressly provided."[48]

The *1933 Montevideo Declaration*, in articles 8–10 shows a progression of a dispute on an international watercourse through graduated 'Steps' or phases of dispute resolution mechanisms.[49] Article 8 contemplates an *ad hoc* body, a "Mixed Technical Commission of technical experts from both sides to pass judgment on the case."[50] This article allows a period of six months for the "Mixed Technical Commission" to act and if no agreement has been reached in this period the members of this "Mixed Technical Commission" shall "set forth their respective opinions, informing the governments thereof."[51] The proceedings of this "Mixed Technical Commission" shall be taken into account in any award of a conciliation tribunal, which under article 9 would be impaneled if an agreement through diplomatic channels is not possible.[52] Such a conciliation tribunal would have three months, with possible extensions, in

48 *American Treaty on Pacific Settlement*, 30 April 1948, 30 UNTS 55, art III at 84 (*Pact of Bogotá*).

49 *Declaration of Montevideo concerning the industrial and agricultural use of international rivers approved by the seventh international conference of American States*, 24 December 1933, 28 American Journal of International Law 59, art 8–10 at 59–60, Pan American Union, Seventh International Conference of American States, Plenary Sessions, Minutes and antecedents, 114 (*1933 Montevideo Declaration*).

50 *Ibid* at art 8 at 60.

51 *Ibid.*

52 *Ibid* at art 9 at 60.

which to act.[53] After a conciliation award the parties would have a month to state whether they accepted the award or not.[54] If the conciliation award was not accepted then at the request of the "interested parties the disagreement shall then be submitted to arbitration."[55] It is worth remarking on the compulsory nature of arbitration contemplated here, but of more importance to the discussion at hand it is necessary to point out how these articles function together to move parties through technical level dispute resolution or avoidance through to more formalized adjudicative measures in arbitration provision of article 10. Here we not only see a clear directional progression through these graduated 'Steps', ensured by clear timelines, but also 'Steps' that build off each other, using the findings of the "Mixed Technical Committee" in the award of the conciliation tribunal.[56]

Article 3(b) of the *Agreement concerning the utilization of the rapids of the Uruguay River in the Salto Grande area* between Argentina and Uruguay,[57] quoted above, illustrates a succinct example of a provision in an international watercourse agreement that displays a clear progression through the dispute resolution framework including the triggering of subsequent 'Steps' when the previous 'Steps' have failed to resolve the matter. In this agreement however we don't see clear limitations in regard to the duration of the 'Steps' so it would seem that it is up to the parties to decide that a 'Step' has failed to produce results.

Though outside the law of international watercourses the WTO's *Understanding on Rules and Procedures Governing the Settlement of Disputes* contained in Annex 2 of the *Marrakesh Agreement Establishing the World Trade Organization* of April 1994 provides for parties progressing through various 'Steps' of its dispute resolution provisions.[58] Often requiring parties to have concluded a previous procedure, once engaged, before undertaking the next one provided for in the understanding.[59] Parties progress through consultations,[60]

53 *Ibid.*
54 *Ibid* at art 10 at 60.
55 *Ibid.*
56 *Ibid.*
57 *Agreement concerning the utilization of the rapids of the Uruguay River in the Salto Grande area*, Argentina and Uruguay, 30 December 1946, 671 UNTS 17, art 3(b).
58 *Understanding on Rules and Procedures Governing the Settlement of Disputes, Marrakesh Agreement Establishing the World Trade Organization, Annex* 2, 15 April 1994, 1869 UNTS 401 articles 4–25.
59 *Understanding on Rules and Procedures Governing the Settlement of Disputes, Marrakesh Agreement Establishing the World Trade Organization, Annex* 2, 15 April 1994, 1869 UNTS 401.
60 *Ibid* at art 4.

ad hoc expert panels[61] and appellate review procedures to resolve their disputes.[62] Parties also may have recourse to good offices, conciliation, mediation,[63] temporary measures[64] or arbitration as alternative dispute resolution mechanisms.[65]

1.5 *Diverse Dispute Resolution Mechanisms*

As part of this work, we looked for a diverse range of distinct 'Steps' and dispute resolution mechanisms. A substantial portion of the discussion in the proceeding chapters has centred around some of the various dispute resolution mechanisms available in regard to disputes on international watercourses. In the chapter on "Disputes and the Law of the Non-Navigational Uses of International Watercourses" we explored many different types of dispute resolution mechanisms such as diplomatic, technical and adjudicative mechanisms which are reflected in the nine (9) criteria used to analyse the two hundred and twenty-five (225) treaties surveyed as part of this work. In particular a lengthy discussion of 'Technical Level' dispute resolution mechanisms was explored in the chapter on "Disputes at a 'Technical Level'" above, this would encompass the recourse to technical expertise and decision making, as well as the distinct technical 'Step' listed as part of the nine (9) criteria. In this section we will explore some aspects of the following criteria used in the assessment of international agreements for this work. In the interest of space an effort will be made to avoid repeating discussions that have occurred above regarding the individual 'Steps' but rather the importance of their interaction and relationship vis-a-vis each other in a 'Stepped Approach' will be explored here. The 'Steps' implicated in this discussion are:

- **Recourse to technical expertise and decision making** – for this criterion dispute resolution provisions were assessed to see if parties to a dispute had explicit recourse to specific technical expertise in the process, for example, the ability to have a technical report made or to consult with an engineer;
- **A distinct technical 'Step'** – this criterion is distinct from the preceding one in that it looks for a specific technical 'Step', separate from juridical, political or diplomatic mechanisms; in some cases it was not always apparent if a mechanism or body was exclusively technical in its composition or work,

61 *Ibid* at art 6.
62 Ibid at art 17.
63 *Ibid* at art 5.
64 *Ibid* at art 22.
65 *Ibid* at art 25.

here the function and makeup of a mechanism or body was analysed based on the surrounding provisions of the treaty to assess if it had predominantly technical functions or composition;

- **A distinct diplomatic 'Step'** – agreements were analysed to see if there was a clearly diplomatic 'Step', i.e. negotiation, mediation, good offices, 'by agreement' etc., parties arguably always have recourse to diplomatic means of dispute resolution but unless it was specifically mentioned in the dispute resolution provision(s) it was not counted as such for our purposes here;
- **A distinct adjudicative 'Step'** – this criterion looked at whether a dispute resolution provision in an agreement provided a distinct 'Step' for adjudicative means of resolving the dispute, such as arbitration or recourse to an international court or tribunal of a distinctly juridical nature.

1.6 *Integrated Mechanisms*

This work looked for three (3) clear types of 'Steps' in the dispute resolution provisions reviewed, a technical 'Step', a diplomatic 'Step', and an adjudicative 'Step'. In the *Agreement concerning the utilization of the rapids of the Uruguay River in the Salto Grande area* between Argentina and Uruguay discussed above we can identify these three (3) 'Steps'. The "Mixed Technical Commission" which is empowered to "deal with all matters relating to the utilization, damming and diversion of the waters of the Uruguay River"[66] is a clear technical 'Step'. If matters cannot be resolved at this technical 'Step' then the parties "shall resolve their disputes by diplomatic procedures"[67] a distinct diplomatic 'Step'. Finally, if the parties are still unable to resolve their disputes the matters are sent to arbitration, a distinct adjudicative 'Step'.

Another succinct example is found in the *Agreement with Final Protocol Regulating the Withdrawal of Water from Lake Constance*:

Article 9

(1) Where the riparian States are unable to reach agreement through discussions in the consultative committee on a matter of the kind referred to in article 8, paragraph (1), agreement shall be sought through the diplomatic channel.

---

66 *Agreement concerning the utilization of the rapids of the Uruguay River in the Salto Grande area*, Argentina and Uruguay, 30 December 1946, 671 UNTS 17, art 2.

67 *Ibid* at art 3(b).

(2) If no agreement is reached through the diplomatic channel, any interested riparian State may require that the case should be submitted to an arbitration commission.[68]

Here we see a three 'Step' process, a first technical 'Step' in the consultative committee followed by a diplomatic 'Step', and finally an adjudicative 'Step' through arbitration.

These three (3) distinct 'Steps' each represent a different type of dispute resolution mechanism suited for a different purpose. These diverse mechanisms are an integral feature of a 'Stepped Approach'. A 'Stepped Approach' derives its strength as a framework by moving through progressive 'Steps' each tailored to a different purpose and utilizing a different type of dispute resolution mechanism.

While it is true that no mechanism of dispute resolution enjoys an inherent preference under general international law,[69] a 'Stepped Approach', by employing diverse dispute resolution mechanisms in a progressive sequence, can avail itself of the strengths of all of its constituent mechanisms while also addressing the weakness inherent to each one, creating a dispute resolution framework that is stronger and more adaptable than the sum of its parts. These integrated mechanisms can also be used to build off each other supplementing the work done at each progressive 'Step'. The *1933 Montevideo Declaration* for example, illustrates this complementary and integrated nature, by using the findings of the "Mixed Technical Committee" in the award of the conciliation tribunal.[70]

1.7 *Compulsory 'Steps'*

- **At least one compulsory 'Step'** – agreements were reviewed to see if they had at least one clearly compulsory dispute resolution 'Step' that obligated a party or the parties to participate, regardless of their consent; the use of the language 'must' or 'shall' or the presence of a 'Step' that could be instigated

68 *Agreement with Final Protocol Regulating the Withdrawal of Water from Lake Constance*, 30 April 1966, 620 UNTS 191, art 9.

69 Kari Hakapää, "Negotiation" (last updated 2013) at para 27, online: *Max Planck Encyclopedias of International Law* <https://opil.ouplaw.com/home/mpil>.

70 *Declaration of Montevideo concerning the industrial and agricultural use of international rivers approved by the seventh international conference of American States*, 24 December 1933, 28 American Journal of International Law 59, art 9 at 60, Pan American Union, Seventh International Conference of American States, Plenary Sessions, Minutes and antecedents, 114 (*1933 Montevideo Declaration*).

by only one of the parties were determined to indicate such a compulsory 'Step'.

As part of this work, we looked for the presence of at least one (1) compulsory 'Step' in the dispute resolution provisions of the international watercourse agreements surveyed. Ninety-five percent (95%) of the agreements had at least one compulsory 'Step'. A fairly significant majority. Most often a compulsory 'Step' was found in relation to diplomatic mechanisms of international dispute resolution. State consent still underlies compulsory dispute resolution provisions, consent being given by the State parties at some point in time to a specific mechanism, such as an international court or body performing an adjudicative function.[71] "Agreement is still both the basis and the aim of every means of dispute settlement; even the so-called 'compulsory' mechanisms require the consent of the parties, albeit expressed before the dispute has actually arisen."[72] The ability to compel State parties to a dispute, regardless of how controversial this idea is to some States,[73] to enter into at least some form of dispute resolution mechanics is an important element in articulating a robust dispute resolution framework for international watercourses.

1.8 *Binding Ultimate 'Step'*

- **A binding ultimate 'Step'** – agreements were looked at to see if the final 'Step' in their dispute resolution process had the power to impose a 'binding' or 'final' determination of the dispute regardless of any agreement or lack of agreement of the parties to the dispute.[74]

---

71 "It is well established in international law that no State can, without its consent, be compelled to submit its disputes with other States either to mediation or to arbitration, or to any other kind of pacific settlement. Such consent can be given once and for all in the form of an obligation freely undertaken, but it can, on the contrary, also be given in a special case apart from any existing obligation." *Status of Eastern Carelia* (1923), Advisory Opinion, PCIJ (Ser B) No 5 at 27; see also the Case concerning the Aerial Incident of July 27th, 1955 (Israel v Bulgaria); Sir Robert Jennings, "Keynote Address" in The International Bureau of the Permanent Court of Arbitration, ed, *Resolution of International Water Disputes* (The Permanent Court of Arbitration/Peace Palace Papers, 2003) 23 at 30.

72 Attila Tanzi, *The Economic Commission for Europe Water Convention and the United Nations Watercourses Convention: An analysis of their harmonized contribution to international water law*, Water Series No 6 (UN, 2015) at 73 [footnote omitted].

73 UNGA, 51st Sess, 62nd Mtg, UN Doc A/C.6/51/SR.62 (1997); UNGA, 51st Sess, 99th Plen Mtg, UN Doc A/51/PV.99 (1997).

74 In some cases, where it was not stated, the binding nature of the mechanism was assumed i.e. the ICJ or arbitration being deemed to be binding. Other mechanisms, such as diplomatic means, were deemed to be non-binding.

The existence of a binding ultimate 'Step' is an important feature in a dispute resolution framework and an interesting criterion for our study. While perhaps the presence or lack thereof of this criterion is not of vital importance to the presence of a 'Stepped Approach' this element found its way into our nine (9) criteria. The ability of a dispute resolution framework to offer an ultimate binding or final resolution to a dispute on an international watercourse was assessed to be an important aspect of such a process.

One hundred and twenty-five (125) of the two hundred and twenty-five (225) treaties reviewed had a binding ultimate 'Step' all of which also possessed a distinct adjudicative 'Step'. Generally speaking, where we find an adjudicative 'Step' we also find that the agreement satisfies the criteria that the ultimate 'Step' is binding. An adjudicative 'Step' generally is associated with a degree of finality[75] through a third party decision of a legally binding nature[76] and is often viewed, as discussed above, as a dispute resolution mechanism of 'last resort'.[77] While the association between the presence of a distinct adjudicative 'Step' and a binding ultimate 'Step' is to be expected, given the finality of adjudicative 'Steps' as mechanisms, there was an exception.[78] The *Agreement between the Government of Canada and the Government of the United States of America for Water Supply and Flood Control in the Souris River Basin*[79] creates a tribunal that is only given advisory powers, whether this provision can properly be called an adjudicative 'Step' is unclear and left for a later debate. Here it has been viewed as an adjudicative 'Step'.

In some agreements, such as the *UN Watercourses Convention*, binding adjudicative mechanisms were included but as part of a suite of options available at a particular 'Step'. Another example of this can be found in Article 18 of the *Agreement for the Establishment of the Organization for the Management and Development of the Kagera River Basin*[80] which refers disputes to the

---

75 Sir Robert Jennings, "Keynote Address" in The International Bureau of the Permanent Court of Arbitration, ed, *Resolution of International Water Disputes* (The Permanent Court of Arbitration/Peace Palace Papers, 2003) 23 at 30–31.

76 Kari Hakapää, "Negotiation" (last updated 2013) at para 28, online: *Max Planck Encyclopedias of International Law* <https://opil.ouplaw.com/home/mpil>.

77 Sir Robert Jennings, "Keynote Address" in The International Bureau of the Permanent Court of Arbitration, ed, *Resolution of International Water Disputes* (The Permanent Court of Arbitration/Peace Palace Papers, 2003) 23 at 31.

78 *Agreement between the Government of Canada and the Government of the United States of America for Water Supply and Flood Control in the Souris River Basin*, 23 October 1989, Can TS 1986 No 36.

79 *Ibid.*

80 *Agreement for the Establishment of the Organization for the Management and Development of the Kagera River Basin*, 24 August 1977, 1089 UNTS 165, art 18.

Commission of Mediation, Conciliation and Arbitration under the *Charter of the Organization of African Unity*.[81] Under the *Organization of African Unity: Protocol of the Commission of Mediation, Conciliation and Arbitration*[82] parties may choose binding arbitration under the protocol of the Commission of Mediation, Conciliation and Arbitration under the, now defunct,[83] Organization for African Unity but this is only one of a series of mechanisms available to the parties under the Commission of Mediation, Conciliation and Arbitration as a suite of options, thus not a clear adjudicative 'Step' nor a clear ultimate 'Step'.

1.9 *Understanding a 'Stepped Approach' through the ILC Process*

Much of the discussion of a 'Stepped Approach' owes a debt to the detailed and excellent work of the ILC on the subject of the non-navigational uses of international watercourses. It is perhaps useful for our discussion in understanding the proposed 'Stepped Approach' to look at the work of the ILC on this subject and the evolution of various draft dispute resolution provisions that were proposed.

In his third report to the ILC Stephen Schwebel put forward in his draft articles a section for the "avoidance and settlement of disputes"[84] that contemplated an innovative and robust "Stepped" or as he termed it an "echelon"[85] approach to the prevention and resolution of disputes on international watercourses. In these proposed articles parties would progress through negotiation and consultations, the creation of an "international commission of inquiry to investigate and report upon the facts relevant to the unresolved difference", more negotiations, conciliation, and finally arbitration or adjudication.[86] It

81 *Charter of the Organization of African Unity*, 25 May 1963, 479 UNTS 39, art XIX.

82 *Organization of African Unity: Protocol of the Commission of Mediation, Conciliation and Arbitration*, 21 July 1964, 3 ILM 6, art XIX.

83 It is worth noting that the Commission of Mediation, Conciliation and Arbitration of the organization of African Unity does not exist anymore. The Organization of African Unity has since been replaced by the African Union, which has, as of today, not replaced the former Commission. See, Susanne Schmeier, *Governing International Watercourses: River Basin Organizations and the sustainable governance of internationally shared rivers and lakes* (Earthscan, 2013) at 262; Abdoul Samboly Ba & Makane Moïse Mbengue, "Le Régime Juridique du Fleuve Sénégal: Aspects du Droit des Cours d'Eau dans un Contexte Régional," in *African Yearbook of International Law*, Volume 12, Issue 1 (2004) 322.

84 Stephen M. Schwebel, "Third report on the law of the non-navigational uses of international watercourses" (UN Doc A/CN.4/348) in *Year Book of the International Law Commission 1982 vol 2 part 1 (1984)* 65 at 186–187 (UN Doc A/CN.4/SER.A/1982/Add.1(Part 1)).

85 *Ibid* at 182.

86 *Ibid* at 186–187 art 16(4).

is only in the final 'Step' that the matter would be termed a dispute, earlier being called a difference. We also see a clear progression laid out in these draft articles that would require parties to progress through, completing previous 'Steps' before progressing to the next, all with relatively clear procedure and timetables based on 'Steps' of clearly delineated scope and duration. We also see clear technical, diplomatic and adjudicative 'Steps'. It is important to note that under Schwebel's proposed articles the 'Technical Level' 'Step' of creating an "international commission of inquiry to investigate and report upon the facts relevant to the unresolved difference" can be triggered by any of the State parties to a dispute, early in the dispute resolution process, allowing the commission to help break a potential impasse between the parties by providing factual findings that could help provide a degree of certainty and move matters along. It would seem that Schwebel's proposed dispute resolution framework would satisfy, or at least largely satisfy, dependant on the proposed annexes which were intended to be affixed, the nine (9) criteria laid out in this work. For our purposes a portion of Article 16 of Schwebel's draft articles is reproduced:

1. Unless the system States concerned otherwise agree,
   (a) Failure after a reasonable period of consultation and negotiations to reach an accommodation of a difference between system States regarding the development, use, protection or control of an international watercourse system entitles any of the system States concerned to call for the creation of an international commission of inquiry to investigate and report upon the facts relevant to the unresolved difference;
   (b) Any system State concerned is, after the call for creation of an international commission of inquiry, entitled to convoke a special period of intensified negotiations not to exceed six months measured from the date of the call for the said commission, during which time the formation of the said commission shall be held in abeyance;
   (c) International commissions of inquiry shall be constituted in accordance with this article and the procedures annexed to these articles at the instance of any system State concerned;
   (d) Upon receipt of the report of an international commission of inquiry, the system States concerned shall renew their negotiations and, with the said report as a basis, endeavour to arrive at a just and equitable resolution of the difference;
   (e) In the event that resolution of the difference by negotiation is not attained within six months after receipt by the system States concerned of the report of the international commission of inquiry,

or the formation or work of said commission has been frustrated so that its report is not rendered, any system State concerned may thereafter refer the matter to conciliation in accordance with the procedure annexed to these articles;

(f) In the event that with the assistance of conciliation, the system States concerned fail to resolve the difference within a reasonable time, any system State concerned may, after notice to all system States concerned and thereafter waiting a minimum of ninety days, declare the matter to be an international dispute and call for arbitration or adjudication of the dispute in accordance with the optional procedures annexed to these articles. This subparagraph shall not be operative where the system States concerned have an applicable mutually binding agreement to arbitrate or adjudicate disputes.[87]

The next ILC rapporteur to pick up the subject of dispute resolution mechanisms in the non-navigational uses of international watercourses and to try their hand at drafting proposed articles was Jens Evensen. In his first report as special rapporteur to the ILC on the subject of the non-navigational uses of international watercourses Evensen put forward a draft chapter on the settlement of disputes with a progressive set of graduated 'Steps'.[88]

As a first 'Step' State parties to a dispute are required to enter into consultations and negotiations, either directly or through a joint institution or through other international or regional third party organs or agencies.[89] If this diplomatic 'Step' fails to produce a resolution of a dispute within a "reasonable period of time" then the parties shall resort to the other procedures laid down in the chapter.[90] As part of the consultation and negotiation procedure under these draft articles parties "may, by agreement, establish a Board of Inquiry of qualified experts for the purpose of establishing the relevant facts pertaining to the dispute in order to facilitate the consultations and negotiations between the parties."[91] By making this "Board of Inquiry" function only through the agreement of the parties we see much of the power of the proposed commission of inquiry under Schwebel's proposed articles removed and its utility as a mechanism to clarify technical issues and help move disputes ahead

87 *Ibid* at 186–187 para 498 art 16.

88 Jens Evensen, "First report on the law of the non-navigational uses of international watercourses" (UN Doc A/CN.4/367) in *Yearbook of the International Law Commission 1983*, vol 2, part 1 (1985) 155 at 190–194 (UN Doc A/CN.4/SER.A/1983/Add.1 (Part 1)).

89 *Ibid* at 190.

90 *Ibid.*

91 *Ibid* at 191.

where parties are at loggerheads seems to be severely curtailed. In addition to a "Board of Inquiry" as part of the consultation and negotiation process, State parties can also by agreement utilize third party mediation to provide impartial non-binding advice to the parties.[92]

Articles 34, 35 and 36 of Evensen's draft articles deal with conciliation[93] and can be viewed as a distinct technical 'Step' in the process. The "Conciliation Commission" under these articles has the power to make recommendations and report.[94]

> The Conciliation Commission shall file its report with the parties within twelve months of its constitution, unless the parties otherwise agree. Its report shall record any agreement reached between the parties and, failing agreement, its recommendations to the parties. Such recommendations shall contain the Commission's conclusions with regard to the pertinent questions of fact and law relevant to the matter in dispute and such recommendations as the Commission deems fair and appropriate for an amicable settlement of the dispute.[95]

We also see clear limitations as to the scope and duration of this specific mechanism. It is again left up to parties to provide for conciliation in their specific agreements or to agree amongst themselves on the basis of a specific dispute to submit the matter to conciliation.[96] This optional aspect of conciliation does seem to undermine the effectiveness of this mechanism. Depending on the specific watercourse agreement, if the parties had previously agreed to permit conciliation this could become a less optional 'Step'. The "report of the Conciliation Commission – including its recommendations to the parties and its conclusions with regard to facts and law – is not binding upon the parties to the dispute unless the parties have agreed otherwise."[97]

Finally, the parties may submit a dispute to binding international adjudication[98] to the "International Court of Justice, to another international court or to a permanent or *ad hoc* arbitral tribunal".[99] This adjudicative 'Step' requires that the parties involved have consented to the jurisdiction of

---

92 *Ibid.*
93 *Ibid* at 191–193.
94 *Ibid* at 192.
95 *Ibid.*
96 *Ibid* at 191.
97 *Ibid* at 193.
98 *Ibid* at 193–194.
99 *Ibid* at 193.

the specified court or tribunal either by a general acceptance of jurisdiction or specifically for the particular dispute. While this provision is optional it is quite common to allow States to consent or refuse the jurisdiction of particular international courts or tribunals.

Evensen's draft articles still embody several elements of a 'Stepped Approach'. The number of optional procedures mean that it would be possible that the only 'Step' in this process would be the obligatory consultation and negotiation 'Step' but it is possible that State parties could avail themselves of three (3) or four (4) 'Steps', including a technical 'Step', a diplomatic 'Step', and an adjudicative 'Step'. There is also recourse to technical experts and decision making at least in an advisory capacity. There appears to be a relatively clear progression through these 'Steps' and for most 'Steps' there are clear limits in scope and/or duration placed upon them. There is also at least one compulsory 'Step' and the ultimate adjudicative 'Step' is binding. While Evensen's draft articles are less focused, succinct or robust than Schwebel's they still arguably represent a 'Stepped Approach' albeit a watered-down version.

McCaffrey was the next rapporteur to deal with the matter proposing a set of his own draft articles in his sixth report to the ILC. In his draft articles we see the clear inspiration of the work of the preceding rapporteurs Schwebel and Evensen, who had proposed draft articles on dispute resolution, a fact that is acknowledged by McCaffrey.[100] McCaffrey provides for technical fact-finding, outside of the dispute resolution provisions of his draft articles, that may be instigated by any "watercourse States for the purpose of establishing facts necessary to the fulfilment of the obligations of watercourse States under the present articles,"[101] to be carried out by a joint body, an *ad hoc* commission of experts, or a commission of inquiry.[102]

The first 'Step' in McCaffrey's proposed dispute resolution framework is a compulsory diplomatic 'Step', consultations and negations to be carried out directly by the parties, through a joint organization created by them, or through another competent third party.[103] Under the auspices of this initial diplomatic 'Step' the parties may avail themselves of a commission of inquiry or third party mediation to assist them with their consultations and negotiations.[104]

100 Stephen C. McCaffrey, "Sixth report on the law of the non-navigational uses of international watercourses" (UN Doc A/CN.4/427 and Add.1) in *Yearbook of the International Law Commission 1990*, vol 2, part 1 (1993) 41 at 77 note 197 (UN Doc A/CN.4/SER.A/1990/Add.1 (Part 1)).

101 *Ibid* at 75–76.

102 *Ibid.*

103 *Ibid* at 78.

104 *Ibid.*

These draft articles provided for a period of six months to resolve a dispute at this 'Step' before the State parties have recourse to the other "procedures for the settlement of disputes provided for in the following articles."[105]

Following the initial diplomatic 'Step', disputes between parties that have not been resolved in the six-month period "shall be submitted by the watercourse States concerned to conciliation as provided in the present article. Conciliation may be initiated by any of the watercourse States concerned by written notification to the other party or parties to the dispute, unless the parties otherwise agree."[106] This appears to be a distinct technical 'Step'. The conciliation commission under these draft articles will then have a period of twelve months from its constitution within which it shall file its report with the parties as well as transmitting a copy of its report to the conference of the parties.[107] "The report shall indicate the findings of the commission concerning questions of law and fact pertinent to the matter in dispute and shall record any agreement reached between the parties or, failing such agreement, the recommendations of the commission concerning the settlement of the dispute."[108] The conciliation commission's report will generally be non-binding unless the parties have agreed otherwise.[109] It is an interesting aspect that McCaffrey includes a requirement, in his provisions on conciliation, "that the report of the conciliation commission be transmitted to the conference of the parties. [...] it is believed that this procedure, while not involving any binding effect of the report, will increase the incentive of the parties to follow the recommendation of the commission."[110] If the conciliation process has not led to a resolution of the dispute, then the receipt of the conciliation commission's report will trigger a renewed negotiation process between the parties on the basis of the report.[111]

Finally, if after a period of six months from the receipt of the conciliation commission's report the negotiations between the parties have still not resulted in a resolution of the dispute then "any of the parties may submit the dispute to binding arbitration by any permanent or *ad hoc* arbitral tribunal that has been accepted by all the parties to the dispute."[112] This adjudicative 'Step' is again based on the consent of the State parties to a particular court or

105 *Ibid.*
106 *Ibid.*
107 *Ibid* at 79.
108 *Ibid.*
109 *Ibid.*
110 *Ibid.*
111 *Ibid.*
112 *Ibid.*

tribunal. As McCaffrey stated "Article 5 does not require the parties to submit their dispute to binding arbitration. The Special Rapporteur agrees with his two predecessors that recourse to previously accepted means of dispute settlement or to an *ad hoc* procedure agreed upon by the parties is more likely to be generally acceptable and to produce a result that will be accepted by the parties to the dispute."[113]

McCaffrey's draft seems to represent a rather robust 'Stepped Approach' to dispute resolution. It possesses a clear set of graduated 'Steps' that include a diplomatic 'Step', a technical 'Step', and an adjudicative 'Step'. This series of 'Steps' have clear limits both in subject matter and duration and there is a clearly articulated progression through these 'Steps'. The parties have recourse to technical experts and decision making through the conciliation process as well as the fact-finding provisions. Here we have at least two compulsory 'Steps' and we can assume that the ultimate adjudicative 'Step' would be binding. These draft articles would meet all nine (9) criteria laid out in this work. McCaffrey's draft articles, by providing fewer optional 'Steps' than Evensen's, empowers a more robust and clear-cut 'Stepped Approach', closer in this regard to Schwebel's draft articles.

The ILC process seems to have let the subject of dispute resolution languish. After McCaffrey provided draft dispute resolution provisions in his sixth-report to the ILC, the matter seems to have not been discussed by the ILC along with the discussions of his sixth and seventh reports,[114] prompting the following special rapporteur to the ILC on the subject of the non-navigational uses of international watercourses, Robert Rosenstock, to comment:

> The Special Rapporteur remains convinced that, at a minimum, a tailored, bare-bones provision on the settlement of disputes is an indispensable component of any convention the Commission would put forward on the current topic.

113 *Ibid.*

114 "At the present session, the Commission had before it the second part of the sixth report (A/CN.4/427/Add.1) and the seventh report (A/CN.4/436) of the Special Rapporteur. The second part of the sixth report contained a chapter on settlement of disputes, which had been introduced at the last session but was not discussed for lack of time. In order to enable the Commission to make the best use of its time, the Special Rapporteur proposed not to take up that chapter. He recommended that the debate should focus on his seventh report and, in particular, on the question of the use of terms." "Report of the Commission to the General Assembly on the work of its forty-third session" (UN Doc A/46/10) in *Yearbook of the International Law Commission 1991* vol 2 part 2 (1994) 1 at 63 para 35 (UN Doc A/CN.4/SER.A/1991/Add.1 (Part 2)).

> While the Special Rapporteur would be more than willing to return *in toto*, should the members so desire, to the scheme contained in Mr. McCaffrey's sixth report (1990), he urges, as an alternative and at a minimum, consideration of the addition in the main body of the draft of simplified article reproduced below.[115]

Special Rapporteur Robert Rosenstock, as indicated in the passage above, drafted his own simplified draft articles on dispute resolution. Rosenstock's simplified draft articles were themselves inspired by the work of his predecessors.

> There was no need for an elaborate system. It would suffice to indicate at some point that there was an obligation to accept a third-party procedure. There would, of course, be a choice between conciliation, arbitration and judicial settlement, each of which had advantages and disadvantages. The Special Rapporteur would, however, not even have to draft provisions, since those prepared by Mr. McCaffrey, who had wisely opted for mandatory conciliation, could serve as a basis for the Commission's work.[116]

We also see some of the tensions regarding the ultimate purpose of the ILC's draft articles being reflected in the proposed dispute resolution provisions. Until late in the ILC's process the draft on the non-navigational uses of international watercourses was not certain as a framework convention but may have also taken the form of model rules.[117] Model rules would have allowed for the inclusion of more specific guidance, but this may not have been advisable given the great diversity of transboundary river basins around the world.[118]

Rosenstock's draft articles, while simplified, still represented a 'Stepped Approach', providing a clear diplomatic 'Step', a technical 'Step', and an adjudicative 'Step' set against a clear progression through these 'Steps' delineated by the clear limitations in scope and duration of the respective 'Steps'. There seems to be recourse to technical expertise and decision making in the

115 Robert Rosenstock, "Second report on the law of the non-navigational uses of international watercourses" (UN Doc A/CN.4/462) in *Year Book of the International Law Commission 1994* vol 2 part 1 (2001) 113 at 115 para 15–16 (UN Doc A/CN.4/SER.A/1994/Add.1(Part 1)) [footnote omitted].

116 "2311th Meeting Thursday, 24 June 1993, at 10.10 A.M." in *Yearbook of the International Law Commission 1993* vol 1 (1995) 93 at 94 para 10 (UN Doc A/CN.4/SER.A/1993).

117 *Ibid* at 94 para 11.

118 *Ibid.*

fact-finding/conciliation process. The ultimate adjudicative 'Step' would again presumably be binding and there is at least one compulsory 'Step', the initial diplomatic 'Step' embodied by the consultations and negotiations process. We see many of the mechanisms embodied in the drafts of earlier rapporteurs reflected here as well as many of the fundamental elements of the 'Stepped Approach'. In rendering the technical 'Step', here the fact-finding/conciliation mechanism, as effectively an optional 'Step', we see a framework closer to Evensen's draft. It is also unclear that this optional 'Step' would be utilized thus creating a two 'Step' process, or a one 'Step' process if the parties had not consented to the jurisdiction of any international tribunal or court. Rosenstock's draft articles are reproduced below:

Article 33: Settlement of disputes

1. Watercourse States shall settle their watercourse disputes by peaceful means.
2. In the absence of an applicable agreement between the States concerned for the settlement of such disputes, the disputes are to be settled in accordance with the following:
   (a) If a dispute arises concerning a question of fact or concerning the interpretation or application of the present articles, the States concerned shall expeditiously enter into consultations and negotiations with a view to arriving at an equitable resolution of the dispute;
   (b) If the States concerned have not arrived at a settlement of the dispute through consultations and negotiations within six months, they shall have recourse to impartial fact-finding or conciliation;
   (c) If after twelve months from the initial request for fact-finding or conciliation or, if there has been agreement to establish a fact-finding or conciliation commission, six months after receipt of a report from the fact-finding or conciliation commission, whichever is later, the parties have been unable to settle the dispute, any of the parties may submit the dispute to binding arbitration by any permanent or ad hoc tribunal that has been accepted by all the parties to the dispute.[119]

119 Robert Rosenstock, "Second report on the law of the non-navigational uses of international watercourses" (UN Doc A/CN.4/462) in *Year Book of the International Law Commission*

The dispute settlement provisions provided by Special Rapporteur Rosenstock ultimately were revised by the drafting committee of the ILC, feeling that "the proposed dispute settlement mechanism should be simple and realistic and should not depart from the overall tone of the draft which was based on consent and cooperation among riparian States."[120] The draft that was submitted to the UN General assembly by the ILC is reproduced below:

Article 33: Settlement of disputes

> In the absence of an applicable agreement between the watercourse States concerned, any watercourse dispute concerning a question of fact or the interpretation or application of the present articles shall be settled in accordance with the following provisions:
> (*a*) If such a dispute arises, the States concerned shall expeditiously enter into consultations and negotiations with a view to arriving at equitable solutions of the dispute, making use, as appropriate, of any joint watercourse institutions that may have been established by them.
> (*b*) If the States concerned have not arrived at a settlement of the disputes through consultations and negotiations, at any time after six months from the date of the request for consultations and negotiations, they shall at the request of any of them have recourse to impartial fact-finding or, if agreed upon by the States concerned, mediation or conciliation.
> (i) Unless otherwise agreed, a Fact-finding Commission shall be established, composed of one member nominated by each State concerned and in addition a member not having the nationality of any of the States concerned chosen by the nominated members who shall serve as Chairman.
> (ii) If the members nominated by the States are unable to agree on a Chairman within four months of the request for the establishment of the Commission, any State concerned may request the Secretary-General of the United Nations to

1994 vol 2 part 1 (1994) 113 at 121 para 41 (UN Doc A/CN.4/SER.A/1994/Add.1(Part 1)) [footnote omitted].

120 Report of the Drafting Committee, "2353rd Meeting Tuesday, 21 June 1994, at 10.10 A.M." in *Yearbook of the International Law Commission 1994* vol 1 (1996) 158 at 171 para 93 (UN Doc A/CN.4/SER.A/1994).

appoint the Chairman. If one of the States fails to nominate a member within four months of the initial request pursuant to paragraph (*b*), any other State concerned may request the Secretary-General of the United Nations to appoint a person who shall not have the nationality of any of the States concerned, who shall constitute a single member Commission.

(iii) The Commission shall determine its own procedure.

(iv) The States concerned have the obligation to provide the Commission with such information as it may require and, on request, to permit the Commission to have access to their respective territory and to inspect any facilities, plant, equipment, construction or natural feature relevant for the purpose of its inquiry.

(v) The Commission shall adopt its report by a majority vote, unless it is a single member Commission, and shall submit that report to the States concerned setting forth its findings and the reasons therefor and such recommendations as it deems appropriate.

(vi) The expenses of the Commission shall be borne equally by the States concerned.

(*c*) If, after twelve months from the initial request for fact-finding, mediation or conciliation or, if a fact-finding, mediation or conciliation commission has been established, six months after receipt of a report from the Commission, whichever is the later, the States concerned have been unable to settle the dispute, they may by agreement submit the dispute to arbitration or judicial settlement.[121]

Ultimately the draft articles on the non-navigational uses of international watercourses were submitted to the UN General assembly by the ILC and reflect quite closely the proposed draft articles of Rosenstock, although the optional technical 'Step' seems to have been replaced with a stronger mechanism that allows recourse to impartial fact-finding at the request of any of the State parties to a dispute.[122] This fact-finding commission has the power to

121 "Report of the Commission to the General Assembly on the work of its forty-sixth session" (UN Doc A/49/10) in *Yearbook of the International Law Commission 1994* vol 2 part 2 (1997) 1 at 133–134 (UN Doc A/CN.4/SER.A/1994/Add.1 (Part 2)).

122 *Ibid* at 133.

make findings of fact, report and make recommendations to the parties.[123] This alteration to the technical 'Step', changing it from a seemingly optional 'Step' to a compulsory 'Step' if requested by one of the parties, brings these drafts closer into conformity with the criteria laid out in regard to a 'Stepped Approach' in this work. The ultimate provisions of the *UN Watercourses Convention* covering dispute resolution in many respects reflects this draft as submitted although we do indeed see the influence towards State consent in some of the changes. The 'Stepped Approach' was ultimately eroded to some degree by allowing State parties a suite of options in Article 33(2)[124] and thus arguably confusing the progression between the various 'Steps'. Of the nine (9) criteria analysed as part of the review of treaties for this work, the *UN Watercourses Convention* satisfied seven (7), a majority of the criteria, only lacking a distinctly adjudicative 'Step' and binding final mechanism.

In briefly examining the progression of proposed draft articles by the various rapporteurs to the ILC, through the ILC's process we can see the importance and consistent presence of some form of a 'Stepped Approach'. By comparing these various drafts, we can see how these provisions would comply more or less with the criteria laid out in this work regarding a 'Stepped Approach'.

2 A 'Stepped Approach' to International Watercourse Disputes in Treaty Practice

As stated above in the methodology section, two hundred and twenty-five (225) treaties were identified containing distinct dispute resolution provisions between State actors[125] since 1900. These treaties were reviewed and scored based on the presence of nine (9) criteria, identified by the author after a review of relevant treaties as important components of an ideal "Stepped Approach":
- **The presence of three (3) or more 'Steps'** – three (3) or more distinct 'Steps' were looked for in the specific provision(s) dealing with the resolution of

123 *Ibid* at 134.

124 *Convention on the Law of Non-Navigational Uses of International Watercourses*, 21 May 1997, 2999 UNTS 77, 36 ILM 700 (*Watercourses Convention*) at 136 art 32 (entered into force 17 August 2014).

125 It is important to note that only distinct provisions addressing disputes between State parties were reviewed. The author attempted to differentiate these from compliance and management mechanisms in the agreements, unless these mechanisms were specifically mentioned in the dispute resolution provisions as applying to disputes between State actors.

disputes between State parties to an agreement during the implementation of the treaty;

- **Steps of limited scope or duration** – agreements were assessed for either subject-matter or time-period limitations in the provision(s) dealing with the resolution of disputes between State parties to an agreement;
- **A clear progression through the 'Steps'** – this criterion assessed whether there was an obvious and clearly articulated progression through the various 'Steps' dealing with the resolution of disputes between State parties to an agreement. For example, provisions which provided parties to a dispute with a series of choices were regarded as a single 'Step';
- **Recourse to technical expertise and decision making** – for this criterion dispute resolution provisions were assessed to see if parties to a dispute had explicit recourse to specific technical expertise in the process, for example, the ability to have a technical report made or to consult with an engineer;
- **A distinct technical 'Step'** – this criterion is distinct from the preceding criteria in that it looks for a specific technical 'Step', separate from juridical, political or diplomatic mechanisms; in some cases it was not always apparent if a mechanism or body was exclusively technical in its composition or work, here the function and makeup of a mechanism or body was analysed based on the surrounding provisions of the treaty to assess if it had predominantly technical functions or composition;
- **A distinct diplomatic 'Step'** – agreements were analysed to see if there was a clearly diplomatic 'Step', i.e. negotiation, mediation, good offices, 'by agreement' etc., parties arguably always have recourse to diplomatic means of dispute resolution but unless it was specifically mentioned in the dispute resolution provision(s) it was not counted as such for our purposes here;
- **A distinct adjudicative 'Step'** – this criterion looked at whether a dispute resolution provision in an agreement provided a distinct 'Step' for adjudicative means of resolving the dispute, such as arbitration or recourse to an international court or tribunal of a distinctly juridical nature;
- **At least one compulsory 'Step'** – agreements were reviewed to see if they had at least one clearly compulsory dispute resolution 'Step' that obligated a party or the parties to participate, regardless of their consent; the use of the language 'must' or 'shall' or the presence of a 'Step' that could be instigated by only one of the parties were determined to indicate such a compulsory 'Step'; and
- **A binding ultimate 'Step'** – agreements were looked at to see if the final 'Step' in their dispute resolution process had the power to impose a 'binding'

> or 'final' determination of the dispute regardless of any agreement or lack of agreement of the parties to the dispute.[126]

Of the two hundred and twenty-five (225) treaties reviewed, nineteen (19)[127] or roughly eight percent (8%) met all nine (9) criteria. One hundred and nineteen

126 In some cases, where it was not stated, the binding nature of the mechanism was assumed i.e. the ICJ or arbitration being deemed to be binding. Other mechanisms, such as diplomatic means, were deemed to be non-binding.

127 *Agreement to Regulate the Level of the Lake of the Woods and Protocol relating thereto*, United States and Canada, 24 February 1925, 43 LNTS 251; *Convention between Spain and Portugal to regulate the hydro-electric development of the international section of the River Douro*, 11 August 1927, LXXXII LNTS 130; *Convention between the Federal Republic of Germany, the French Republic, and the Grand-Duchy of Luxembourg on the subject of Moselle canalization*, 27 October 1956, 2375 UNTS 3; *Agreement between the government of the French Republic and the Spanish government relating to Lake Lanoux*, 12 July 1958, 796 UNTS 217; *Treaty between the Kingdom of the Netherlands and the Federal Republic of Germany concerning the course of the common frontier, the boundary waters, real property situated near the frontier, traffic crossing the frontier on land and via inland waters, and other frontier questions*, 8 April 1960, 508 UNTS 148 (*Frontier Treaty*); *The Indus Waters Treaty 1960* (*with annexes*), 19 September 1960, 419 UNTS 125 (*Indus Waters Treaty*); *Treaty between Canada and the United States of America relating to co-operative development of the water resources of the Columbia River Basin*, 17 January 1961, 542 UNTS 246; *Protocol between the government of the Federal Republic of Germany, the French Republic and the Grand Duchy of Luxembourg concerning the establishment of an international commission to protect the Moselle against pollution*, 20 December 1961, 940 UNTS 217; Agreement between the Socialist Federal Republic of Yugoslavia and the Romanian People's Republic concerning the construction and operation of the Iron Gates Water Power and Navigation System on the River Danube, 30 November 1963, 512 UNTS 42; Convention between the Socialist Federal Republic of Yugoslavia and the Romanian People's Republic concerning the execution of works for the Iron Gates Water Power and Navigation System on the River Danube, 30 November 1963, 512 UNTS 152; *Convention to regulate the hydroelectric development of the international sections of the river Douro and its tributaries* (*with additional protocol*), *Spain and Portugal, 16 July 1964, 1288 UNTS 191; Exchange of Notes* (*with attachments*) *constituting an agreement authorizing the Canadian Entitlement Purchase Agreement provided for under the Treaty relating to co-operative development of the water resources of the Columbia River Basin*, Canada and the United States of America, 16 September 1964, 542 UNTS 244, Can TS 1964 No 2; *Treaty between the Republic of Austria and the Czechoslovak Socialist Republic concerning the regulation of water management questions relating to frontier waters*, 7 December 1967, 728 UNTS 313; *Statute of the river Uruguay, signed at Salto*, Argentina and Uruguay, 26 February 1975, 1295 UNTS 339 (*Statute of the river Uruguay*); *Treaty on the Lesotho Highlands Water Project between the Government of the Kingdom of Lesotho and the Government of the Republic of South Africa*, 24 October 1986, https://www.fao.org/faolex/results/details/en/c/LEX-FAOC015909/; *Protocol IV to the treaty on the Lesotho Highlands Water Project – supplementary arrangements regarding phase IA*, 19 November 1991, http://gis.nacse.org/tfdd/tfdddocs/498ENG.pdf; *Protocol VI to the Treaty on the Lesotho Highlands Water Project Supplementary Arrangements Regarding the System of Governance for the Project, Lesotho and South Africa, 4 June 1999*, https://www.fao.org/faolex/results/details/en/c/LEX-FAOC216572; *Niger Basin Water Charter*

TABLE 3 Number and percentage of treaties at each score

Presence of 'Stepped Approach' (1–9)	Number of treaties at each score (X%)
9	19 (8%)
8	9 (4%)
7	26 (12%)
6	20 (9%)
5	45 (20%)
4	29 (13%)
3	25 (11%)
2	46 (20%)
1	6 (3%)
Total number of treaties with a dispute resolution mechanism	225 (100%)

(119) or roughly fifty-three percent (53%) met five (5) or more criteria. The breakdown of treaties by assessed score is illustrated in Table 3. The percentages given are the percentage of the two hundred and twenty-five (225) treaties reviewed.

As evidenced by the results represented in Table 3 most treaties reviewed partially fulfilled the nine (9) criteria laid out. These nine (9) criteria should be viewed as an idealized 'Stepped Approach' based on the author's review of the relevant treaties. It is of course possible to say that an agreement which partially fulfills the nine (9) criteria may have a 'Stepped Approach' to disputes, but for the interests of this discourse it seems useful to have an idealized benchmark against which to measure these agreements.

If we break down the scores by region we see some regional variation from our more general numbers above, generally though the numbers remain relatively consistent. We see that Europe as a region has the highest number of its treaties that meet all nine (9) criteria with ten (10) treaties representing roughly eleven percent (11%) of their eighty-eight (88) treaties with dispute resolution mechanisms in the database. North America had the highest proportion of its treaties that met all nine (9) criteria with three (3) treaties representing roughly twenty-three percent (23%). Asia as a region had the smallest proportion of its treaties meet all nine criteria with one (1) treaty amounting to approximately two percent (2%) of all of the Asian regional agreements

(*La Charte de L'eau du Bassin du Niger*), *30 April 2008*, http://www.abn.ne/images/documents/Charte_Eau/niger_basin_water_charter_certified_copy.pdf.

TABLE 4 Number and percentage of treaties at each score by region[a]

Presence of 'Stepped' approach (1–9)	Number of treaties at each score (X%)	S. America (X%)	N. America (X%)	General (X%)	Europe (X%)	Asia (X%)	Africa (X%)
9	**19 (8%)**	**1 (5%)**	**3 (23%)**	0	**10 (11%)**	**1 (2%)**	**4 (7%)**
8	9 (4%)	2 (11%)	0	0	3 (3%)	2 (4%)	2 (3%)
7	26 (12%)	1 (5%)	1 (8%)	1 (50%)	8 (9%)	6 (13%)	9 (16%)
6	20 (9%)	1 (5%)	0	0	7 (8%)	3 (7%)	9 (16%)
5	45 (20%)	**2 (11%)**	**4 (31%)**	0	**19 (22%)**	**4 (9%)**	**16 (28%)**
4	29 (13%)	4 (21%)	2 (15%)	0	13 (15%)	5 (11%)	5 (9%)
3	25 (11%)	1 (5%)	1 (8%)	0	13 (15%)	4 (9%)	6 (10%)
2	46 (20%)	5 (26%)	2 (15%)	1 (50%)	12 (14%)	20 (44%)	6 (10%)
1	6 (3%)	2 (11%)	0	0	3 (3%)	0	1 (2%)
Total	225 (100%)	19 (100%)	13 (100%)	2 (100%)	88 (100%)	45 (100%)	58 (100%)

a The regions used are based upon those used in the TFDD and reflect the continents of the world as such the middle east for example is categorised as part of Asia. The regions also reflect the area affected by the treaty and not necessarily the region of the parties, for example many colonial era treaties are grouped with the area affected by the treaty rather than the home continent of the colonial powers.

with dispute resolution mechanisms measured in this work. Europe had forty-seven (47) agreements that had a score of five (5) or more, representing roughly fifty-three percent of its total agreements (53%). Africa as a region had the highest proportion of agreements that received a score of five (5) or more at forty (40), amounting to sixty-nine percent (69%) of its total agreements. North America was close behind with sixty-two percent (62%) of its agreements with a score of five (5) or above. Asia and South America were the only regions that had a majority of their agreements with a score of less than five (5), with twenty-nine (29) or sixty-four percent (64%) and twelve (12) agreements or roughly sixty-three percent (63%) below that mark respectively. This data can be seen reflected in Table 4. The percentages given on that table are the percent of the total agreements reviewed from that region at each score.

Certainly, a certain degree of regional variation and practice can be expected. It is certainly worth noting the high proportion of the North

American agreements that met all nine (9) criteria as well as the high percentage of African agreements that were scored at five (5) or above. The high proportion of Asian and South American agreements that were below a score of five (5) can also in part be attributed to the prevalence of diplomatic only dispute resolution 'Steps' in many of these agreements, Asia for example has forty-four percent (44%) of its treaties with a score of two (2) capturing many of these types of treaties with only a compulsory diplomatic 'Step'. Still too much should perhaps not be read into these regional variations given the rather limited data with which we are comparing them, it certainly would be easy to miss contributing factors at this macro scale.

It is also instructive for us to compare our results with the total number of agreements on international watercourses by region.[128] This data can be found in Table 5. The percentages given are the percentages of the total agreements listed, whether that be all international watercourse agreements regardless of whether they have a dispute resolution provision, the total number assessed by this work to have a dispute resolution provision or those nineteen (19) that met all nine (9) of the criteria for a 'Stepped Approach'. We can see for example that North America as a region represents roughly thirteen percent (13%) of all international watercourse agreements but only roughly six percent (6%) of international watercourse agreements with a dispute resolution provision. Both North America and Europe show an increase in their proportion of agreements that met all nine (9) criteria for a 'Stepped Approach' compared to their proportional share of the total number of international watercourse treaties and the number of treaties with a dispute resolution provision. Both the south America and Asia regions show a proportionally lower representation in agreements that met all nine (9) criteria for a 'Stepped Approach' than they have for the total number of treaties and the number of treaties with a dispute resolution provision. The Asia region also show a strong drop in their share of treaties that met all nine (9) criteria relative to their share of the total number of agreements and number of treaties with a dispute resolution provision. The Africa region seems to be relatively consistent across the board with a slight increase in their proportion of treaties that have a dispute resolution provision. It is important to remember that some regions have a greater representation in total agreements on international watercourses. Europe for instance has a much higher representation generally in number of agreements on

128 For this a modified database was used from the years 1900–2010 based on the TFDD with some duplicate treaties removed and some additional treaties added based on cross referencing against the table of 219 treaties compiled in Christina Leb, *Cooperation in the Law of Transboundary Water Resources* (Cambridge University Press, 2013) at 263–298.

TABLE 5 Breakdown by region of the total number of international watercourse agreements, agreements with dispute resolution provisions and those that met all the criteria for a 'Stepped Approach'

Region/Continent	Total number of treaties[a] (X%)	Number of treaties with a dispute resolution provision (X%)	Number of treaties that met all criteria (X%)
S. America	56 (9%)	19 (8%)	1 (5%)
N. America	79 (13%)	13 (6%)	3 (16%)
General	7 (1%)	2 (1%)	0
Europe	223 (37%)	88 (39%)	10 (53%)
Asia	117 (19%)	45 (20%)	1 (5%)
Africa	125 (21%)	58 (26%)	4 (21%)
Total	607 (100%)	225 (100%)	19 (100%)

a For this a database beginning at 1900 AD was used, created through the cross referencing of the various treaty sources described in the methodology section, and the author's own knowledge.

international watercourses. It is useful to keep these facts in mind when comparing regions in regard to their fulfillment of the nine (9) 'Stepped Approach' criteria. To some degree it may be more informative to compare regions against themselves across these data sets rather than comparing regions against each other.

It is important for our purposes to note the not inconsequential proportion of agreements that met all nine (9) criteria certainly enough to indicate a degree of deliberate State practice in crafting international watercourse agreements. It is also worth noting again that the majority of international agreements reviewed carried a moderate to high degree of adoption of the selected criteria. This may also be in part due to the heavy domination in number of treaties reviewed with a distinct dispute resolution provision that were from either the Europe or Africa regions, roughly sixty-five percent (65%). Whether we would say that all of these international agreements which showed a moderate to high degree of adoption of the selected criteria reflected a 'Stepped Approach' is not clear without a close reading of the individual treaties in question on a case-by-case basis. What we can say is this majority reflects a degree of acceptance of the criteria which a 'Stepped Approach' would ideally possess.

3 Why a 'Stepped Approach' to Disputes Is Important in the Law of the Non-navigational Uses of International Watercourses

To assist our discussion, it may be useful to view a few examples of dispute resolution provisions in existing international watercourse agreements that exhibit a 'Stepped Approach'. The examples selected have met all nine (9) of the criteria used to evaluate the two hundred and twenty-five (225) international agreements as part of this work. An attempt has been made to reproduce the dispute resolution provisions in their entirety to allow the reader to see for themselves how a 'Stepped Approach' could look and to observe how the various 'Steps' interact with each other.

The *Indus Waters treaty*:[129]

(1) Any question which arises between the Parties concerning the interpretation or application of this Treaty or the existence of any fact which, if established, might constitute a breach of this Treaty shall first be examined by the Commission, which will endeavour to resolve the question by agreement.

(2) If the Commission does not reach agreement on any of the questions mentioned in Paragraph (1), then a difference will be deemed to have arisen, which shall be dealt with as follows:

(a) Any difference which, in the opinion of either Commissioner, falls within the provisions of Part 1 of Annexure F[1] shall, at the request of either Commissioner, be dealt with by a Neutral Expert in accordance with the provisions of Part 2 of Annexure F;

(b) If the difference does not come within the provisions of Paragraph (2) (a), or if a Neutral Expert, in accordance with the provisions of Paragraph 7 of Annexure F, has informed the Commission that, in his opinion, the difference, or a part thereof, should be treated as a dispute, then a dispute will be deemed to have arisen which shall be settled in accordance with the provisions of Paragraphs (3), (4) and (5):

Provided that, at the discretion of the Commission, any difference may either be dealt with by a Neutral Expert in accordance with the Provisions of Part 2 of Annexure F or be deemed to be a dispute to be settled in

129 *The Indus Waters Treaty 1960 (with annexes)*, 19 September 1960, 419 UNTS 125.

accordance with the provisions of Paragraphs (3), (4) and (5), or may be settled in any other way agreed upon by the Commission.

(3) As soon as a dispute to be settled in accordance with this and the succeeding paragraphs of this Article has arisen, the Commission shall, at the request of either Commissioner, report the fact to the two Governments, as early as practicable, stating in its report the points on which the Commission is in agreement and the issues in dispute, the views of each Commissioner on these issues and his reasons therefor.

(4) Either Government may, following receipt of the report referred to in Paragraph (3), or if it comes to the conclusion that this report is being unduly delayed in the Commission, invite the other Government to resolve the dispute by agreement. In doing so it shall state the names of its negotiators and their readiness to meet with the negotiators to be appointed by the other Government at a time and place to be indicated by the other Government. To assist in these negotiations, the two Government may agree to enlist the services of one or more mediators acceptable to them.

(5) A court of Arbitration shall be established to resolve the dispute in the manner provided by Annexure G[1]
   (a) upon agreement between the Parties to do so; or
   (b) at the request of either Party, if, after negotiations have begun pursuant to Paragraph (4), in its opinion the dispute is not likely to be resolved by negotiations or mediation; or
   (c) at the request of either Party, if, after the expiry of one month following receipt by the other Government of the invitation referred to in Paragraph (4), that Party comes to the conclusion that the other Government is unduly delaying the negotiations.

(6) The Provisions of Paragraphs (3), (4) and (5) shall not apply to any difference while it is being dealt with by a Neutral Expert.[130]

Here we have article IX of the *Indus Waters Treaty* which is an excellent example of a 'Stepped Approach' and indeed served as a template for a 'Stepped Approach' in approaching this research and identifying the nine (9) criteria

130 *Ibid* at art IX.

used in the assessment of other international watercourse agreements. It has been termed an "innovative multi-tier dispute resolution system".[131]

The approach here begins with "any question"[132] arising being examined internally by the "Permanent Indus Commission".[133] Given the technical nature of this "Permanent Indus Commission" this can be characterized as a distinct technical 'Step' while also being capable of fulfilling a diplomatic role between the two governments. The Commissioners, who are ordinarily high-ranking engineers competent in the field of hydrology and water-use, serve as the primary representatives of their respective Governments. If after good faith attempts to resolve a "question" in accordance with Article IX(1) the "Commission" is unable to resolve the matter, then under Article IX, an impasse transforms a "question" into a "difference"[134] which will be dealt with by either a "Neutral Expert" or deemed a "dispute".[135]

The neutral expert shall deal with a "difference" if the difference falls within the provisions of Part 1 of Annexure F in the opinion of either Commissioner and either Commissioner has made a request for the "difference" to be dealt with by a neutral expert.[136] Accordingly a matter does not need to be referred to a neutral expert before being deemed a "dispute" and forwarded to a Court of Arbitration, this question has been at issue in recent disputes between India and Pakistan.[137] The functions of using a "Neutral Expert"[138] can also be viewed as a distinct technical 'Step'. Here also the scope of this 'Step' is limited by Annexure F,[139] particularly the technical questions contained in Part I that are qualified to be put to a neutral expert.[140] "The decision of the Neutral Expert on all matters within his competence shall be final and binding, in respect of the

131 Makane Moïse Mbengue and Rukmini Das, *Use of Experts in International Freshwater Disputes* (Brill Research Perspectives in International Water Law, 2019) at 9.

132 *The Indus Waters Treaty 1960 (with annexes)*, 19 September 1960, 419 UNTS 125, art IX (1),(2) (*Indus Waters Treaty*).

133 *Ibid* at art VIII.

134 *Indus Waters Treaty Arbitration (Pakistan v India)* (6 July 2023), Award on the Competence of the Court, PCA Case No 2023-01 at para 171, (Permanent Court of Arbitration), online: <https://pca-cpa.org/en/cases/284/>.

135 *The Indus Waters Treaty 1960 (with annexes)*, 19 September 1960, 419 UNTS 125, art IX (2) (*Indus Waters Treaty*).

136 *Indus Waters Treaty Arbitration (Pakistan v India)* (6 July 2023), Award on the Competence of the Court, PCA Case No 2023-01 at para 191, (Permanent Court of Arbitration), online: <https://pca-cpa.org/en/cases/284/>.

137 *Ibid* at para 195–198.

138 "A Neutral Expert shall be a highly qualified engineer [...]." *The Indus Waters Treaty 1960 (with annexes)*, 19 September 1960, 419 UNTS 125, Annexure F, Part 2 (*Indus Waters Treaty*).

139 *Ibid* at Annexure F.

140 *Ibid* at Annexure F, Part 1.

particular matter on which the decision is made, upon the Parties and upon any Court of Arbitration established under the provisions of Article IX (5)."[141]

According to the PCA for a "dispute" to be deemed to have arisen one of two circumstances need to have occurred: the "difference" does not fall within the provisions of paragraph (2)(a) or after having been referred to a neutral expert the neutral expert under paragraph 7 of Annexure F has determined that the "difference" is outside their competence, which is restricted to technical matters.[142] If a "dispute"[143] arises then the "[Permanent Indus Commission] shall, at the request of either Commissioner, report the fact to the two Governments, as early as practicable, stating in its report the points on which the Commission is in agreement and the issues in dispute, the views of each Commissioner on these issues and his reasons therefor."[144] This can properly be viewed either as a distinct technical 'Step' or as a reporting function of the "Commission" emanating from the previous two technical 'Steps'. At this point the State parties to a dispute may enter into negotiations or mediation, upon receipt of the report or if one of the States concerned decides that that the report is being unduly delayed.[145] This is a distinct diplomatic 'Step'. This diplomatic 'Step' is limited in duration by Article IX (5)[146] which allows parties to prompt the following adjudicative 'Step' by agreement, if either of the parties feel that the dispute is not likely to be resolved by diplomatic means (once negotiations or mediation have already begun), or if after a period of one month from the receipt of an invitation to negotiate one party determines that the other is unduly delaying the diplomatic 'Step'.[147] The final 'Step' in this dispute resolution framework is forwarding a dispute to a court of Arbitration, as provided in Annexure G, for resolution.[148] A distinct binding adjudicative 'Step'.[149]

We see that the *Indus Waters Treaty* complies with all nine (9) criteria set forward in this work. It has four (4) to five (5) distinct graduated 'Steps' depending

141 *Ibid* at Annexure F, Part 2 (11).

142 *Indus Waters Treaty Arbitration* (*Pakistan v India*) (6 July 2023), Award on the Competence of the Court, PCA Case No 2023-01 at para 194, (Permanent Court of Arbitration), online: <https://pca-cpa.org/en/cases/284/>.

143 *The Indus Waters Treaty 1960* (*with annexes*), 19 September 1960, 419 UNTS 125, art IX (2) (*Indus Waters Treaty*).

144 *Ibid* at art IX (3).

145 *Ibid* at art IX (4).

146 *Ibid* at art IX (5).

147 *Ibid.*

148 *Ibid.*

149 *Ibid* at Annexure G (23).

on how you view the reporting powers of the "Permanent Indus Commission" under Article IX (3).[150] These steps are limited in scope and duration, although some 'Steps' do not set hard timelines which could prove problematic to moving matters along, although generally the agreement allows one party to force matters to the next 'Step' if they feel a certain 'Step' is being frustrated or unduly delayed.[151] The PCA in their recent judgment on the competence of the court in the *Indus Waters Treaty Arbitration* (*Pakistan v India*) (6 July 2023) remarked on the 'stepped' nature of the Treaty's dispute resolution mechanisms:

> Article IX(1) requires the Parties – within the Commission – to attempt resolution through agreement. If agreement cannot be reached, Article IX(2)(a) provides either Commissioner with the option of invoking the services of a neutral expert, but that option must be exercised through an actual request for the appointment of a neutral expert by the two Governments (or failing that, by the World Bank). If the option provided in Article IX(2)(a) is not exercised, then Article IX(2)(b) provides the alternative option of invoking the services of a court of arbitration. This stepwise procedure ensures that the Parties will attempt to reach prompt consensual resolution, but if they do not, they can seek the form of third-party resolution best suited to their needs.[152]

The 'Steps' are compulsory throughout, evidenced by the use of the word "shall", and the 'Steps' can generally be triggered by any one of the State parties. This ability of either party to trigger the 'Steps' has been an important element in regard to the use of neutral experts and arbitration in recent PCA jurisprudence as it is viewed as a means of preventing a "procedural impasse" by one party attempting to block the use of an Arbitral Court.[153] The PCA rightly found that allowing a party to use the dispute resolution provisions of the Treaty to erect "unnecessary obstacles" would be inconsistent with the overarching goal of the Treaty's dispute resolution provisions.[154] Returning to our nine (9) cri-

150 *Ibid* at art IX (3).

151 *Ibid* at art IX (4), (5)(b), (c).

152 *Indus Waters Treaty Arbitration* (*Pakistan v India*) (6 July 2023), Award on the Competence of the Court, PCA Case No 2023-01 at para 199, (Permanent Court of Arbitration), online: <https://pca-cpa.org/en/cases/284/>.

153 *Ibid* at para 201.

154 *Ibid* at para 211.

teria the Treaty also has distinct technical, diplomatic and adjudicative 'Steps' and the ultimate 'Step' is binding arbitration.[155]

The *Indus Waters Treaty* has endured and operated despite a difficult relationship between the riparians including during periods of armed conflict between them.[156] The *Indus Waters Treaty* provides an excellent showcase of a robust and resilient 'Stepped Approach' dispute resolution framework.

Treaty on the Lesotho Highlands Water Project between the Government of the Kingdom of Lesotho and the Government of the Republic of South Africa:[157]

Article 16: The Prevention and Settlement of Disputes

[…]

(4) In the event of a dispute arising, either Party or the Parties jointly or the Lesotho Highlands Development Authority or the Trans-Caledon Tunnel Authority, may request the Joint Permanent Technical Commission to conduct an investigation and to present a written report containing its recommendations to both Parties, the Lesotho Highlands Development Authority and the Trans-Caledon Tunnel Authority.

(5) The Joint Permanent Technical Commission shall conduct the investigation and present its written report in terms of paragraph (4) with all reasonable dispatch. If the Joint Permanent Technical Commission cannot consider the matter within fourteen calendar days, it shall notify the referring party and, where appropriate, request an extension of time for consideration of the matter.

---

155 *The Indus Waters Treaty 1960 (with annexes)*, 19 September 1960, 419 UNTS 125, Annexure G (23) (*Indus Waters Treaty*).

156 "Fortunately, the two South Asian countries between which relations are perhaps the most delicate, India and Pakistan, have a treaty governing the principal watercourse system they share, the Indus, which has continued to function for over a half-century despite wars between them. Indus Waters Treaty 1960, 419 UNTS 125. The arbitration provisions of the treaty were invoked by Pakistan in the Indus Waters Kishenganga Arbitration […]." Stephen C. McCaffrey, *The Law of International Watercourses*, 3rd ed (Oxford University Press, 2019).

157 *Treaty on the Lesotho Highlands Water Project between the Government of the Kingdom of Lesotho and the Government of the Republic of South Africa*, 24 October 1986, https://www.fao.org/faolex/results/details/en/c/LEX-FAOC015909/ (*Treaty on the Lesotho Highlands Water Project*).

(6) The Joint Permanent Technical Commission may either report that no actions called for or may make recommendations calling for measures to be taken by one of the Parties, the Parties jointly, the Lesotho Highlands Development Authority or the Trans-Caledon Tunnel Authority, or may report that the matter is of such a nature that recourse to more formal procedures is called for.

(7) In the event of a dispute not being resolved by means of any action taken in accordance with the provisions of paragraphs (4), (5) and (6), it shall be made the subject of negotiation between the Parties.

(8) If a dispute cannot be resolved by negotiation between the Parties, such dispute shall be submitted to the Arbitral Tribunal as hereinafter provided.

(9) The Parties may jointly institute arbitration proceedings on the basis of an agreement to that effect between them which agreement shall set forth the nature of the dispute and the names of the arbitrators appointed by each Party.

Provided that any Party may institute arbitration proceedings by giving written notice thereof to the other Party which notice shall set forth the nature of the dispute and the name of the arbitrator appointed by such Party.

[...]

(15) Notwithstanding anything to the contrary contained in this Article, the Parties may at any time agree to refer a dispute to arbitration.

[...]

(17)

(a) The award of the Arbitral Tribunal shall be in writing and signed by the members who voted for it and shall constitute the award of the Tribunal, and a signed counterpart of such award shall be transmitted to each Party;

(b) The award of the Arbitral Tribunal shall be definitive and binding on the Parties, and they shall duly and expeditiously give effect thereto.[158]

The *Treaty on the Lesotho Highlands Water Project between the Government of the Kingdom of Lesotho and the Government of the Republic of South Africa*[159] is

158 *Ibid* at art 16.

159 *Treaty on the Lesotho Highlands Water Project between the Government of the Kingdom of Lesotho and the Government of the Republic of South Africa*, 24 October 1986, https://www

in many respects an excellent example of a 'Stepped Approach' to disputes on international watercourses. It meets all nine (9) of the criteria laid out in this work. Parts of Article 16 reproduced above have been abbreviated due to the requirements of space and for ease of reference by the reader. The "Lesotho Highlands Development Authority" and the "Trans-Caledon Tunnel Authority" are the authorities entrusted with the implementation of the treaty within the territory of the respective parties.[160] Either of these authorities or the respective State parties to the agreement may, either jointly or individually, "request the Joint Permanent Technical Commission to conduct an investigation and to present a written report containing its recommendations [...]."[161] Here we commence with a distinct technical 'Step', which is limited by Article 16 (5) in duration to a period defined as "with all reasonable dispatch"[162] this is further clarified by stating that if the "Commission cannot consider the matter within fourteen calendar days, it shall notify the referring party and, where appropriate, request an extension of time for consideration of the matter."[163] The scope of this technical 'Step' is further limited by Article 16 (6) which limits the scope of authority of the Commission to reporting "that no actions called for or may make recommendations calling for measures to be taken by one of the Parties, the Parties jointly, the Lesotho Highlands Development Authority or the Trans-Caledon Tunnel Authority, or may report that the matter is of such a nature that recourse to more formal procedures is called for."[164] There is also a clear recourse to technical expertise and decision making; not only is there a clear "Joint Permanent Technical Commission" but the agreement allows this "Commission" to "appoint technical experts and consultants to provide expert opinion and advice whenever this appears to be necessary."[165]

If this technical 'Step' fails to resolve the matter then the dispute "shall be made the subject of negotiation between the Parties."[166] Here we have a clear diplomatic 'Step' and a clear progression from the exhausted previous technical 'Step'. If negotiations fail to produce a resolution then the matter "shall be

.fao.org/faolex/results/details/en/c/LEX-FAOC015909/ (*Treaty on the Lesotho Highlands Water Project*).

160 *Ibid* at art 7, 8.

161 *Ibid* at art 16 (4).

162 *Ibid* at art 16 (5).

163 *Ibid* at art 16 (5).

164 *Ibid* at art 16 (6).

165 *Ibid* at art 9(23).

166 *Ibid* at art 16 (7).

submitted to the Arbitral Tribunal [...]."[167] Here we have a clear adjudicative 'Step' and again a clear progression from the exhausted previous 'Step'. Not only does this agreement exhibit the three distinct graduated 'Steps' looked for as part of this study, there is a clear progression from one 'Step' to the next upon the failure of the previous 'Step' to resolve the matter. While the technical 'Step' does have clear limitations of scope and duration the diplomatic 'Step' lacks clear limitations. The adjudicative 'Step' is a bit open ended as the arbitral tribunal is empowered to set its own procedure[168] but does possess some procedural tools that can prevent a deadlock.[169] There are several compulsory 'Steps' in this framework, including the technical and diplomatic 'Steps'. The final adjudicative 'Step' is also expressly binding.[170]

The *Niger Basin Water Charter*:[171]

> Article 29: Amicable Settlement
>
> In the event of a dispute between two or several State Parties concerning the interpretation or the application of the present Charter, the Parties shall seek a settlement by the good offices of the Authority, mediation or conciliation, or by any other peaceful means of dispute settlement.
>
> Article 30: Resort to the Permanent Technical Committee
>
> If no solution has been found on completion of the good offices, mediation and conciliation procedures, the dispute shall be submitted to the Permanent Technical Committee which shall propose a settlement to the Council of Ministers and the Summit of the Heads of State and Government after six (6) months from the time the Executive Secretariat request it to propose a settlement.

---

167 *Ibid* at art 16 (8).

168 *Ibid* at art 16 (14) (b).

169 "All decisions of the Arbitral Tribunal shall be by a majority vote of the members but in the event of there being no majority vote, the President shall have a casting vote in addition to a deliberative vote;" *Ibid* at art 16 (14) (e).

170 *Ibid* at art 16 (15) (b).

171 *Niger Basin Water Charter* (*La Charte de L'eau du Bassin du Niger*), *30 April 2008*, http://www.abn.ne/images/documents/Charte_Eau/niger_basin_water_charter_certified_copy.pdf.

Article 31: Sub-regional and Jurisdictional Settlement

> In the event of no satisfactory settlement at this level, the Parties to the dispute shall refer the matter to the Conciliation Commission of the African Union as a first step, before any referral to the International Court of Justice.[172]

The *Niger Basin Water Charter*[173] met all of the nine (9) criteria set out in this work and is an interesting example of a 'Stepped Approach' to disputes on international watercourses for our purposes, particularly because it is a regional multilateral agreement. The initial 'Step' of this dispute resolution framework is in fact quite general in its scope providing a suite of dispute resolution mechanisms for State parties to choose from.[174] It is similar in this sense to Article 33(2) of the *UN Watercourses Convention*.[175] This 'Step' also does not possess clear limitations of scope or duration other than to say that "If no solution has been **found on completion of the good offices, mediation and conciliation procedures**, the dispute shall be submitted to the Permanent Technical Committee".[176] The "Permanent Technical Committee"[177] can be seen to represent either a distinct technical 'Step' in the process or, due to its advisory function to the Council of Ministers and the Summit of the Heads of State, as recourse to technical expertise and decision making under a distinct diplomatic 'Step'. In any case the "Permanent Technical Committee" does possess recourse to technical expertise and decision making.[178] The

172 *Ibid* at chapter IX.

173 *Niger Basin Water Charter* (*La Charte de L'eau du Bassin du Niger*), *30 April 2008*, http://www.abn.ne/images/documents/Charte_Eau/niger_basin_water_charter_certified_copy.pdf.

174 *Ibid* at chapter IX, art (29).

175 *Convention on the Law of Non-Navigational Uses of International Watercourses, 21 May 1997, 2999 UNTS 77, 36 ILM 700* (*Watercourses Convention*) at 136–138 art 33(2) (*entered into force 17 August 2014*).

176 *Niger Basin Water Charter* (*La Charte de L'eau du Bassin du Niger*), *30 April 2008*, http://www.abn.ne/images/documents/Charte_Eau/niger_basin_water_charter_certified_copy.pdf, chapter IX, art (30) (emphasis added).

177 *Ibid* at chapter V.

178 *Ibid*; see Article 18 in particular which states "In pursuance of its missions, the Permanent technical Committee is supported by the Niger Basin Observatory, the National Focal Structures, the Sub-basin Commissions, the Regional Advisory Unit and the Panel of Experts. [...]." *Niger Basin Water Charter* (*La Charte de L'eau du Bassin du Niger*), *30 April 2008*, http://www.abn.ne/images/documents/Charte_Eau/niger_basin_water_charter_certified_copy.pdf, chapter V, art (18).

"Permanent Technical Committee" is triggered by the failure of the previous 'Step' to resolve the dispute and shall recommend a resolution "after six (6) months from the time the Executive Secretariat request it to propose a settlement",[179] showing a clear limitation in the duration of this 'Step'. The scope of the "Permanent Technical Committee" is also limited in its function, it is empowered only to submit a proposed settlement to the Council of Ministers and the Summit of the Heads of State. Whether you chose to view the Council of Ministers and the Summit of the Heads of State as a distinct 'Step' from the "Permanent Technical Committee" it is nonetheless a distinctly diplomatic 'Step' albeit one without clear limitations of scope or duration. "In the event of no satisfactory settlement at this level, the Parties to the dispute shall refer the matter to the Conciliation Commission of the African Union".[180] Here we have a clear technical 'Step' triggered by the failure of the previous 'Step' to resolve the dispute.[181] Upon the failure of this 'Step' to resolve the dispute the matter is then referred to the ICJ[182] which is a binding adjudicative 'Step'.

This agreement uses several compulsory 'Steps' as evidenced by the repeated use of the word "Shall". It displays clear graduated 'Steps' and a clear progression through those 'Steps'. It also displays the three distinct 'Steps' our study looked for and recourse to technical expertise and decision making. It also possesses a binding final 'Step'. It, however, leaves several 'Steps' without clear limits in duration or scope which could prove to be problematic, although the "Permanent Technical Committee" possesses limitations in both scope and duration.

---

179 *Niger Basin Water Charter (La Charte de L'eau du Bassin du Niger), 30 April 2008*, http://www.abn.ne/images/documents/Charte_Eau/niger_basin_water_charter_certified_copy.pdf, chapter IX, art (30).

180 *Ibid* at chapter IX, art (31); It is worth noting that the Commission of Mediation, Conciliation and Arbitration does not exist anymore. The Organization of African Unity has since been replaced by the African Union, which has, as of today, not replaced the former Commission. See, Susanne Schmeier, *Governing International Watercourses: River Basin Organizations and the sustainable governance of internationally shared rivers and lakes* (Earthscan, 2013) at 262; Abdoul Samboly Ba & Makane Moïse Mbengue, "Le Régime Juridique du Fleuve Sénégal: Aspects du Droit des Cours d'Eau dans un Contexte Régional," in *African Yearbook of International Law*, Volume 12, Issue 1 (2004) 322.

181 *Niger Basin Water Charter (La Charte de L'eau du Bassin du Niger), 30 April 2008*, http://www.abn.ne/images/documents/Charte_Eau/niger_basin_water_charter_certified_copy.pdf, chapter IX, art (30).

182 *Ibid* at chapter IX, art (3).

3.1 *Clear Progression through the 'Steps' Can Help Create a Predictable and Stable Dispute Resolution Procedure That Provides Opportunities for the Resolution of Disputes*

A 'Stepped Approach' to international watercourse dispute resolution can help to create a predictable and stable framework for State parties to resolve their disputes. A predictable and stable dispute resolution framework can help State parties anticipate the resolution of disputes and hopefully allow them to avoid unnecessary disputes and incentivise resolution. It can also help State parties understand the procedural path that disputes will take helping them better evaluate the potential costs and expected duration of a dispute.

A dispute resolution framework that possesses regular or standardized 'Steps' allows parties to predict the path that disputes will take through the framework while also allowing them to anticipate what manner of information and arguments might be advanced at each stage, helping the parties to strategize and plan. This can also help State parties to separate some issues of a dispute by addressing different aspects of a dispute at different 'Steps' in the process, allowing some issues to be resolved earlier in the process and distilling the dispute down to the core contentious issues as the matter moves through the process.

It is important to have clearly defined 'Steps' based on limitations of scope and duration to help parties to understand the scope and duration of each respective 'Step'. As we see for example in the operation of the "Joint Permanent Technical Commission", under the *Treaty on the Lesotho Highlands Water Project between the Government of the Kingdom of Lesotho and the Government of the Republic of South Africa*,[183] where we have a clear technical 'Step' delineated in both duration and scope by reasonable limitations.

Where we don't have clear limitations of a 'Step' in either scope or duration there is a risk of disputes stalling at a particular mechanism if the parties are unable to resolve the matter or unwilling to move forward in the dispute resolution process. For example, the first 'Step' of the *Niger Basin Water Charter* Chapter IX, Article 29[184] could prove problematic to the progression of disputes through the dispute resolution framework due to its general structure

183 *Treaty on the Lesotho Highlands Water Project between the Government of the Kingdom of Lesotho and the Government of the Republic of South Africa*, 24 October 1986, https://www.fao.org/faolex/results/details/en/c/LEX-FAOC015909/, art 16 (4)–(6).

184 *Niger Basin Water Charter* (*La Charte de L'eau du Bassin du Niger*), *30 April 2008*, http://www.abn.ne/images/documents/Charte_Eau/niger_basin_water_charter_certified_copy.pdf, chapter IX, art (29).

providing a suite of options between various dispute resolution mechanisms with no clear limitations of scope or duration, by allowing parties to park disputes in this first general 'Step'.

Some limitations can be set by procedural requirements such as in Article 21 of the 1964 *Convention to regulate the hydroelectric development of the international sections of the river Douro and its tributaries* between Spain and Portugal[185] where the "International Commission" fulfils a management as well as a 'Technical Level' function. This body, if unable to reach a decision, votes again at the following session and if the matter cannot be resolved then the dispute is forwarded to the State parties for negotiation. "The decisions of the International Commission shall be adopted by a majority vote. Where the votes are equally divided, the matter at issue shall be put to a new vote at a subsequent meeting and, if no agreement is then reached, the Commission shall refer the dispute to the two Governments."[186] Perhaps the most innovative aspect of the approach showcased in the *Indus Waters Treaty* is how matters are classified as a "question",[187] "difference",[188] or "dispute"[189] depending where they are in the process. This manner of classifying the matter being dealt with allows a certain gatekeeper function preventing matters from going to the ultimate 'Step' immediately, this helps issues to be resolved at earlier stages without being classified as a "dispute" while also helping to propel matters through the dispute resolution framework in a predictable manner.

For a stable and predictable 'Stepped Approach' dispute resolution framework we also look for a uniform progression through the 'Steps'. It is in this sense that a suite of options, like we see in Article 33(2) of the *UN Watercourses Convention*[190] and Article 18 of the *Agreement for the Establishment of the Organization for the Management and Development of the Kagera River Basin*,[191] which refers disputes to the Commission of Mediation, Conciliation and

185 *Convention to regulate the hydroelectric development of the international sections of the river Douro and its tributaries (with additional protocol), Spain and Portugal, 16 July 1964, 1288 UNTS 191*, art 21 at 216.

186 *Ibid.*

187 *The Indus Waters Treaty 1960 (with annexes)*, 19 September 1960, 419 UNTS 125, art IX (1),(2) (*Indus Waters Treaty*).

188 *Ibid at* art IX (2),(6) (*Indus Waters Treaty*).

189 *Ibid at* art IX (2)–(5) (*Indus Waters Treaty*).

190 *Convention on the Law of Non-Navigational Uses of International Watercourses*, 21 May 1997, 2999 UNTS 77, 36 ILM 700 (*Watercourses Convention*) at 136 art 32 (entered into force 17 August 2014).

191 *Agreement for the Establishment of the Organization for the Management and Development of the Kagera River Basin*, 24 August 1977, 1089 UNTS 165, art 18.

Arbitration under the *Charter of the Organization of African Unity*,[192] does not afford a clear or uniform progression through the various mechanisms. These grab bags of options can be useful for State parties to choose from a diverse range of dispute resolution mechanisms to best tailor a mechanism to their specific dispute but it may often be hard for State parties to a dispute to find a favourable option that fits the interests and positions of both parties. A suite of options would arguably confuse the progression between the various 'Steps'. A 'Stepped Approach' by contrast can help provide the strength found in a diversity of dispute resolution mechanisms but also a degree of procedural regularity and impartiality, allowing the parties to progress through the 'Steps', gaining the benefits of each successive 'Step' and the cumulative benefits of the set of 'Steps' progressed through until a matter can be resolved. In having a predictable and uniform progression through the 'Steps' a degree of procedural standardization and fairness can be achieved.

3.2 *Diverse 'Steps' Help to Create a Flexible Dispute Resolution Framework*

By integrating several types of diverse dispute resolution mechanisms into a progressive 'Stepped Approach' a dispute resolution framework can be built that is stronger than the sum of its parts. The ability to utilize different dispute resolution mechanisms can assist parties in breaking deadlocks and avoiding the risk of a dispute becoming eternally locked in the stasis of a process that has met a roadblock and grown stale. Sometimes a fresh approach can allow parties to divorce themselves from certain problematic positions and allow a dispute to move forward. In an area as technical as the law of the non-navigational uses of international watercourses the ability to utilize diverse methods to address disputes, to clarify the issues at hand and to ascertain the relevant facts can be of great help in moving matters forward in a peaceful and constructive manner.

Diplomatic and adjudicative 'Steps' present more traditional dispute resolution characteristics. Their utility has been observed and these types of mechanisms are rather ubiquitous in international agreements that possess dispute resolution provisions. Diplomatic 'Steps' present flexible mechanisms for resolving disputes through the exercise of diplomacy and State consent and agreement; these very attributes, however, can be a weakness of these types of mechanisms if State parties are too entrenched in their positions. In contrast adjudicative 'Steps' provide more structured and forceful mechanisms

192 *Charter of the Organization of African Unity*, 25 May 1963, 479 UNTS 39, art XIX.

for dispute resolution that may be able to force a dispute to a binding conclusion but also can cause reservations in some State parties faced with the prospect of giving up autonomy to a third party mechanism. Technical 'Steps' can prove valuable in finding rational fact-based solutions but often can overlook broader diplomatic or legal considerations and thus are generally confined to advisory functions. These three types of 'Steps' each possess unique strengths and weaknesses.

Although it has already been discussed at some length, it is worth noting that a 'Stepped Approach' can prove invaluable in integrating 'Technical Level' dispute resolution mechanisms along with diplomatic and adjudicative 'Steps' into a progressive dispute resolution framework. Given the technical nature of the law of the non-navigational uses of international watercourses, the presence of 'Technical Level' mechanisms for dispute resolution and avoidance is an important element in a 'Stepped Approach' to disputes on international watercourses. As discussed in the chapter on "Disputes at a 'Technical Level'", 'Technical Level' dispute resolution and avoidance on international watercourses allows for subsequent 'Steps' in a 'Stepped Approach' to function more efficiently in part by helping to identify the issues at stake, divert matters away from other 'Steps' by resolving them at a 'Technical Level' and creating a factual basis for later 'Steps' to work upon. Through the incorporation of 'Technical Level' mechanisms and through the very act of moving through the progressive 'Steps' of a 'Stepped Approach' parties may also become more aware of the existence of technical issues or questions underlying their disputes.

The integration of a technical 'Step' relatively early in a 'Stepped Approach' dispute resolution framework can help to alleviate pressure on the later 'Steps' by diverting and settling disputes on a technical basis early on, by avoiding the politicization and hardening of disputes, by helping to establish the substantive rights of the parties, and by establishing a factual basis that may form an important foundation for the resolution of international watercourse disputes at subsequent 'Steps'. As part of a 'Stepped Approach' 'Technical Level' mechanisms serve an integral role in supplementing and complementing the functions of more traditional 'Diplomatic Level' and 'Adjudicative Level' mechanisms. In the next section we will explore in greater detail a 'Stepped Approach' to the settlement of international watercourse disputes.

The integration of these three types of 'Steps' can be seen clearly in international watercourse agreements that employ a 'Stepped Approach' to dispute resolution. For example, the 1963 *Agreement between the Socialist Federal Republic of Yugoslavia and the Romanian People's Republic concerning the construction and operation of the Iron Gates Water Power and Navigation System on the River Danube*[193] utilizes a "Mixed Commission" established by Article 11 of the agreement:

> [w]ith a view to maintaining permanent co-operation and co-ordination and ensuring the fulfilment and application of the provisions of the Agreement, Conventions and Protocols concerning the Iron Gates System, the Contracting Parties shall establish, as a mixed organ of the two Governments, the Mixed Yugoslav-Romanian Commission for the Iron Gates, hereinafter referred to as 'the Mixed Commission'.[194]

The scope of the Mixed Commission is limited by the *Statute of the Mixed Yugoslav-Romanian Commission for the Iron Gates*[195] and by the *Agreement Between the Socialist Federal Republic of Yugoslavia and the Romanian People's Republic Concerning the Construction and Operation of the Iron Gates Water Power and Navigation System on the River Danube*.[196]

Article 21 of the agreement articulates the 'Stepped Approach' framework to dispute resolution.

> 1. Any difference relating to the interpretation or application of the provisions of this Agreement, or of the Conventions and Protocols concerning the Iron Gates System, and any other dispute of a legal nature relating to the construction or operation of the System shall be settled by the Mixed Commission.
> 2. Where differences cannot be settled in the Mixed Commission, they shall be submitted to the two Governments for settlement by diplomatic means.
> 3. Where agreement cannot be reached on the settlement of differences in accordance with paragraph 2 of this article, the Contracting Parties undertake to settle the said differences by arbitration and,

---

193 *Agreement between the Socialist Federal Republic of Yugoslavia and the Romanian People's Republic concerning the construction and operation of the Iron Gates Water Power and Navigation System on the River Danube*, 30 November 1963, 512 UNTS 42.

194 *Ibid* at art 11 at 52.

195 *Statute of the Mixed Yugoslav-Romanian Commission for the Iron Gates*, 30 November 1963, 513 UNTS 154.

196 *Agreement Between the Socialist Federal Republic of Yugoslavia and the Romanian People's Republic Concerning the Construction and Operation of the Iron Gates Water Power and Navigation System on the River Danube*, 30 November 1963, 512 UNTS 42.

for that purpose, to take all necessary steps to set up an arbitral commission within the shortest possible time.

4. The Contracting Parties agree to employ the following procedure in the cases referred to in paragraph 3 of this article: within a period of one month after the submission of a request by either Party, each Government shall appoint an arbitrator; the arbitrators shall endeavour to settle the difference; if the two arbitrators fail to agree on a settlement of the difference within a period of three months, they shall select an umpire who is a national of neither of the two States; if the two arbitrators fail to agree on the selection of an umpire within a period of two months, the umpire shall be appointed by the Government of a third State or by the executive organ of an international organization; in the last-mentioned case, the third State or international organization shall be selected by agreement between the two Governments within the shortest possible time.[197]

Under article 21(1) of the agreement[198] the first step is through the operation of the "Mixed Commission". The Mixed Commission has distinctly technical functions and also has a "Board for the Settlement of differences" provided for in the *Statute of the Mixed Yugoslav-Romanian Commission for the Iron Gates*.[199] This board will, at least in part, be composed of jurists.[200] The Mixed Commission may also request the Design Review Board[201] to deliver an opinion regarding differences of a technical matter and in some cases even settle such differences.[202] This "Mixed Commission" is a distinct technical 'Step' and also has clear recourse to technical expertise and decision makers. "Each national group [of the Mixed Commission] may have advisers and experts."[203]

197 *Ibid* at art 21 at 64.

198 *Ibid* at art 21 (1) at 64.

199 *Statute of the Mixed Yugoslav-Romanian Commission for the Iron Gates*, 30 November 1963, 513 UNTS 154, art 3, (2)(b).

200 *Ibid* at art 7, (2)(b).

201 *Ibid* at art 3, (2)(a).

202 "(d) It shall deliver an opinion, at the request of the Mixed Commission, on any matter of a technical nature connected with the designing of the structures and works of the Iron Gates System; (e) At the request of the Mixed Commission, it shall deliver an opinion on differences concerning technical matters between the Chief Design Agencies or between the Investors; it shall settle such differences where the Mixed Commission authorizes it to do so." *Ibid* at art 6 (d), (e).

203 *Ibid* at art 2(3).

Where "differences cannot be settled in the Mixed Commission" they "shall" be forwarded to the parties for settlement by diplomatic mechanisms.[204] Here we have a distinct diplomatic 'Step'. If the difference persists matters must then be forwarded for arbitration, a distinct adjudicative 'Step'.[205] In article 21 of this agreement[206] we see the three key dispute resolution 'Steps' looked for in this work arrayed in a progressive 'Stepped Approach'. Each 'Step' must be engaged and fail to produce a result before the matter moves on to the next 'Step'. It is important to see such 'Steps' arrayed alongside each other to observe their interaction and integration.

An example of the flexibility that is provided by different mechanisms through the diverse 'Steps' of a 'Stepped Approach' can also be exhibited in the flexibility that can be found in a single 'Step'. In the 1964 *Convention to regulate the hydroelectric development of the international sections of the river Douro and its tributaries* between Spain and Portugal, the final 'Step' in the dispute resolution framework is an adjudicative one, a compulsory reference of the dispute for decision before an arbitral tribunal presided over by an umpire.[207] This arbitral tribunal can tailor its expertise to the nature of the issue before it.

> If the dispute refers to a legal question, the umpire shall be a legal expert appointed by the International Court of Justice at The Hague; if the question is of a technical nature, the umpire shall be an engineer appointed by the Zurich Poly-technical Institute, in both cases at the request of the two Governments.
>
> Where the two Governments do not agree as to whether the dispute is of a legal or technical nature, this previous question shall be decided by The Hague Court itself.[208]

The idea of integrating different and diverse types of dispute resolution mechanisms is not a new one. "An integrated approach to watercourse disputes that takes all of the existing means and procedures for conflict resolution, including

204 *Agreement between the Socialist Federal Republic of Yugoslavia and the Romanian People's Republic concerning the construction and operation of the Iron Gates Water Power and Navigation System on the River Danube*, 30 November 1963, 512 UNTS 42, art 21 (2) at 64.

205 *Ibid* at art 21 (3), (4) at 64.

206 *Ibid* at art 21 at 64.

207 *Convention to regulate the hydroelectric development of the international sections of the river Douro and its tributaries (with additional protocol), Spain and Portugal, 16 July 1964, 1288 UNTS 191*, art 21 at 216.

208 *Ibid.*

adjudication and arbitration, into account finds support in basic international law."[209] As discussed above, the spectre of an impending adjudicated decision on a matter may help precipitate fruitful negotiations and the resolution of a dispute, but negotiations can also supplement the adjudicative process by helping to clarify issues and articulate the positions of the parties. Such was the observation of the tribunal in the *Lac Lanoux* arbitration.[210] Similarly technical mechanisms can also aid in helping to provide clarification of issues and a factual basis for future negotiations or adjudication. For that matter, a similar argument can be made that adjudication can help facilitate future settlement of a dispute simply by helping to define issues and the respective legal positions and rights of the parties. Employing mechanisms with differing strengths and weaknesses in a progressive 'Stepped Approach' provides an effective dispute resolution framework which is greater than the sum of its parts.

3.3 *'Steps' May Complement Each Other*

As discussed, primarily in regard to technical 'Steps', a 'Stepped Approach' to disputes on international watercourses allows an integrated approach to dispute resolution incorporating various, complementing mechanisms of dispute resolution.

> Considering the peaceful settlement of disputes as a continuum of mechanisms, it is possible to point to the complementarity between different aspects. In this sense, for example, negotiations can complement adjudication at different stages of a dispute, prior to, during, and after a dispute goes to court or arbitration. To ensure that dispute settlement is as effective as it can be in the area of water, a wide range of dispute settlement tools will need to be drawn upon.[211]

---

209 Attila Tanzi, *The Economic Commission for Europe Water Convention and the United Nations Watercourses Convention: An analysis of their harmonized contribution to international water law*, Water Series No 6 (UN, 2015) at 73 [footnote omitted].

210 "Il est délicat d'apprécier s'il a été satisfait à une telle obligation. Mais, sans se substituer aux Parties, le juge es ten measure de procéder à cette apprécitaion sur la base des éléments fournis par les négciations." *Affaire du Lac Lanoux* (*France v Spain*) (1957), Judgment, 12 RIAA 281 at 315; "It is delicate to appreciate whether such an obligation has been satisfied. But, without taking the place of the Parties, the judge is in a position to carry out such an assessment on the basis of the elements provided by the negotiations." [translated by Author].

211 Laurence Boisson de Chazournes, "The Settlement of Disputes through Judicial Means (Article 33(10) and Annex on Arbitratin)" in Laurence Boisson de Chazournes et al eds,

It can be argued that the very nature of a 'Stepped Approach' to disputes framework, by integrating various types of mechanisms and procedural 'Steps', can create a complementary progressive system that addresses disputes at different levels. Such a framework allows 'Steps' to build off each other. For example, the adjudicative 'Step' in the 1964 *Convention to regulate the hydroelectric development of the international sections of the river Douro and its tributaries* between Spain and Portugal mentioned above builds off earlier 'Steps' by composing the arbitral tribunal with members of the "International Commission themselves and presided over by an umpire."[212] This "International Commission" is charged to "Regulate the Hydro-electric Development of the International Sections of the River Douro and its Tributaries, the special function of which shall be to monitor the exercise of the rights recognized bilaterally and to solve the judicial or technical problems to which such rights may give rise."[213] This body serves to resolve disputes at a technical 'Step' earlier in the dispute resolution process by majority vote.[214] In this way the members of the "International Commission", who then comprise the arbitral tribunal in the ultimate adjudicative 'Step', are able to bring their prior experience and knowledge of the dispute to bear through a different mechanism and guided by an expert umpire.

We also can see evidence of the complementary nature of 'Steps' in a 'Stepped Approach' in the *Indus Waters* Treaty. Here it is the work of the 'Technical Level' dispute resolution mechanisms that can assist later 'Steps'. For example, the reporting function of the "Commission" under Article IX (3) of the *Indus Waters Treaty* can help distill the pertinent issues in dispute as well as the viewpoints, summarizing the previous 'Steps' so that the later 'Steps' can build from them and fulfill their functions more efficiently.

The presence of multiple 'Steps' can also help parties transition between dispute resolution mechanisms in a complementary manner. For instance, the Technical 'Step' in the *UN Watercourses Convention*[215] can help act as a tran-

---

The UN Convention on the Law of the Non-Navigational Uses of International Watercourses: A Commentary (Oxford University Press, 2018) 364 at 378 [footnote omitted].

212 *Convention to regulate the hydroelectric development of the international sections of the river Douro and its tributaries (with additional protocol), Spain and Portugal, 16 July 1964, 1288 UNTS 191*, art 21 at 216.

213 *Ibid* at art 14 at 214.

214 *Ibid.*

215 *Convention on the Law of Non-Navigational Uses of International Watercourses*, 21 May 1997, 2999 UNTS 77, 36 ILM 700 (*Watercourses Convention*) at 136–138 art 33(3)–(9) (entered into force 17 August 2014).

sition between the diplomatic processes such as negotiation and mediation and the more adjudicative processes such as submitting a matter to an international court or arbitral tribunal. "The 1997 UN Watercourses Convention [...] endorses the compulsory fact-finding procedure, which bridges the gap between purely diplomatic means, entirely dependent upon the discretion of the parties to the dispute, and binding third-party dispute resolution."[216] These technical mechanisms can also help supplement the rest of the dispute resolution framework, like negotiation or mediation, to help the parties reach a peaceful solution founded on a factual basis,[217] this seems to be the intention contemplated in the *UN Watercourses Convention*'s article 33 as the matter is not concluded by the fact-finding commission but rather parties are required to "consider in good faith" the report and recommendations of the commission.[218]

3.4 *Progression through the 'Steps' Can Help Divert Matters Away from More Costly and Time-Consuming Mechanisms, Creating a More Efficient Dispute Resolution System*

Structuring dispute resolution and avoidance frameworks so that parties advance to later 'Steps' only when earlier 'Steps' have failed to yield results can help give a clear progression to dispute provisions. This can also alleviate pressure on later 'Steps', such as adjudicative mechanisms, by allowing matters to progress through preliminary 'Steps' in the hope of resolution, serving as a manner of diversion away from adjudicative 'Steps'. "The [UN] Charter reflects the normal obligation to attempt settlement through the diplomatic channel, which is sometimes demanded as a procedural prerequisite to third-party determination of the rights and duties of the parties."[219] At the seminar held in Vancouver, Canada in 1961 on "The Development and Administration of the

216 Sergei Vinogradov, Patricia Wouters and Patricia Jones, *Transforming Potential Conflict into Cooperation Potential: The Role of International Water Law* (UNESCO-IHP, PCCP, 2003) at 66.

217 Jens Evensen, "First report on the law of the non-navigational uses of international watercourses" (UN Doc A/CN.4/367) in *Yearbook of the International Law Commission 1983*, vol 2, part 1 (1985) 155 at 191 (UN Doc A/CN.4/SER.A/1983/Add.1 (Part 1)).

218 *Convention on the Law of Non-Navigational Uses of International Watercourses*, 21 May 1997, 2999 UNTS 77, 36 ILM 700 (*Watercourses Convention*) at 136–138 art 33(8) (entered into force 17 August 2014).

219 The International Law Association, "*Helsinki Rules on the Uses of the Waters of International Rivers*" ('*Helsinki Rules*') in *Report of the Fifty-Second Conference of the International Law Association Held at Helsinki, August 14–20, 1966*, vol 52 (1967) 484, Comment to art XXX at 522.

International River Basin" it was held that "the interpretation of a particular agreement or treaty is best left to administrative commissions or organizations and only when it is not possible to settle subsequent differences over application or interpretation should differences be referred to a special arbitration tribunal or to the International Court of Justice."[220] The *Pact of Bogotá* Article IV specifies that "Once any pacific procedure has been initiated, whether by agreement between the parties or in fulfillment of the present Treaty or a previous pact, no other procedure may be commenced until that procedure is concluded."[221] Such an approach allows an individual 'Step' to operate and helps to establish an organized progression through the 'Steps'. It is possible to have multiple dispute resolution mechanisms function in a single 'Step', for instance the draft articles Stephen Schwebel put before the ILC contained an international commission of inquiry as part of the diplomatic 'Step' to consult and negotiate.[222]

By providing a progressive framework that requires matters to work their way through the 'Steps' more opportunities for resolution are created. The procedural and substantive differences in the respective 'Steps' helps to view disputes in different contexts and can help resolve matters hopefully before the positions of the parties become too entrenched. Such a mechanism is important in an area of international law concerning such a vital resource and of such a technical nature. "[International law] should also provide for a wide range of mechanisms not only for the settlement of water disputes but also for addressing 'issues' and stalemates or deadlocks before they become serious disputes."[223] For example, the fact-finding mechanism articulated in the *UN Watercourses Convention* was intended to deal with disputes before they posed a threat to 'international peace and security' and could have an important

220 J.D. Chapman, ed, *The International River Basin: Proceedings of a Seminar on the Development and Administration of the International River Basin*, held under the auspices of the Regional Training Centre for United Nations Fellows (University of British Columbia, 1963) at 25.

221 *American Treaty on Pacific Settlement*, 30 April 1948, 30 UNTS 55, art IV at 84 (*Pact of Bogotá*).

222 Stephen M. Schwebel, "Third report on the law of the non-navigational uses of international watercourses" (UN Doc A/CN.4/348) in *Year Book of the International Law Commission 1982 vol 2 part 1 (1984)* 65 at 186–187 para 498 art 16 (UN Doc A/CN.4/SER.A/1982/Add.1(Part 1)).

223 Surya P. Subedi, "Resolution of International Water Disputes: Challenges for the 21st Century" in The International Bureau of the Permanent Court of Arbitration, ed, *The Permanent Court of Arbitration/Peace Palace Papers Resolution of International Water Disputes* (Kluwer Law International, 2003) 33 at 47.

dispute avoidance role by articulating the factual basis underlying a matter before a true dispute had even crystalized.[224]

In cultivating a 'Stepped Approach' to disputes on international watercourses it is important to have a progressive set of 'Steps'. Multiple 'Steps' can help to increase the opportunities for the resolution of disputes between the parties. It is often observed that matters are resolved on the courthouse steps. This is to say that the very process of adjudication and the looming threat of an adjudicated decision outside the hands of the parties can help promote parties to seek an agreed resolution to a dispute. A 'Stepped Approach' by utilizing multiple diverse 'Steps' in a stable and predictable framework, can help promote agreement between the parties in a similar way. The use of adjudicative 'Steps' later in the process can help provide a similar incentive to resolve matters by agreement rather than submit to the uncertainty of an adjudicated judgment imposed by an impartial third party. The operation of procedures that allow for the use of diverse mechanisms for dispute resolution can mean that some mechanisms, like adjudication, may be seldom used, this may not be a rejection of any particular mechanism but rather a sign of the success of the other processes available in resolving the matter.[225] Through a standardized and predictable progression of diverse dispute resolution mechanisms a 'Stepped Approach' can help the parties remove areas of contention and find common ground. The very fact of interacting through the various 'Steps' and examining the issues in different contexts can help bring the parties together in much the same way that the prospect of an impending adjudicated decision may bring about a resolution when the parties interact with each other "on the courthouse steps".

224 "Fact-finding as envisaged in the draft articles [...] could come into play well before any threat to international peace and security arose, and indeed prior to the emergence of a 'dispute'." Stephen C. McCaffrey, "Sixth report on the law of the non-navigational uses of international watercourses" (UN Doc A/CN.4/427 and Add.1) in *Yearbook of the International Law Commission 1990*, vol 2, part 1 (1993) 41 at 68 para 51 (UN Doc A/CN.4/SER.A/1990/Add.1 (Part 1)).

225 C.B. Bourne, "Mediation, Conciliation and Adjudication in the Settlement of International Drainage Basin Disputes" (1971) 9 Canadian Yearbook of International Law 114, at 144.

4 Importance of a 'Stepped Approach' to Disputes, in Recent International Cases

As discussed above this work does not seek to "prove" the superiority of a 'Stepped Approach' for all disputes in regard to international watercourses. A 'Stepped Approach' will not always be the best approach for any situation, but it should be viewed as a useful tool. Indeed, trying to "prove" such a concept poses many problems not least of which is the very subjective nature of evaluating the effectiveness of a particular dispute resolution mechanism or the result of a particular dispute. Viewpoints can diverge widely on this. Even the selection of specific case studies can be fraught with subjective bias. With this in mind, the author will briefly discuss two recent international cases that in the author's opinion can help illustrate the usefulness of a 'Stepped Approach' to disputes, but by no means are they offered to definitively "prove" that a 'Stepped Approach' works as a panacea for all disputes on international watercourses.

4.1 *Indus Waters Treaty Arbitration* (*Pakistan v India*) (2023)

In 2023 the PCA had the opportunity to review the dispute resolution mechanisms under the *Indus Waters Treaty*[226] in light of a new process brought by Pakistan on 19 August 2016. Much of this discussion has been covered above on the section dealing with the *Indus Waters Treaty* and will not be reproduced here. The current issues at play are tied to efforts to develop hydro-electric plants in the Indus River Basin by India. Some of the related issues were addressed by the PCA in the *Indus Waters Kishenganga Arbitration*[227] but ongoing disagreement following that decision in 2013 has led Pakistan to institute proceedings before the PCA and for India to follow suit by empowering a neutral expert[228] both under the authority of the *Indus Waters Treaty*[229] (the neutral expert appointed the PCA as registry and Secretariat) in regard to the same matters, creating two parallel processes. Both processes were instituted under the Treaty by the World Bank as the parties were not in agreement. India

226 *The Indus Waters Treaty 1960 (with annexes)*, 19 September 1960, 419 UNTS 125.

227 *Indus Waters Kishenganga Arbitration (Pakistan v India)* (20 December 2013), Final Award, 31 RIAA 309, (Permanent Court of Arbitration).

228 *Indus Waters Treaty Neutral Expert Proceedings (India v Pakistan)*, PCA Case No 2023-14, (Permanent Court of Arbitration), online: <https://pca-cpa.org/en/cases/297/>.

229 *The Indus Waters Treaty 1960 (with annexes)*, 19 September 1960, 419 UNTS 125, art IX, Annexure F, and Annexure G (*Indus Waters Treaty*).

has continued to question the competency of the PCA arbitral proceedings and had not attended before the arbitral Court prior to the judgement.

This current moment finds the *Indus Waters Treaty* and its parties in a precarious position. It is important to note that the *Indus Waters Treaty*, and its institutional mechanisms have endured fraught moments before and continued to operate as envisaged even during times of armed conflict between the parties.[230] The dispute resolution mechanisms under the Treaty have been relatively well used in the past, for example the use of the neutral expert functions utilized in the 2007 neutral expert decision on the Baglihar Hydro-electric Plant,[231] and the use of a Court of Arbitration in the *Kishenganga Arbitration*. Currently despite the friction between the two parties and India's refusal to participate in the arbitral process this author would argue that the provisions and mechanisms of the treaty continue to operate largely as envisaged, and by and large much of the tension in regard to these issues between the parties has been funnelled into the various dispute resolution 'Steps' under the Treaty. For this author it is an example of the successful operation of a 'Stepped Approach' to disputes.

The Court in its award on competence did find that the *Indus Waters Treaty* possessed a "graded" or "stepwise" dispute resolution procedure but not in the "rigid sense that India urges";[232] instead the Court found that this procedure "ensures that the Parties will attempt to reach prompt consensual resolution, but if they do not, they can seek the form of third-party resolution best suited to their needs".[233] Thus the 'Stepped Approach' here allows parties a degree of flexibility through further mechanisms for the resolution of disputes where they have reached an impasse. In the *Indus Waters Kishenganga Arbitration (Pakistan v India) (18 February 2013)* Partial Award, the Court found that the purpose of the dispute resolution provisions of the *Indus Waters Treaty* contained

230 "Fortunately, the two South Asian countries between which relations are perhaps the most delicate, India and Pakistan, have a treaty governing the principal watercourse system they share, the Indus, which has continued to function for over a half-century despite wars between them. Indus Waters Treaty 1960, 419 UNTS 125. The arbitration provisions of the treaty were invoked by Pakistan in the Indus Waters Kishenganga Arbitration […]." Stephen C. McCaffrey, *The Law of International Watercourses*, 3rd ed (Oxford University Press, 2019).

231 *Baglihar Hydro-electric Plant (Pakistan v India)*, Neutral Expert Determination on the Baglihar Hydro-electric Plant dated 12 February 2007.

232 *Indus Waters Treaty Arbitration (Pakistan v India)* (6 July 2023), Award on the Competence of the Court, PCA Case No 2023-01 at para 199, see also para 277 (Permanent Court of Arbitration), online: <https://pca-cpa.org/en/cases/284/>.

233 *Ibid* at para 199.

in Article IX "is to provide a comprehensive framework for the resolution of disagreements between the Parties arising from the Treaty".[234] Viewing a 'Stepped Approach' as a "framework" that allows for a resilient yet flexible dispute resolution process is an excellent illustration of the potential utility of a 'Stepped Approach' to dispute resolution on international watercourses. It is also noteworthy that the PCA in its recent award on the competence of the Court has found that parallel processes, such as the neutral expert functions and the court of arbitration,[235] even in regard to related questions, are "entirely possible under the Treaty"; adding an interesting facet to the implementation of a 'Stepped Approach' under the Treaty.

The Court also found that the process had allowed the parties to refine or "focus" the issues and their positions, particularly it allowed Pakistan to understand that the disagreements that it initially characterized as technical design choices were disagreements on the requirements of the Treaty.[236] The Court continued by remarking that the process had allowed Pakistan to realize when it deemed a "difference" to have arisen that "the contours of that difference had evolved over time and became more focused in the months that followed".[237] The Court also noted that through the process Pakistan had withdrawn some of its objections or resolved some of its disagreements as it refined its position through the technical exchange in the Commission,[238] an incredibly important feature of a 'Stepped Approach' which ideally allows for more efficient and effective dispute resolution at later 'Steps'.

One question arises pertaining to the usefulness of a 'Stepped Approach' in connection with this new process and the earlier 2013 *Indus Waters Kishenganga Arbitration* as it seems two arbitrations have instituted where one might have sufficed. Several of the items in this current dispute were brought up between the parties prior to the *Indus Waters Kishenganga Arbitration* but were separated at the time and were left unresolved by the *Indus Waters Kishenganga Arbitration Partial Award*.[239] The winnowing down of the issues that left these matters unaddressed at the time, seem to represent one of the benefits of the

234 *Indus Waters Kishenganga Arbitration* (*Pakistan v India*) (18 February 2013), Partial Award, 31 RIAA 55 at paras 126–139, (Permanent Court of Arbitration).

235 *Indus Waters Treaty Arbitration* (*Pakistan v India*) (6 July 2023), Award on the Competence of the Court, PCA Case No 2023-01 at paras 313–314, (Permanent Court of Arbitration), online: <https://pca-cpa.org/en/cases/284/>.

236 *Ibid* at para 184.

237 *Ibid* at para 188.

238 *Ibid* at para 71, 86.

239 *Ibid* at para 83.

proposed 'Stepped Approach' as the issues were refined by the parties through the original *Indus Waters Kishenganga Arbitration* process, but now the parties are in the process of engaging in a separate process to deal with them. This is indeed time consuming and regrettable in hindsight, but it also arguably represents a proper function of a 'Stepped Approach'. The fact that some issues were deemed better suited to technical or diplomatic resolution at the time,[240] represent the ability parties have to tailor the resolution process to the particular dispute in a 'Stepped Approach' and reflects the ability of parties to change their assessment of the situation and potential disputes. It is an excellent example of how a 'Stepped Approach' can provide flexibility to the parties and prevent deadlocks. The ability to utilize a tiered system of dispute resolution 'Steps' shows the flexible and adaptable approach the parties can turn to, an approach that limits the duration and scope of individual 'Steps' allowing the parties to progress through them and break any potential deadlocks. The process here also provided for another opportunity to resolve these matters at these technical and diplomatic 'levels' in arguably a less contentious and possibly a less politicized mechanism, diverting the matters away from adjudication. The 'Stepped Approach' provided by the *Indus Waters Treaty*, and used in this current arbitration and the *Kishenganga Arbitration* also shows how one party can compel some degree of dispute resolution and that there is the possibility of an ultimate and binding 'Step'. The predictable and stable framework provided here by a 'Stepped Approach' allows the parties to understand and chart their path through the process, here the parties disagree on the correct operation of the 'Steps' yet they continue to generally engage with each other through the process.

4.2 *Dispute over the Status and Use of the Waters of the Silala (Chile v Bolivia)* (2022)[241]

The issues initially in the *Dispute over the Status and Use of the Waters of the Silala* (*Chile v Bolivia*) ("*Silala Waters Case*") began in a rather straightforward manner. The key focus was around whether the "Silala Waters" flowing from Bolivia into Chile were an international watercourse and thus subject to the

240 *Ibid* at paras 71, 83.

241 It is important to note that the author acted as a legal advisor to the Government of Chile on the *Dispute over the Status and Use of the Waters of the Silala* (*Chile v Bolivia*), Judgment of 1 December 2022, [2022] ICJ 614. The views expressed here are entirely those of the author in his individual capacity and do not necessarily reflect the positions or opinions of any of the parties to the dispute.

law of international watercourses. The parties themselves had no governing international watercourse agreement between them[242] and as such the question would be whether customary international watercourse law would apply and to what extent.

As an aside it may seem like an odd choice to talk about a case that did not involve a watercourse treaty containing specific dispute resolution provisions when talking about a 'Stepped Approach' to international watercourse disputes in treaty practice, but the ICJ process itself works much like a 'Stepped Approach' with its written and oral submissions and prescribed process and discernible timelines. The use of technical experts also acts in many ways as a technical dispute resolution mechanism through the written submissions process. This argument may leave the reader wondering about the need for a 'Stepped Approach' enshrined in treaty provisions given that many of these aspects might be addressed through the adjudicative process. The answer is twofold: many parties are reluctant to engage in third party adjudication such as before the ICJ where the process is largely out of the parties' hands and the decision of the adjudicator is uncertain and binding on the parties; and the adjudicative process can be quite an investment in terms of time and resources. By utilizing earlier 'Steps' where parties have more control to refine the positions and arguments of the parties or to divert and resolve some matters can help to make the adjudicative process more efficient and the dispute resolution process more approachable.

There are many interesting aspects of the *Silala Waters Case*. The case will not be explored in great depth here but one aspect does stand out in the context of a 'Stepped Approach' to international watercourse disputes, and that is the apparent convergence of the parties' technical or factual positions during the oral hearings. The ICJ process began on the 1st of June 2016 when Chile initiated proceedings seeking a declaratory judgment pertaining to the international aspect of the Silala waters and their use.[243] There were two rounds of written submissions, including an additional filing by Chile and requests by both parties for additional data and documentation, as well as an oral hearing.[244] In total the matter took approximately six (6) and a half years from

242 The jurisdiction of the Court was founded on the American Treaty on Pacific Settlement, 30 April 1948, 30 UNTS 55 (*Pact of Bogotá*).

243 *Dispute over the Status and Use of the Waters of the Silala* (*Chile v Bolivia*), Judgment of 1 December 2022, [2022] ICJ 614 at para 1.

244 *Ibid* at paras 1–27.

the initiation of the ICJ process until a judgment was rendered by the Court on the 1st of December 2022.

Over the course of the written submission process and the exchange of the submissions of the technical experts of both sides the positions of the parties moved closer together. By the time of the oral hearings phase it became apparent to the Court that the positions of the parties had substantially converged, particularly the position of Bolivia regarding the status of the Silala waters and the application of international law, moving substantially closer to that of Chile in many respects. The Court noted that:

> [T]he positions of the Parties with respect to the legal status of the Silala waters and the rules applicable under customary international law have converged in the course of the proceedings. During the oral proceedings, Bolivia has on several occasions expressed its agreement with Chile's claim that despite the "artificial enhancement" of the surface flow of the Silala River the Silala waters qualify in their entirety as an international watercourse under customary international law and stated that, therefore, customary international law applies both to the "naturally flowing" waters and the "artificially enhanced" surface flow of the Silala.[245]

Ultimately though the Court found in regard to most of the claims and counter-claims that the parties' positions had converged and that there was no longer an object to most of them, declining to render a further judgement in regard to these claims and counter-claims of the parties, save for two which it rejected.[246] The Court did make some interesting pronouncements reinforcing existing several of the tenants of existing customary international watercourse law[247] as well as acknowledging the international nature of the Silala stating that the "Court considers that modifications that increase the surface flow of a watercourse have no bearing on its characterization as an international watercourse … [t]here is no doubt that the Silala is an international watercourse and, as such, subject in its entirety to customary international law, as both Parties now agree".[248] Through this process we can see the ameliorating effect of the 'Stepped' dispute resolution process through the many 'Steps' of written

245 *Ibid* at para 40 [footnotes omitted].
246 *Ibid* at para 163.
247 *Ibid* at paras 92–102.
248 *Ibid* at paras 93–94.

submissions, the impending deadline of an oral hearing and judgment which arguably refined and pushed the parties' positions closer together.

Whether this result is a "success" in terms of international dispute resolution is arguable. From the perspective of seeking a final and authoritative judgment, this case may be seen to fall somewhat short, on the other hand ultimately both parties embraced positions they were apparently comfortable with which brought them largely into agreement, at least in the eyes of the Court.[249] Ultimately both parties escaped a possibly negative judgment and ostensibly reached a settlement of the dispute. This is not perhaps a process that most States will wish to emulate given the time and cost associated with litigation before the ICJ, as judge *Ad Hoc* Simma observes in his separate opinion:

> States do not institute proceedings before the World Court at the drop of a hat. The cases they bring to the Court are usually of considerable importance legally and politically and the volume of preparation and work involved is significant, sometimes enormous. Hundreds of professionals may be involved. Technical or scientific expertise may be mobilized. The Court owes it to the parties to render well-reasoned judgments which settle their disputes with binding force, and, where appropriate, offers them guidance on their rights and obligations. Reflecting on the Court's deliberative process, the then President of the Permanent Court of International Justice, Max Huber, once compared the Court's decisions to "ships which are intended to be launched on the high seas of international criticism". It is a pity that today the Court chose to launch an empty vessel.[250]

249 Judge *Ad Hoc* Simma does state "This brings me to my third and final set of observations. States appearing before the Court have a legitimate interest in seeking declaratory judgments that may ensure recognition of a situation at law, once and for all and with binding force. In order to be binding, this recognition must be clothed in the operative part of the judgment, which alone is binding on the parties. I am troubled that the present Judgment might be read as sending the signal that any position may be held, however untenable, so long as this position is abandoned at the eleventh hour of the judicial proceedings. In this regard, I see a difference between a dispute that has disappeared because the parties genuinely have come to agree in the course of the proceedings, and a dispute that has been hollowed out by one party wishing to evade a declaratory judgment and the legal effects ensuing therefrom". *Dispute over the Status and Use of the Waters of the Silala (Chile v Bolivia)*, Separate Opinion of Judge *Ad Hoc* Simma of 1 December 2022, [2022] ICJ 677 at 18.

250 *Ibid* at 20 [footnotes omitted].

The *Silala Waters Case*, while not a complete 'Stepped Approach' to dispute resolution, showcases many of the strengths of such an approach. By providing a stable and predictable process, the parties were able to chart their path through the process. In allowing for written submissions and the exchange of technical data, the parties were in some way able to step outside of the politicization of the dispute to come closer to each other on the factual basis of the dispute and thus clarify the position of the parties, narrowing down the potential issues before the court. In this case the Court found that the parties agreed to such an extent that their positions had converged, essentially diverting the matter away from adjudication. Having written submissions leading to oral hearings and an ultimate binding adjudicative decision, all with fixed timelines, allowed the matter to move through the process building off the various 'Steps' and helping to break what had been a deadlock between the parties on the issue of the Silala waters. The potential motivating factor of an impending ultimate judgement on the matter should also not be underestimated.

CHAPTER 4

Conclusions

What is a 'Stepped Approach' to disputes on international watercourses and what is its utility to resolving disputes under the law of the non-navigational uses of international watercourses?

This work attempted to answer these questions by examining what Stephen McCaffrey termed a "graduated series of stages"[1] and which we have called a 'Stepped Approach' to disputes on international watercourses. For our purposes a 'Stepped Approach' to disputes on international watercourses encompasses a dispute resolution and avoidance system dealing with an international watercourse and composed of a set of graduated discrete 'Steps', phases, or echelons of limited scope or duration with a relatively clear progression from one 'Step' to another.

Two hundred and twenty-five (225) treaties were identified containing distinct dispute resolution provisions between State actors[2] from 1900. These treaties were reviewed and scored based on the presence of nine (9) criteria identified by the author after a review of relevant treaties as important components of an ideal "Stepped Approach".

As evidenced by the results represented in Table 3, most treaties reviewed partially fulfilled the nine (9) criteria laid out. Of the two hundred and twenty-five (225) treaties reviewed, nineteen (19) or roughly eight percent (8%) met all nine (9) criteria. One hundred and nineteen (119) or roughly fifty-three percent (53%) met five (5) or more criteria.

In regard to distinct 'Steps' a diplomatic 'Step' is the most utilized, being found in eighty-eight percent (88%) of treaties with a dispute resolution provision assessed. Adjudication as a 'Step' is also quite common being found in roughly fifty-seven percent (57%) of the agreements. A technical 'Step' is the least utilized, being utilized as a distinct 'Step' in only approximately twenty-one percent (21%) of the agreements reviewed. This heavy emphasis

1 Stephen C. McCaffrey, "Sixth report on the law of the non-navigational uses of international watercourses" (UN Doc A/CN.4/427 and Add.1) in *Yearbook of the International Law Commission 1990*, vol 2, part 1 (1993) 41 at 66 para 42 (UN Doc A/CN.4/SER.A/1990/Add.1 (Part 1)).

2 It is important to note that only distinct provisions addressing disputes between State parties were reviewed. The author attempted to differentiate these from compliance and management mechanisms in the agreements, unless these mechanisms were specifically mentioned in the dispute resolution provisions as applying to disputes between State actors.

 | DOI:10.1163/9789004736771_007

on the traditional mechanism of dispute resolution in international law: diplomatic and adjudicative processes, does not seem surprising.

A compulsory 'Step' was found in ninety-five percent (95%) of the agreements and fifty-six percent (56%), showed an ultimate or final 'Step' that was binding in its decision. One hundred and fifty-six agreements, roughly sixty-nine percent (69%), utilized two or more 'Steps' and sixty-two, or twenty-eight percent (28%) of treaties reviewed had three or more 'Steps'.[3] While a minority of agreements had three or more 'Steps' the number of agreements that incorporated two or more 'Steps' represented a majority and fifty-two percent (52%) of the treaties scored five (5) or above on the nine (9) criteria evaluated. This seems to show a broad basis of support in State practice for at least a minimum level of integrating various dispute resolution mechanisms into international agreements dealing with transboundary water resources. The level of integration would in fact be higher but this research did not account for provisions which provided parties with a suite or 'menu' of mechanisms from which to choose.[4]

In the chapter on "Disputes and the Law of the Non-Navigational Uses of International Watercourses" an attempt was made to place the broader question of a 'Stepped Approach' into the context of international watercourse disputes and the law of the non-navigational uses of international watercourses. We saw that there is growing stress on global water supplies due to environmental changes, growing industrial and agricultural use, as well as the pressure of increasing global populations. These pressures on global water supplies result in increased competition by riparian States over this vital resource. Despite this increasing competition international cooperation over shared water resources is the rule rather than the exception. Nevertheless, it is important to build robust and resilient dispute resolution and avoidance frameworks in anticipation of increasing disputes over shared freshwater resources. To that end there are many diplomatic, technical, and adjudicative dispute resolution mechanisms available to address disputes on international watercourses. Benefits can be achieved by integrating the use of several of these mechanisms into a dispute resolution framework.

3 For the purpose of this work, three or more 'Steps' constituted the threshold for determining a graduated framework of 'Steps' as part of a 'Stepped Approach'.

4 In this work distinct 'Steps' were measured. Where a provision allowed for a suite of options such as in article 33(2) of the *UN Watercourses Convention*, these were not measured. This means that an agreement could provide for several mechanisms in a 'menu' for the parties that are not accounted for. This work also did not count general provisions that allowed parties to consent to the jurisdiction of the ICJ or another international court or tribunal as a distinct 'Step' as it was not a given that parties would elect to do so.

In the chapter on "Disputes at a 'Technical Level'" we looked further into the increasingly technical nature of disputes on international watercourses and the need for specialized 'Technical Level' dispute resolution mechanisms to facilitate the resolution of disputes on international watercourses. Here 'Technical Level' dispute resolution was defined as a phase or 'Step' primarily concerned with factual and technical issues, systems or functions or dominated by technical experts such as scientists or engineers. It is defined by the expert nature of those assessing the matter but also what they are assessing, primarily technical, scientific and factual considerations. 'Technical Level' dispute resolution mechanisms in international watercourse agreements can be either *Ad Hoc* or permanent but their most common form is through the operation of joint organizations to address technical questions or disputes.[5] 'Technical Level' dispute resolution mechanisms are generally of more utility early in the process of dispute resolution and can prove essential to the efficiency of a 'Stepped Approach'. 'Technical Level' dispute resolution on international watercourses allows for subsequent 'Steps' in a 'Stepped Approach' to function more efficiently, in part by helping to identify the issues at stake, divert matters away from other 'Steps' by resolving them at a 'Technical Level' and creating a factual basis for later 'Steps' to work in. "Many disputes turn essentially on disagreements over facts and their evaluation, rather than on questions of law."[6]

The discussion in the chapter on "A 'Stepped Approach' to Disputes Regarding the Non-Navigational Uses of International Watercourses" centred around the conception and features of a 'Stepped Approach', discussing how the selected nine (9) criteria were embodied in existing international agreements and the ILC process which led to the *UN Watercourses Convention*. In briefly examining the progression of proposed draft articles by the various rapporteurs to the ILC we can see the importance and consistent presence of some form of a 'Stepped Approach'. By comparing these various drafts, we can see to what extent these provisions would comply with the criteria laid out in this work regarding a 'Stepped Approach'. Much of the discussion in this work on a 'Stepped Approach' owes a debt to the detailed and excellent work of the ILC on the subject of the non-navigational uses of international watercourses.

5 Stephen C. McCaffrey, "Sixth report on the law of the non-navigational uses of international watercourses" (UN Doc A/CN.4/427 and Add.1) in *Yearbook of the International Law Commission 1990*, vol 2, part 1 (1993) 41 at 78 (UN Doc A/CN.4/SER.A/1990/Add.1 (Part 1)); a similar passage appears in Stephen C. McCaffrey, *The Law of International Watercourses*, 3rd ed (Oxford University Press, 2019) at 575.

6 John Collier and Vaughan Lowe, *The Settlement of Disputes in International Law* (Oxford University Press, 1999) at 91.

This chapter also explored the benefits of employing a 'Stepped Approach' to disputes on international watercourses by looking to examples from international agreements. We discussed how a 'Stepped Approach' can:

- create a predictable and stable dispute resolution procedure by cultivating a clear progression of 'Steps';
- help create a flexible and adaptable framework that is greater than the sum of its parts by using diverse dispute resolution mechanisms in different 'Steps';
- complement other 'Steps' in the process, allowing State parties to build off the work of each progressive 'Step'.
- help divert matters away at lower 'Steps', particularly at 'Technical Levels', to create a more efficient dispute resolution system and alleviate pressure on more formalized dispute resolution procedures such as adjudication which can require more time and resources.

The general lessons learned discussed above are not necessarily confined to disputes involving international water resources and certainly can be applied more broadly to international environmental disputes, particularly those of a technical nature.

In this same chapter on "A 'Stepped Approach' to Disputes Regarding the Non-Navigational Uses of International Watercourses" we concluded by examining recent international disputes to see what these cases could illustrate about the importance and usefulness of employing a 'Stepped Approach' to disputes involving international water resources. In general case studies can be quite subjective in regard to illustrating the 'effectiveness' of dispute resolution mechanisms but still we can draw some general illustrations of the potential usefulness of such a 'Stepped Approach' from these recent cases as they pertain to the general lessons learned outlined above.

This work has focused on legal mechanisms for dispute resolution, but as discussed previously, the author has taken a rather broad interpretation of what qualifies as a "dispute" or "dispute resolution" often encapsulating what would often be termed as "dispute avoidance" or cooperative/preventative actions particularly under the discussion around 'Technical Level' dispute resolution and joint mechanisms. The 'Stepped Approach' discussed here does incorporate many elements of dispute avoidance particularly in its ability to divert maters away from more formal dispute resolution mechanisms such as adjudication. It is important to understand the context of international watercourse disputes and the importance of cooperative mechanisms and engagement between riparian parties which can help avoid and prevent disputes before they have essentially crystalized. For the most part this is the most effective manner of addressing potential disputes involving international water resources.

In focusing on dispute resolution and avoidance mechanisms contained in international treaty practice it is important to not lose sight of the political, economic, social, and cultural realities of many international watercourse disputes. Legal mechanisms can provide useful tools for addressing such disputes and they have been the focus of our discussion here to allow us to examine them in detail, but these broader realities inform the development of disputes and their progression through the various legal mechanisms. Many disputes often do not reach legal mechanisms for dispute resolution but are instead dropped or addressed in other more expedient, informal, or cost-effective ways. Many practical considerations will factor into State parties' decisions to pursue the settlement of disputes through particular legal mechanisms, such as projected timelines and costs, domestic political concerns, geopolitical relationships, as well as the degree of control that a party can maintain over the process. "Fundamentally, however, the variety and number of such mechanisms suggest states' compelling trust in dispute settlement based on the rule of law, whose necessity to the protection of fresh water remains crucial."[7]

Certainly, more work can be undertaken in regard to the work begun here. An analysis at a more micro basin specific level may provide more illuminating State practice under existing 'Stepped Approaches'. Also, more analysis of factors that may contribute to the prevalence of 'Stepped Approaches' such as the purpose of watercourse agreements or the nature of joint organizations that exist between riparians. While left general in its definition, a 'Stepped Approach'[8] to dispute resolution in the law of international watercourses has existed and persists in this vital yet specialized area of law. By defining the contours of a 'Stepped Approach' more clearly and by providing additional datasets and details this work can hopefully contribute towards further enquiries into a 'Stepped Approach' to dispute resolution on international watercourses.

7 Laurence Boisson de Chazournes, Fresh Water in International Law, 2nd ed (Oxford University Press, 2021) at 339.

8 "[E]chelon" Stephen M. Schwebel, "Third report on the law of the non-navigational uses of international watercourses" (UN Doc A/CN.4/348) in *Year Book of the International Law Commission 1982 vol 2 part 1 (1984)* 65 at 182 (UN Doc A/CN.4/SER.A/1982/Add.1(Part1)); "[S]tepwise dispute -resolution system" Stephen C. McCaffrey, *The Law of International Watercourses*, 3rd ed (Oxford University Press, 2019) at 577; "[S]taged procedure for the avoidance and resolution of disputes" Stephen C. McCaffrey, *The Law of International Watercourses*, 3rd ed (Oxford University Press, 2019) at 578–579; "[S]eries of stages, or echelons" Stephen C. McCaffrey, "Sixth report on the law of the non-navigational uses of international watercourses" (UN Doc A/CN.4/427 and Add.1) in *Yearbook of the International Law Commission 1990*, vol 2, part 1 (1993) 41 at 72 para 75 (UN Doc A/CN.4/SER.A/1990/Add.1 (Part 1)); "[P]hased approach" Sergei Vinogradov, Patricia Wouters and Patricia Jones, *Transforming Potential Conflict into Cooperation Potential: The Role of International Water Law* (UNESCO-IHP, PCCP, 2003) at 63.

What is a 'Stepped Approach' to disputes on international watercourses? This work has defined a 'Stepped Approach' as a dispute resolution system dealing with an international watercourse and composed of a set of graduated discrete 'Steps', phases, or echelons of limited scope or duration with a relatively clear progression from one 'Step' to another. This work has also created an analytical framework of nine (9) criteria to help identify the presence of a 'Stepped Approach' in existing international agreements and to analyze those 'Stepped Approaches' as well as identifying a database of two hundred and twenty-five (225) treaties with distinct dispute resolution provisions between State actors.[9] The established practice in the field, as illustrated by the work of the ILC, international agreements, and the work of international courts and tribunals showcases that a 'Stepped Approach' to dispute resolution enjoys a vibrant role in international watercourse dispute resolution.

What is the utility of a 'Stepped Approach' to resolving disputes under the law of the non-navigational uses of international watercourses? It is important to appreciate that each basin and set of riparians present their unique needs and circumstances. While a 'Stepped Approach' may not be the best dispute resolution framework for all basins or riparians, it can present many elements that could prove advantageous to the settlement of increasingly technical and important international watercourse disputes. In allowing a dispute resolution framework that incorporates several separate yet complementary dispute resolution mechanisms this framework can be flexible and adaptable to the needs of riparians. By providing a clear progression through these mechanisms such an approach can create a stable and predictable dispute resolution process for riparians that can save time and costs by diverting matters away from more costly forms of dispute resolution early in the process, identifying the issues at stake, and creating a factual basis for later 'Steps' to work in. Above all, this 'Stepped Approach' provides an important and ongoing process or structure for riparians to engage with each other regarding disputes over shared water resources. In better understanding what is meant by a 'Stepped Approach', its potential utility, and the established practice regarding it in the field, it can be better employed and tailored to the specific needs of riparians and basins.

9 It is important to note that only distinct provisions addressing disputes between State parties were reviewed. The author attempts to differentiate these from compliance and management mechanisms in the agreements, unless these mechanisms were specifically mentioned in the dispute resolution provisions as applying to disputes between State actors.

Appendix A: Table of Treaties Examined

Rating	Treaty name	Date	Region	Graduated steps (3 or more)	Steps of limited scope and duration
7	*Final working agreement relative to the Sirhind Canal between Great Britain and Patiala, Jind and Nabha.*	1903-08-12	Asia	0	1
5	*Agreement between Great Britain and the Independent State of the Congo, modifying the Agreement signed at Brussels, May 12, 1894, relating to the Spheres of Influence of Great Britain and the Independent State of the Congo in East and Central Africa.*	1906-05-09	Africa	0	0
6	*Agreement between the British Government and the Panna State regarding jurisdiction and other matters connected with the working of the Ken Canal.*	1908-09-30	Asia	0	1
5	*Treaty Relating to Boundary Waters, and Questions Arising Between the United States and Canada (Boundary Waters Treaty).*	1909-01-11	North America	0	0
5	*Convention to fix the boundary between the Colonies of Suriname and French Guiana.* (France and Netherlands)	1915-09-30	South America	0	0

 | DOI:10.1163/9789004736771_008

Clear progression through steps	Recourse to technical expertise and decision making	A distinct technical step	A distinct diplomatic step	A distinct adjudicative step	A compulsory step	Ultimate step is binding
1	1	1	0	1	1	1
1	0	0	1	1	1	1
1	1	0	0	1	1	1
0	1	1	0	1	1	1
1	0	0	1	1	1	1

(*cont.*)

Rating	Treaty name	Date	Region	Graduated steps (3 or more)	Steps of limited scope and duration
3	*Peace Treaty and Protocol.* (Lithuania and Soviet Government of Russia)	1920-07-12	Europe	0	0
8	*Convention on certain points connected with the mandates for Syria and the Lebanon, Palestine and Mesopotamia.* (Great Britain and France)	1920-12-23	Asia	0	1
2	*Convention Concerning the Delimitation of the Frontier Between Austria and Czechoslovakia and Various Questions Connected Therewith.*	1921-03-10	Europe	0	0
8	*Convention Instituting the Definitive Statute of the Danube.*	1921-07-23	Europe	0	1
5	*Convention instituting the Statute of Navigation of the Elbe, with Protocol of signature.*	1922-02-22	Europe	0	0
4	*Treaty for the Regulation of the Rhine from the Confluence of the Ill to the Lake of Constance.* (Austria and Switzerland)	1924-11-19	Europe	0	0

Clear progression through steps	Recourse to technical expertise and decision making	A distinct technical step	A distinct diplomatic step	A distinct adjudicative step	A compulsory step	Ultimate step is binding
0	0	0	0	1	1	1
1	1	1	1	1	1	1
0	0	0	1	0	1	0
1	1	1	1	1	1	1
1	0	0	1	1	1	1
0	0	0	1	1	1	1

(*cont.*)

Rating	Treaty name	Date	Region	Graduated steps (3 or more)	Steps of limited scope and duration
4	*Convention concerning the International Legal Regime of the Waters of the Pasvik (Patsjoki) and the Jakobselv (Vuoremajoki), with Protocol.* (Finland and Norway)	1925-02-14	Europe	0	0
9	*Agreement to Regulate the Level of the Lake of the Woods and Protocol relating thereto.* (United States and Canada)	1925-02-24	North America	1	1
3	*Agreement between South Africa and Portugal regulating the use of the water of the Kunene River for the purposes of generating hydraulic power and inundation and irrigation in the Mandated Territory of South West Africa.*	1926-07-01	Africa	0	0
5	*Convention for the Settlement of Relations Between Switzerland and France on the Subject of Certain Clauses of the Legal Regime of the Future Derivation of Kembs, France and Switzerland.*	1926-08-27	Europe	1	0

Clear progression through steps	Recourse to technical expertise and decision making	A distinct technical step	A distinct diplomatic step	A distinct adjudicative step	A compulsory step	Ultimate step is binding
0	0	0	1	1	1	1
1	1	1	1	1	1	1
0	0	0	0	1	1	1
0	0	0	1	1	1	1

(*cont.*)

Rating	Treaty name	Date	Region	Graduated steps (3 or more)	Steps of limited scope and duration
3	*Convention between Belgium and Portugal regarding various questions of economic interest of the colonies Belgian Congo and Angola.*	1927-07-20	Africa	0	0
9	*Convention between Spain and Portugal to regulate the hydro-electric development of the international section of the River Douro.*	1927-08-11	Europe	1	1
3	*Convention regarding the Maintenance and Administration of the Frontier Waterways, with Final Protocol.* (Germany and Lithuania)	1928-01-29	Europe	0	0
5	*Treaty of peace, friendship and of arbitration.* (Dominican Republic and Haiti)	1929-02-20	North America	0	0
5	*Exchange of Notes Regarding the Use of Waters of the Nile for Irrigation Purposes.* (Egypt and Great Britain)	1929-05-07	Africa	1	0
4	*Treaty between Chile and Peru for the settlement of the dispute regarding Tacna and Arica.*	1929-06-03	South America	0	0

Clear progression through steps	Recourse to technical expertise and decision making	A distinct technical step	A distinct diplomatic step	A distinct adjudicative step	A compulsory step	Ultimate step is binding
0	0	0	0	1	1	1
1	1	1	1	1	1	1
0	0	0	0	1	1	1
1	0	0	1	1	1	1
0	0	0	1	1	1	1
0	0	0	1	1	1	1

(*cont.*)

Rating	Treaty name	Date	Region	Graduated steps (3 or more)	Steps of limited scope and duration
5	*Convention Between Switzerland and France on the Subject of the Concession of the Chatelot Waterfall.*	1930-11-19	Europe	1	0
3	*Agreement Between the United Kingdom and Belgium Regarding Water Rights on the Boundary Between Tanganyika and Ruanda-Urundi.*	1934-11-22	Africa	0	0
5	*Utilization of Waters of the Colorado and Tijuana Rivers and of the Rio Grande.* (Mexico and the United States of America)	1944-02-03	North America	0	0
4	*Treaty of friendship and neighbourly relations, and six annexed protocols, signed at Ankara.* (Iraq and Turkey)	1946-03-29	Asia	0	0
8	*Agreement concerning the utilization of the rapids of the Uruguay River in the Salto Grande area.* (Argentina and Uruguay)	1946-12-30	South America	1	0
5	*Convention Regarding the Regime of Navigation on the Danube.*	1948-08-18	Europe	0	0

Clear progression through steps	Recourse to technical expertise and decision making	A distinct technical step	A distinct diplomatic step	A distinct adjudicative step	A compulsory step	Ultimate step is binding
0	0	0	1	1	1	1
0	0	0	0	1	1	1
1	1	1	1	0	1	0
1	0	0	1	1	1	0
1	1	1	1	1	1	1
1	0	0	1	1	1	1

(*cont.*)

Rating	Treaty name	Date	Region	Graduated steps (3 or more)	Steps of limited scope and duration
5	*Exchange of Notes Constituting an Agreement Between the Great Britain and Egypt Regarding the Construction of the Owen Falls Dam, Uganda.*	1949-05-31	Africa	0	0
4	*Agreement Between Switzerland and Italy on the Subject of the Concession of Hydraulic Forces of the Reno Di Lei, with Additional Protocol.*	1949-06-18	Europe	0	0
3	*State Treaty between the Grand Duchy of Luxembourg and the Land Rhineland-Palatinate in the Federal Republic of Germany concerning the construction of a hydro-electric power plant on the Sauer (Sûre) at Rosport/Ralingen.*	1950-04-25	Europe	0	0
3	*Agreement between the Government of the Republic of Austria and the Government of the Federal Republic of Germany and of the Free State of Bavaria concerning the Donaukraftwerk-Jochenstein-Aktiengesellschaft (Danube power-plant and Jochenstein joint-stock company).*	1952-02-13	Europe	0	0

Clear progression through steps	Recourse to technical expertise and decision making	A distinct technical step	A distinct diplomatic step	A distinct adjudicative step	A compulsory step	Ultimate step is binding
1	0	0	1	1	1	1
0	0	0	1	1	1	1
0	0	0	0	1	1	1
0	0	0	0	1	1	1

(*cont.*)

Rating	Treaty name	Date	Region	Graduated steps (3 or more)	Steps of limited scope and duration
7	*Agreement between the Republic of Syria and the Hashemite Kingdom of Jordan concerning the utilization of the Yarmuk waters.*	1953-06-04	Asia	1	0
3	*Treaty between the Swiss Confederation and the Republic of Austria for the regulation of the Rhine from the mouth of the Ill to Lake Constance.*	1954-04-10	Europe	0	0
3	*Agreement between the Government of India and Government of Nepal on the Kosi Project.*	1954-04-25	Asia	0	0
3	*Convention Concerning Water Economy Questions Relating to the Drava.* (Austria and Yugoslavia)	1954-05-25	Europe	0	0
5	*Agreement concerning water economy questions in respect of the frontier sector of the Mura and the frontier waters of the Mura (the Mura Agreement).* (Austria and Yugoslavia)	1954-12-16	Europe	0	0

Clear progression through steps	Recourse to technical expertise and decision making	A distinct technical step	A distinct diplomatic step	A distinct adjudicative step	A compulsory step	Ultimate step is binding
1	1	0	1	1	1	1
0	0	0	0	1	1	1
0	0	0	0	1	1	1
0	0	0	0	1	1	1
1	0	0	1	1	1	1

(*cont.*)

Rating	Treaty name	Date	Region	Graduated steps (3 or more)	Steps of limited scope and duration
3	*Agreement between Yugoslavia and Romania concerning questions of water control on water control systems and watercourses on or intersected by the state frontier, together with the statute of the Yugoslav-Romanian Water Control Commission.*	1955-04-07	Europe	0	0
3	*Agreement between Yugoslavia and Hungary together with the statute of the Yugoslav-Hungarian water economy commission.*	1955-08-08	Europe	0	0
4	*Convention Between Italy and Switzerland Concerning the Regulation of Lake Lugano.*	1955-09-17	Europe	0	0
5	*Treaty* (*with annexes*) *concerning the regulation of water economy questions in the frontier region.* (Hungary and Austria)	1956-04-09	Europe	0	0
9	*Convention between the Federal Republic of Germany, the French Republic, and the Grand-Duchy of Luxembourg on the subject of Moselle canalization.*	1956-10-27	Europe	1	1

Clear progression through steps	Recourse to technical expertise and decision making	A distinct technical step	A distinct diplomatic step	A distinct adjudicative step	A compulsory step	Ultimate step is binding
1	0	0	1	0	1	0
1	0	0	1	0	1	0
0	0	0	1	1	1	1
1	1	1	1	0	1	0
1	1	1	1	1	1	1

(*cont.*)

Rating	Treaty name	Date	Region	Graduated steps (3 or more)	Steps of limited scope and duration
8	Convention between the Federal Republic of Germany and the French Republic on the management of the upper course of the Rhine between Basel and Strasbourg and protocol annexed to the convention, signed at Luxembourg.	1956-10-27	Europe	1	1
3	*Agreement concerning water economy questions, together with the statue of the Yugoslav-Albanian water economic Commission and the Protocol concerning fishing in frontier lakes and rivers.* (Albania and Yugoslavia)	1956-12-05	Europe	0	0
5	*Convention between the Swiss Confederation and the Italian Republic on the subject of utilization of the hydraulic force of the Spol and additional protocol.*	1957-05-27	Europe	0	0
4	*Agreement Concerning Water Economy Questions Between Bulgaria and Yugoslavia.*	1958-04-04	Europe	0	0

Clear progression through steps	Recourse to technical expertise and decision making	A distinct technical step	A distinct diplomatic step	A distinct adjudicative step	A compulsory step	Ultimate step is binding
1	1	1	0	1	1	1
1	0	0	1	0	1	0
1	0	0	1	1	1	1
1	0	0	1	1	1	0

(*cont.*)

Rating	Treaty name	Date	Region	Graduated steps (3 or more)	Steps of limited scope and duration
3	*State Treaty between the Grand Duchy of Luxembourg and the Land Rhineland Palatinate in the Federal Republic of Germany, concerning the construction of hydroelectric power installations on the Our (with Annexes).*	1958-07-10	Europe	0	0
9	*Agreement between the government of the French Republic and the Spanish government relating to Lake Lanoux.*	1958-07-12	Europe	1	1
3	*Agreement Concerning the Regulation of Lake Inari by Means of the Kaitakoski Hydroelectric Power Station and Dam.*	1959-04-29	Europe	0	0
2	*Agreement Between Greece and Yugoslavia Concerning Hydro-economic Questions.*	1959-06-18	Europe	0	0
4	*Indo-Pakistan Agreement (with appendices) on East Pakistan border disputes.*	1959-10-23	Asia	0	0
5	*Agreement on the Gandak Irrigation and Power Project.* (India and Nepal)	1959-12-04	Asia	0	0

Clear progression through steps	Recourse to technical expertise and decision making	A distinct technical step	A distinct diplomatic step	A distinct adjudicative step	A compulsory step	Ultimate step is binding
0	0	0	0	1	1	1
1	1	1	1	1	1	1
1	0	0	1	0	1	0
0	0	0	0	1	0	1
0	0	0	1	1	1	1
1	0	0	1	1	1	1

(*cont.*)

Rating	Treaty name	Date	Region	Graduated steps (3 or more)	Steps of limited scope and duration
9	*Treaty between the Kingdom of the Netherlands and the Federal Republic of Germany concerning the course of the common frontier, the boundary waters, real property situated near the frontier, traffic crossing the frontier on land and via inland waters, and other frontier questions.*	1960-04-08	Europe	1	1
9	*The Indus Waters Treaty 1960 (with annexes).*	1960-09-19	Asia	1	1
9	*Treaty between Canada and the United States of America relating to co-operative development of the water resources of the Columbia River Basin.*	1961-01-17	North America	1	1
9	*Protocol between the government of the Federal Republic of Germany, the French Republic and the Grand Duchy of Luxembourg concerning the establishment of an international commission to protect the Moselle against pollution.*	1961-12-20	Europe	1	1

Clear progression through steps	Recourse to technical expertise and decision making	A distinct technical step	A distinct diplomatic step	A distinct adjudicative step	A compulsory step	Ultimate step is binding
1	1	1	1	1	1	1
1	1	1	1	1	1	1
1	1	1	1	1	1	1
1	1	1	1	1	1	1

(*cont.*)

Rating	Treaty name	Date	Region	Graduated steps (3 or more)	Steps of limited scope and duration
2	*Protocol concerning the establishment of an international commission to protect the Saar against pollution, signed at Paris.* (France and Germany)	1961-12-20	Europe	0	0
2	*Exchange of notes constituting an agreement establishing a Joint Commission for the development of the Mirim Lagoon.* (Brazil and Uruguay)	1963-04-26	South America	0	0
4	*Convention Relating to the General Development of the Senegal River Basin.*	1963-07-26	Africa	0	0
5	*Convention concerning the Émosson Hydroelectric Facility (with exchanges of letters).* (France and Switzerland)	1963-08-23	Europe	0	0
6	*Act Regarding Navigation and Economic Co-operation between the States of the Niger Basin.*	1963-10-26	Africa	1	0
9	*Convention between the Socialist Federal Republic of Yugoslavia and the Romanian People's Republic concerning the execution of works for the Iron Gates Water Power and Navigation System on the River Danube.*	1963-11-30	Europe	1	1

Clear progression through steps	Recourse to technical expertise and decision making	A distinct technical step	A distinct diplomatic step	A distinct adjudicative step	A compulsory step	Ultimate step is binding
0	0	0	1	0	1	0
0	0	0	1	0	1	0
0	0	0	1	1	1	1
1	0	0	1	1	1	1
0	1	0	1	1	1	1
1	1	1	1	1	1	1

(*cont.*)

Rating	Treaty name	Date	Region	Graduated steps (3 or more)	Steps of limited scope and duration
9	*Agreement between the Socialist Federal Republic of Yugoslavia and the Romanian People's Republic concerning the construction and operation of the Iron Gates Water Power and Navigation System on the River Danube.*	1963-11-30	Europe	1	1
3	*Exchange of notes (with attachment) constituting an agreement regarding sale of Canada's entitlement to downstream benefits under the Treaty relating to co-operative development of the water resources of the Columbia River Basin.* (Canada and USA)	1964-01-22	North America	0	0
4	*Convention Relating to the Statute of the Senegal River.*	1964-02-07	Africa	0	0
5	*Agreement between Finland and the Soviet Union Concerning Frontier Watercourses.*	1964-04-24	Europe	1	0
5	*Convention and Statute relating to the Development of the Chad Basin, Fort Lamy.*	1964-05-22	Africa	0	0

Clear progression through steps	Recourse to technical expertise and decision making	A distinct technical step	A distinct diplomatic step	A distinct adjudicative step	A compulsory step	Ultimate step is binding
1	1	1	1	1	1	1
0	0	0	0	1	1	1
1	0	0	0	1	1	1
1	1	0	1	0	1	0
0	1	0	1	1	1	1

(*cont.*)

Rating	Treaty name	Date	Region	Graduated steps (3 or more)	Steps of limited scope and duration
9	*Convention to regulate the hydroelectric development of the international sections of the river Douro and its tributaries (with additional protocol).* (Portugal and Spain)	1964-07-16	Europe	1	1
9	*Exchange of Notes (with attachments) constituting an agreement authorizing the Canadian Entitlement Purchase Agreement provided for under the Treaty relating to co-operative development of the water resources of the Columbia River Basin.* (Canada and USA)	1964-09-16	North America	1	1
1	*Agreement Concerning the Niger River Commission and the Navigation and Transport on the River Niger.*	1964-11-25	Africa	0	0
9	*Agreement with Final Protocol Regulating the Withdrawal of Water from Lake Constance.*	1966-04-30	Europe	1	1
5	*Revised Agreement between the Government of India and His Majesty's Government of Nepal Concerning the Kosi Project.*	1966-12-19	Asia	0	0

Clear progression through steps	Recourse to technical expertise and decision making	A distinct technical step	A distinct diplomatic step	A distinct adjudicative step	A compulsory step	Ultimate step is binding
1	1	1	1	1	1	1
1	1	1	1	1	1	1
0	1	0	0	0	0	0
1	1	1	1	1	1	1
1	0	0	1	1	1	1

(*cont.*)

Rating	Treaty name	Date	Region	Graduated steps (3 or more)	Steps of limited scope and duration
5	*Franco-Italian Convention Concerning the Supply of Water to the Commune of Menton.*	1967-09-28	Europe	0	0
9	*Treaty between the Republic of Austria and the Czechoslovak Socialist Republic concerning the regulation of water management questions relating to frontier waters.*	1967-12-07	Europe	1	1
4	*Agreement concerning the establishment of a River Administration in the Rajka-Gönyü sector of the Danube (with exchange of letters).* (Czechoslovakia and Hungary)	1968-02-27	Europe	0	0
8	*Agreement regulating the use and development of the water resources of the international reaches of the rivers Miño, Limia, Tajo, Guadiana, and Chanza and of their tributaries (with additional protocol).* (Portugal and Spain)	1968-05-29	Europe	1	1
5	*African Convention on the Conservation of Nature and Natural Resources.*	1968-09-15	Africa	0	0

Clear progression through steps	Recourse to technical expertise and decision making	A distinct technical step	A distinct diplomatic step	A distinct adjudicative step	A compulsory step	Ultimate step is binding
1	0	0	1	1	1	1
1	1	1	1	1	1	1
1	1	0	1	0	1	0
1	1	0	1	1	1	1
0	1	0	1	1	1	1

(*cont.*)

Rating	Treaty name	Date	Region	Graduated steps (3 or more)	Steps of limited scope and duration
5	*Agreement Between the People's Republic of Bulgaria and the Republic of Turkey Concerning Cooperation in the Use of Waters of Rivers Flowing Through the Territory of Both Countries.*	1968-10-23	Europe	0	0
6	*Convention between the French Republic and the Federal Republic of Germany concerning development of the Rhine between Strasbourg/Kehl and Lauterbourg/Neuburgweier.*	1969-07-04	Europe	0	0
1	*Exchange of letters constituting an agreement amending the Agreement relating to Lake Lanoux (with arrangement concerning the lake's development) of 12 July 1958.* (France and Spain)	1970-01-27	Europe	0	0
2	*Convention for the study of the use of the resources of the Paraá river.* (Argentina and Paraguay)	1971-06-18	South America	0	0

Clear progression through steps	Recourse to technical expertise and decision making	A distinct technical step	A distinct diplomatic step	A distinct adjudicative step	A compulsory step	Ultimate step is binding
1	1	1	1	0	1	0
1	1	0	1	1	1	1
0	1	0	0	0	0	0
0	0	0	1	0	1	0

(*cont.*)

Rating	Treaty name	Date	Region	Graduated steps (3 or more)	Steps of limited scope and duration
5	*Agreement between the government of the Socialist Republic of Romania and the government of the Union of Soviet Socialist Republics on the joint construction of the Stînca-Costesti hydraulic engineering scheme on the river Prut and the establishment of the conditions for its operation (with protocols).*	1971-12-16	Europe	0	0
5	*Convention relating to the Statute of the Senegal River.*	1972-03-11	Africa	0	0
5	*Convention establishing the Senegal River Basin Organization.*	1972-03-11	Africa	0	0
5	*Agreement between the government of the Republic of Finland and the government of the Union of Soviet Socialist Republics concerning the production of electric power in the part of the Vuoksi River bounded by the Imatra and Svetogorsk hydroelectric stations.*	1972-07-12	Europe	1	0
2	*Statute of the Indo-Bangladesh Joint Rivers Commission.*	1972-11-24	Asia	0	0

Clear progression through steps	Recourse to technical expertise and decision making	A distinct technical step	A distinct diplomatic step	A distinct adjudicative step	A compulsory step	Ultimate step is binding
1	1	1	1	0	1	0
0	1	0	1	1	1	1
0	1	0	1	1	1	1
1	1	0	1	0	1	0
0	0	0	1	0	1	0

(*cont.*)

Rating	Treaty name	Date	Region	Graduated steps (3 or more)	Steps of limited scope and duration
2	*Treaty Between the Federative Republic of Brazil and the Republic of Paraguay Concerning the Hydroelectric Utilization of the Water Resources of the Paraná River Owned in Condominium by the Two Countries, from and Including the Salto Grande de Sete Quedas or Salto del Guairá, to the Mouth of the Iguassu River (Treaty of Itaipú).*	1973-04-26	South America	0	0
2	*Agreement Revising the Agreement Concerning the Niger River Commission and the Navigation and Transport on the River Niger of 25 November 1964.*	1973-06-15	Africa	0	0
6	*Agreement Creating a Development Fund of the Chad Basin Commission.*	1973-10-10	Africa	0	0
2	*Treaty of Yacyretá.* (Argentina and Paraguay)	1973-12-03	South America	0	0
9	*Statute of the river Uruguay, signed at Salto (Statute of the river Uruguay).* (Argentina and Uruguay)	1975-02-26	South America	1	1
7	*Treaty Concerning the State Frontier and Neighbourly Relations Between Iran and Iraq.*	1975-06-13	Asia	1	1

Clear progression through steps	Recourse to technical expertise and decision making	A distinct technical step	A distinct diplomatic step	A distinct adjudicative step	A compulsory step	Ultimate step is binding
0	0	0	1	0	1	0
0	1	0	1	0	0	0
1	1	0	1	1	1	1
0	0	0	1	0	1	0
1	1	1	1	1	1	1
1	0	0	1	1	1	1

(*cont.*)

Rating	Treaty name	Date	Region	Graduated steps (3 or more)	Steps of limited scope and duration
6	*Supplementary Convention to the Convention concerning the development of the Rhine between Strasbourg/ Kehl and Lauterbourg/ Neuburgweier of 4 July 1969.* (France and Germany)	1975-07-16	Europe	0	0
7	*Agreement between Iran and Iraq concerning the use of frontier watercourses.*	1975-12-26	Asia	1	1
6	*Agreement between the government of the Federal Republic of Germany and the government of the Grand Duchy of Luxembourg concerning the maintenance, restoration and operation of the section of the Moselle common to the two States.*	1976-09-14	Europe	0	1
5	*Convention on the Protection of the Rhine Against Chemical Pollution.*	1976-12-03	Europe	0	0
5	*Convention on the Protection of the Rhine Against Pollution by Chlorides.*	1976-12-03	Europe	0	0
7	*Treaty on Cooperation for the Utilization of the Natural Resources and the Development of the Mirim Lagoon Basin.* (Brazil and Uruguay)	1977-07-07	South America	1	1

Clear progression through steps	Recourse to technical expertise and decision making	A distinct technical step	A distinct diplomatic step	A distinct adjudicative step	A compulsory step	Ultimate step is binding
1	1	0	1	1	1	1
1	0	0	1	1	1	1
1	0	0	1	1	1	1
1	0	0	1	1	1	1
1	0	0	1	1	1	1
1	1	1	1	0	1	0

(*cont.*)

Rating	Treaty name	Date	Region	Graduated steps (3 or more)	Steps of limited scope and duration
4	*Agreement for the Establishment of the Organization for the Management and Development of the Kagera River Basin.*	1977-08-24	Africa	0	0
3	*Treaty Concerning the Construction and Operation of the Gabčíkovo-Nagymaros System of Locks.* (Czechoslovak Socialist Republic and the Hungarian People's Republic)	1977-09-16	Europe	0	0
7	*Agreement on Sharing of the Ganges Waters at Farakka and on Augmenting Its Flows.* (Bangladesh and India)	1977-11-05	Asia	1	1
7	*The Convention Relating to the Creation of the Gambia River Basin Development Organization.*	1978-06-30	Africa	1	0
7	*Convention Relating to the Status of the River Gambia.*	1978-06-30	Africa	1	0
2	*Protocol of the Agreement between the Republic of Guinea and the Republic of Guinea Bissau on the Management of the Koliba-Korubal River (Koliba-Korubal River Basin Protocol).*	1978-10-21	Africa	0	0

Clear progression through steps	Recourse to technical expertise and decision making	A distinct technical step	A distinct diplomatic step	A distinct adjudicative step	A compulsory step	Ultimate step is binding
1	1	0	1	0	1	0
1	0	0	1	0	1	0
1	1	1	1	0	1	0
1	1	0	1	1	1	1
1	1	0	1	1	1	1
0	0	0	1	0	1	0

(*cont.*)

Rating	Treaty name	Date	Region	Graduated steps (3 or more)	Steps of limited scope and duration
7	*Convention Concerning the Legal Status of Common Works.*	1978-12-21	Africa	1	0
4	*Convention between the Kingdom of Belgium and the Grand-Duchy of Luxembourg on the subject of the water of the Sûre.*	1980-03-17	Europe	0	0
2	*Treaty for the developing the shared water resources of the frontier sections of the Uruguay river and its tributary, the Pepiri-Guaçu (Pepirí-Guazú) River.* (Brazil and Argentina)	1980-05-17	South America	0	0
5	*Convention Creating the Niger Basin Authority.*	1980-11-21	Africa	0	0
6	*Convention concerning improvement of the common River Lys between Deulemont and Menin (with annexes).* (Belgium and France)	1982-02-03	Europe	0	0
5	*Indo-Bangladesh memorandum of understanding on the sharing of Ganga waters at Farakka.* (Bangladesh and India)	1982-10-07	Asia	1	0

Clear progression through steps	Recourse to technical expertise and decision making	A distinct technical step	A distinct diplomatic step	A distinct adjudicative step	A compulsory step	Ultimate step is binding
1	1	0	1	1	1	1
0	0	0	1	1	1	1
0	0	0	1	0	1	0
1	0	0	1	1	1	1
1	1	0	1	1	1	1
1	1	0	1	0	1	0

(*cont.*)

Rating	Treaty name	Date	Region	Graduated steps (3 or more)	Steps of limited scope and duration
6	*Convention modifying and completing the Supplementary Convention of 16 July 1975 to the Convention between the French Republic and the Federal Republic of Germany concerning development of the Rhine between Strasbourg/Kehl and Lauterbourg/Neuburgweier. Signed at Paris on 4 July 1969 (with Supplementary Protocol).*	1982-12-06	Europe	0	0
4	*Treaty relating to the Skagit River and Ross Lake, and the Seven Mile Reservoir on the Pend d'Oreille River.* (Canada and USA)	1984-04-02	North America	0	0
4	*Convention between the government of the French Republic and the government of the Grand Duchy of Luxembourg for the realization and exploitation of certain industrial settlements on the Moselle.*	1986-03-12	Europe	0	0

Clear progression through steps	Recourse to technical expertise and decision making	A distinct technical step	A distinct diplomatic step	A distinct adjudicative step	A compulsory step	Ultimate step is binding
1	1	0	1	1	1	1
1	0	0	0	1	1	1
0	0	0	1	1	1	1

(*cont.*)

Rating	Treaty name	Date	Region	Graduated steps (3 or more)	Steps of limited scope and duration
9	*Treaty on the Lesotho Highlands Water Project between the Government of the Kingdom of Lesotho and the Government of the Republic of South Africa.*	1986-10-24	Africa	1	1
3	*Agreement Between the Republic of Zimbabwe and the Republic of Zambia Concerning the Utilization of the Zambesi River.*	1987-07-28	Africa	0	0
4	*Agreement between the Republic of Syria and the Hashemite Kingdom of Jordan concerning the utilization of the Yarmuk waters.*	1987-09-03	Asia	0	0
5	*Revised convention Pertaining to the Creation of the Niger Basin Authority.*	1987-10-29	Africa	0	0
5	*Agreement between the Federal Republic of Germany and the European Economic Community, on the one hand, and the Republic of Austria, on the other, on cooperation on management of water resources in the Danube Basin.*	1987-12-01	Europe	0	0

Clear progression through steps	Recourse to technical expertise and decision making	A distinct technical step	A distinct diplomatic step	A distinct adjudicative step	A compulsory step	Ultimate step is binding
1	1	1	1	1	1	1
0	0	0	0	1	1	1
1	1	0	1	0	1	0
1	0	0	1	1	1	1
1	0	0	1	1	1	1

(*cont.*)

Rating	Treaty name	Date	Region	Graduated steps (3 or more)	Steps of limited scope and duration
2	*Exchange of notes constituting an agreement concerning the construction of a joint ring levee (with plan).* (Canada and USA)	1988-08-30	North America	0	0
7	*Agreement between the Government of Canada and the Government of the United States of America for Water Supply and Flood Control in the Souris River Basin.*	1989-10-23	North America	1	0
4	*Agreement concerning the establishment of the Regional Coordination Committee on drinking water and sanitation institutions of Central America, Panama and the Dominican Republic.*	1989-10-23	North America	0	0
4	*Agreement concerning the regulations governing Lake Saimaa and the Vuoksi River (with annexes).* (Finland and Union of Soviet Socialist Republics)	1989-10-26	Europe	0	0

Clear progression through steps	Recourse to technical expertise and decision making	A distinct technical step	A distinct diplomatic step	A distinct adjudicative step	A compulsory step	Ultimate step is binding
0	0	0	1	0	1	0
1	1	1	1	1	1	0
0	0	0	1	1	1	1
1	1	0	1	0	1	0

(*cont.*)

Rating	Treaty name	Date	Region	Graduated steps (3 or more)	Steps of limited scope and duration
6	*Agreement Between the Federal Republic of Nigeria and the Republic of Niger Concerning the Equitable Sharing in the Development, Conservation and Use of their Common Water Resources.*	1990-07-18	Africa	0	1
3	*Agreement Between the Government of Botswana and the Republic of Namibia on the Establishment of a Joint Water Commission.*	1990-11-13	Africa	0	0
9	*Protocol IV to the treaty on the Lesotho Highlands Water Project – supplementary arrangements regarding phase IA.* (Lesotho and South Africa)	1991-11-19	Africa	1	1
3	*Agreement Between the Republic of Kazakhstan, the Kyrgyz Republic, the Republic of Tajikistan, Turkmenistan, and the Republic of Uzbekistan on Cooperation in the Field of Joint Management of the Use and Conservation of Water Resources of Interstate Sources* (*Almaty Agreement*).	1992-02-18	Asia	0	0

Clear progression through steps	Recourse to technical expertise and decision making	A distinct technical step	A distinct diplomatic step	A distinct adjudicative step	A compulsory step	Ultimate step is binding
1	1	0	0	1	1	1
0	1	0	1	0	1	0
1	1	1	1	1	1	1
0	1	0	1	0	1	0

(cont.)

Rating	Treaty name	Date	Region	Graduated steps (3 or more)	Steps of limited scope and duration
6	*Treaty on the Development and Utilization of the Water Resources of the Komati River Basin Between the Government of the Kingdom of Swaziland and the Government of the Republic of South Africa.*	1992-03-13	Africa	0	1
6	*Treaty on the Establishment and Functioning of the Joint Water Commission Between the Government of the Kingdom of Swaziland and the Government of the Republic of South Africa.*	1992-03-13	Africa	0	1
2	*Convention on the Protection and Use of Transboundary Watercourses and International Lakes* (UNECE Water Convention).	1992-03-17	General	0	0
5	*Convention on the Protection of the Marine Environment of the Baltic Sea Area.*	1992-04-09	Europe	1	0
7	*Ancillary agreement to the deed of undertaking and relevant agreements entered into between the Lesotho Highlands Development Authority and the government of the Republic of South Africa.*	1992-08-31	Africa	0	1

Clear progression through steps	Recourse to technical expertise and decision making	A distinct technical step	A distinct diplomatic step	A distinct adjudicative step	A compulsory step	Ultimate step is binding
1	0	0	1	1	1	1
1	0	0	1	1	1	1
0	0	0	1	0	1	0
1	0	0	1	1	0	1
1	1	0	1	1	1	1

(*cont.*)

Rating	Treaty name	Date	Region	Graduated steps (3 or more)	Steps of limited scope and duration
4	*Agreement between the government of the Republic of Namibia and the government of the Republic of South Africa on the establishment of a permanent water commission.*	1992-09-14	Africa	0	0
5	*Agreement on the development and utilisation of the water resources of the Komati River Basin between the government of the Republic of South Africa and the government of KaNgwane.*	1992-10-07	Africa	0	0
7	*Treaty between the Czech Republic Government and the Slovak Republic Government on mutual relations and principles of cooperation in agriculture, food industry, forestry, and water economy under the conditions of the customs union.*	1992-11-23	Europe	1	0

Clear progression through steps	Recourse to technical expertise and decision making	A distinct technical step	A distinct diplomatic step	A distinct adjudicative step	A compulsory step	Ultimate step is binding
1	1	1	1	0	0	0
1	0	0	1	1	1	1
0	1	1	1	1	1	1

(*cont.*)

Rating	Treaty name	Date	Region	Graduated steps (3 or more)	Steps of limited scope and duration
1	*Exchange of Notes relating to the creation of the Binational Autonomous Authority of the Basin of the Lake Titicaca System, Desaguadero River, Lake Poopó, Salar de Coipasa* (*TDPS*). (Bolivia and Peru)	1993-06-21	South America	0	0
5	*Agreement Concerning the Establishment of a Border Environment Cooperation Commission and a North American Development Bank.* (Mexico and USA)	1993-11-18	North America	0	0
2	*Agreement between the government of the People's Republic of China and the government of Mongolia on the protection and utilization of transboundary waters.*	1994-04-29	Asia	0	0
7	*Convention on Cooperation for the Protection and Sustainable Use of the River Danube.*	1994-06-29	Europe	0	1
5	*Convention for the Establishment of the Lake Victoria Fisheries Organization with Annex and Final Act.*	1994-06-30	Africa	0	0

Clear progression through steps	Recourse to technical expertise and decision making	A distinct technical step	A distinct diplomatic step	A distinct adjudicative step	A compulsory step	Ultimate step is binding
0	1	0	0	0	0	0
1	0	0	1	1	1	1
0	0	0	1	0	1	0
1	1	0	1	1	1	1
1	0	0	1	1	1	1

(*cont.*)

Rating	Treaty name	Date	Region	Graduated steps (3 or more)	Steps of limited scope and duration
5	*Agreement by exchange of notes between the Republic of Argentina and the Republic of Paraguay adopting the statute of the binational commission administering the lower basin of the Pilcomayo river .*	1994-08-05	South America	0	1
2	*Agreement Between the Governments of the Republic of Angola, the Republic of Botswana and the Republic of Namibia on the Establishment of a Permanent Okavango River Basin Water Commission (OKACOM).*	1994-09-15	Africa	0	0
6	*Agreement between Lebanon and Syria on the distribution of water of Al-Asi River rising in Lebanon.*	1994-09-20	Asia	0	0
2	*Treaty of peace between the state of Israel and the Hashemite Kingdom of Jordan (with annexes, agreed minutes and maps).*	1994-10-26	Asia	0	0

Clear progression through steps	Recourse to technical expertise and decision making	A distinct technical step	A distinct diplomatic step	A distinct adjudicative step	A compulsory step	Ultimate step is binding
1	1	0	1	0	1	0
0	0	0	1	0	1	0
1	1	1	1	1	0	1
0	0	0	1	0	1	0

(*cont.*)

Rating	Treaty name	Date	Region	Graduated steps (3 or more)	Steps of limited scope and duration
5	*Agreement between the Federal Ministry for the Environment, Nature Conservation and Nuclear Safety of the Federal Republic of Germany and the Ministry of the Environment of the Czech Republic on the implementation of the joint environmental protection pilot project "Municipal Wastewater Treatment Plants North Bohemia".*	1994-12-19	Europe	0	0
1	*Agreement constituting the trilateral commission for the development of the Pilcomayo river basin.*	1995-02-09	South America	0	0
4	*Agreement on the Cooperation for the Sustainable Development of the Mekong River Basin.*	1995-04-05	Asia	1	0
4	*Agreement for the multiple use of the resources of the upper basin of the Bermejo River Basin and of the Río Grande de Tarija: creation of the binational commission.* (Argentina and Bolivia)	1995-06-09	South America	0	0
5	*Protocol on Shared Watercourse Systems in the Southern African Development Community* (SADC) *Region.*	1995-08-28	Africa	0	0

Clear progression through steps	Recourse to technical expertise and decision making	A distinct technical step	A distinct diplomatic step	A distinct adjudicative step	A compulsory step	Ultimate step is binding
1	0	0	1	1	1	1
0	0	0	1	0	0	0
0	1	0	1	0	1	0
0	0	0	1	1	1	1
1	0	0	1	1	1	1

(*cont.*)

Rating	Treaty name	Date	Region	Graduated steps (3 or more)	Steps of limited scope and duration
6	*Israeli-Palestine Liberation Organization: Interim agreement on the West Bank and the Gaza Strip, with selected Annexes.*	1995-09-28	Asia	1	0
4	*Agreement between the government of Hellenic Republic and the government of the Republic of Bulgaria for the use of the Nestos River waters.*	1995-12-22	Europe	0	0
2	*Joint Water Commission terms of reference.* (Mozambique and South Africa)	1996-01-01	Africa	0	0
8	*Treaty Concerning the Integrated Development of the Mahakali River including Sarada Barrage, Tanakpur Barrage and Pancheshwar Project.* (India and Nepal)	1996-02-12	Asia	0	1
1	*Convention concerning the collection, storage and discharge of waste from ships navigating along the Rhine and other inland waters.*	1996-09-09	Europe	0	0
7	*Treaty on Sharing of the Ganga/Ganges Waters at Farakka.* (Bangladesh and India)	1996-12-12	Asia	1	1

Clear progression through steps	Recourse to technical expertise and decision making	A distinct technical step	A distinct diplomatic step	A distinct adjudicative step	A compulsory step	Ultimate step is binding
0	1	0	1	1	1	1
1	1	0	1	0	1	0
0	0	0	1	0	1	0
1	1	1	1	1	1	1
0	0	0	0	0	1	0
1	1	1	1	0	1	0

(*cont.*)

Rating	Treaty name	Date	Region	Graduated steps (3 or more)	Steps of limited scope and duration
7	*Convention on the Law of Non-Navigational Uses of International Watercourses* (UN Watercourses Convention).	1997-05-21	General	1	1
2	*Agreement Between the Government of the Russian Federation and the Government of the Republic of Estonia Concerning Cooperation in the Protection and Rational Use of Transboundary Waters.*	1997-08-20	Europe	0	0
3	*Agreement between the Government of Romania and the Government of Ukraine on cooperation in the field of border water management.*	1997-09-30	Europe	0	0
2	*Treaty between the Republics of El Salvador, Guatemala and Honduras for the execution of the Trifinio Plan.*	1997-10-31	North America	0	0
1	*Agreement between the Republic of Turkey and the Republic of Bulgaria on determination of the boundary in the mouth area of the Mutludere/Rezovska River and delimitation of the maritime areas between the two States in the Black Sea.*	1997-12-04	Europe	0	0

Clear progression through steps	Recourse to technical expertise and decision making	A distinct technical step	A distinct diplomatic step	A distinct adjudicative step	A compulsory step	Ultimate step is binding
1	1	1	1	0	1	0
0	0	0	1	0	1	0
1	0	0	1	0	1	0
0	0	0	1	0	1	0
0	0	0	1	0	0	0

(*cont.*)

Rating	Treaty name	Date	Region	Graduated steps (3 or more)	Steps of limited scope and duration
5	*Agreement between the Governments of the Republic of Kazakhstan, the Kyrgyz Republic, and the Republic of Uzbekistan on the Use of Water and Energy Resources of the Syr Darya Basin.*	1998-03-17	Asia	0	0
2	*Agreement Between the Government of the Republic of Kazakhstan, the government of the Kyrgyz Republic and the government of the Republic of Uzbekistan on Cooperation in the area of Environment and Rational Nature Use.*	1998-03-17	Asia	0	0
4	*Regulations for the administration of the Zarumiilla canal and the use of its waters.* (Ecuador and Peru)	1998-10-26	South America	0	0
6	*Agreement on Cooperation for the Protection and Sustainable Use of the Waters of the Spanish-Portuguese Hydrographic Basins.* (Portugal and Spain)	1998-11-30	Europe	1	0
5	*Convention on the Protection of the Rhine.*	1999-04-12	Europe	0	0

Clear progression through steps	Recourse to technical expertise and decision making	A distinct technical step	A distinct diplomatic step	A distinct adjudicative step	A compulsory step	Ultimate step is binding
1	0	0	1	1	1	1
0	0	0	1	0	1	0
0	1	1	1	0	1	0
0	1	0	1	1	1	1
1	0	0	1	1	1	1

(*cont.*)

Rating	Treaty name	Date	Region	Graduated steps (3 or more)	Steps of limited scope and duration
9	*Protocol VI to the Treaty on the Lesotho Highlands Water Project Supplementary Arrangements Regarding the System of Governance for the Project.* (Lesotho and South Africa)	1999-06-04	Africa	1	1
6	*Treaty for the establishment of the East African Community* (signed at Arusha).	1999-11-30	Africa	1	1
2	*Agreement between the Government of the Republic of Kazakhstan and the Government of the Kyrgyz Republic on utilization of the water facilities of interstate use on the Chu and Talas Rivers.*	2000-02-11	Asia	0	0
5	*Revised Protocol on Shared Watercourses in the Southern African Development Community* (SADC).	2000-08-07	Africa	0	0
5	*Agreement Between the Governments of the Republic of Botswana, the Kingdom of Lesotho, the Republic of Namibia, and the Republic of South Africa on the Establishment of the Orange-Senqu River Commission.*	2000-11-03	Africa	0	0

Clear progression through steps	Recourse to technical expertise and decision making	A distinct technical step	A distinct diplomatic step	A distinct adjudicative step	A compulsory step	Ultimate step is binding
1	1	1	1	1	1	1
1	0	0	0	1	1	1
0	0	0	1	0	1	0
1	0	0	1	1	1	1
1	0	0	1	1	1	1

(*cont.*)

Rating	Treaty name	Date	Region	Graduated steps (3 or more)	Steps of limited scope and duration
3	*Agreement between the Government of the Republic of Kazakhstan and the Government of the People's Republic of China on Cooperation in the Use and Protection of Transboundary Rivers.*	2001-09-12	Asia	0	0
2	*Agreement for the sharing of the Great Southern River Basin waters and the building of a joint dam on it.*	2002-04-20	Asia	0	0
6	*Water Charter of the Senegal River.*	2002-05-28	Africa	1	0
6	*Tripartite Interim Agreement for Cooperation on the Protection and Sustainable Utilization of the Water Resources of the Incomati and Maputo Watercourses (IIMA).*	2002-08-29	Africa	0	1
7	*Framework Agreement on the Sava River Basin Between Bosnia and Herzegovina, Croatia, Slovenia and the Federal Republic of Yugoslavia.*	2002-12-03	Europe	1	1
7	*Protocol on the Navigation Regime to the Framework Agreement on the Sava River Basin.*	2002-12-03	Europe	1	1
2	*International Treaty for the Meuse.*	2002-12-03	Europe	0	0

Clear progression through steps	Recourse to technical expertise and decision making	A distinct technical step	A distinct diplomatic step	A distinct adjudicative step	A compulsory step	Ultimate step is binding
0	1	0	1	0	1	0
1	0	0	1	0	0	0
1	0	0	1	1	1	1
1	0	0	1	1	1	1
1	1	1	1	0	1	0
1	1	1	1	0	1	0
0	0	0	1	0	1	0

(*cont.*)

Rating	Treaty name	Date	Region	Graduated steps (3 or more)	Steps of limited scope and duration
2	*Agreement between the Government of the Hellenic Republic and the Government of the Republic of Albania on the establishment of the permanent Greek-Albanian commission on transboundary freshwater issues.*	2003-04-03	Europe	0	0
2	*Framework Convention of the protection and sustainable development of the Carpathians.*	2003-05-22	Europe	0	0
4	*Convention on the Sustainable Management of Lake Tanganyika.*	2003-06-12	Africa	1	0
6	*African Convention on the Conservation of Nature and Natural Resources.*	2003-07-11	Africa	0	1
7	*Protocol for Sustainable Development of Lake Victoria Basin.*	2003-11-29	Africa	1	1
2	*Memorandum of Understanding between the Republic of Niger and the Republic of Mali relating to the construction of the Taoussa dams in Mali and Kandadji dams in Niger.*	2004-06-06	Africa	0	0

Clear progression through steps	Recourse to technical expertise and decision making	A distinct technical step	A distinct diplomatic step	A distinct adjudicative step	A compulsory step	Ultimate step is binding
0	0	0	1	0	1	0
0	0	0	1	0	1	0
0	1	0	1	0	1	0
1	0	0	1	1	1	1
1	0	0	1	1	1	1
0	0	0	1	0	1	0

(*cont.*)

Rating	Treaty name	Date	Region	Graduated steps (3 or more)	Steps of limited scope and duration
2	*Agreement between the council of ministers of the Republic of Albania and the Government of the Republic of Macedonia for the protection and sustainable development of Lake Ohrid and its watershed.*	2004-06-17	Europe	0	0
5	*Agreement on the Establishment of the Zambezi Watercourse Commission.*	2004-07-13	Africa	0	0
8	*Convention on the Status of the Volta River and Establishment of the Volta Basin Authority.*	2007-01-19	Africa	1	0
9	*Niger Basin Water Charter.*	2008-04-30	Africa	1	1
7	*Protocol on Prevention of the Water Pollution Caused by Navigation to the Framework Agreement on the Sava River Basin.*	2009-06-01	Europe	1	1
4	*Agreement for the Establishment of the Binational Commission for the Integrated Management of Water Resources of the Transboundary Hydrographic Basin of the Zarumilla River.* (Ecuador and Peru)	2009-10-22	South America	0	0

Clear progression through steps	Recourse to technical expertise and decision making	A distinct technical step	A distinct diplomatic step	A distinct adjudicative step	A compulsory step	Ultimate step is binding
0	0	0	1	0	1	0
1	0	0	1	1	1	1
1	1	1	1	1	1	1
1	1	1	1	1	1	1
1	1	1	1	0	1	0
1	1	0	1	0	1	0

(*cont.*)

Rating	Treaty name	Date	Region	Graduated steps (3 or more)	Steps of limited scope and duration
2	*Agreement between Finland and Sweden Concerning Transboundary Rivers.*	2009-11-11	Europe	0	0
2	*Memorandum of Understanding in the field of remediation of water quality between the Government of the Republic of Turkey and the Government of the Syrian Arab Republic.*	2009-12-23	Asia	0	0
2	*Memorandum of Understanding between the Government of Turkey and the Government of the Syrian Arab Republic on establishment of a pumping station for withdrawal of water from Tigris River.*	2009-12-23	Asia	0	0
4	*Agreement on the Protection and Sustainable Development of the Prespa Park Area.*	2010-02-02	Europe	1	0
7	*Agreement on the Nile Basin Cooperative Framework.*	2010-05-14	Africa	1	1
7	*Protocol on Flood Protection to the Framework Agreement on the Sava River Basin.*	2010-06-01	Europe	1	1

Clear progression through steps	Recourse to technical expertise and decision making	A distinct technical step	A distinct diplomatic step	A distinct adjudicative step	A compulsory step	Ultimate step is binding
0	0	0	1	0	1	0
0	0	0	1	0	1	0
0	0	0	1	0	1	0
0	1	0	1	0	1	0
1	1	1	1	0	1	0
1	1	1	1	0	1	0

(cont.)

Rating	Treaty name	Date	Region	Graduated steps (3 or more)	Steps of limited scope and duration
2	*Agreement between the Government of the Republic of South Africa and the Government of the Kingdom of Swaziland on water supply across the border between South Africa and Swaziland.*	2010-07-23	Africa	0	0
8	*Guarani Aquifer Agreement (Acuerdo sobre el Acuífero Guaraní).*	2010-08-02	South America	1	1
3	*Agreement between the Government of the Russian Federation and the Government of the Republic of Azerbaijan on the Rational Management and Protection of the Water Resources of the Transboundary River Samur.*	2010-09-03	Asia	0	0
4	*Agreement between the Government of the Russian Federation and the Government of the Republic of Kazakhstan on joint management of transboundary waterbodies.*	2010-09-07	Asia	0	0

Clear progression through steps	Recourse to technical expertise and decision making	A distinct technical step	A distinct diplomatic step	A distinct adjudicative step	A compulsory step	Ultimate step is binding
0	0	0	1	0	1	0
1	1	0	1	1	1	1
0	1	0	1	0	1	0
1	1	0	1	0	1	0

(*cont.*)

Rating	Treaty name	Date	Region	Graduated steps (3 or more)	Steps of limited scope and duration
2	*Memorandum of Understanding between the Government of the Republic of Turkey and the Government of the Islamic Republic of Iran on Natural Resources and Watershed Management.*	2010-09-29	Asia	0	0
2	*Agreement between the Government of the Republic of Tajikistan and the Government of the Islamic Republic of Afghanistan on cooperation in the development and management of water resources of the Pyanj and Amu Darya rivers.*	2010-10-25	Asia	0	0
6	*Statute of the Binational Commission for the Integrated Management of Water Resources of the Transboundary Hydrographic Basin of the Zarumilla River.*	2010-11-05	South America	1	0
2	*Agreement between the Government of the Republic of Kazakhstan and the People's Republic of China on water quality protection of transboundary waters.*	2011-02-22	Asia	0	0

Clear progression through steps	Recourse to technical expertise and decision making	A distinct technical step	A distinct diplomatic step	A distinct adjudicative step	A compulsory step	Ultimate step is binding
0	0	0	1	0	1	0
0	0	0	1	0	1	0
1	1	1	1	0	1	0
0	0	0	1	0	1	0

(cont.)

Rating	Treaty name	Date	Region	Graduated steps (3 or more)	Steps of limited scope and duration
7	*Water Charter for the Lake Chad Basin (Charte de l'Eau du Bassin du Lac Tchad).*	2012-04-30	Africa	1	0
2	*Agreement on cooperation between the Republic of Portugal and the Kingdom of Spain related to the International Park of Tagus River.*	2012-05-09	Europe	0	0
4	*Agreement between the Cabinet of Ministers of Ukraine and the Government of the Republic of Moldova on cooperation in the sphere of protection and sustainable development of the Dniester river basin.*	2012-11-29	Europe	0	0
2	*Agreement between Norway and Finland on a Norwegian-Finnish Water District.*	2013-10-30	Europe	0	0
8	*Memorandum of Understanding for the establishment of a Consultation Mechanism for the Integrated Management of the Water Resources of the Iullemeden, Taoudeni/Tanezrouft Aquifer Systems (ITAS).*	2014-03-28	Africa	1	0

Clear progression through steps	Recourse to technical expertise and decision making	A distinct technical step	A distinct diplomatic step	A distinct adjudicative step	A compulsory step	Ultimate step is binding
1	1	0	1	1	1	1
0	0	0	1	0	1	0
1	1	0	1	0	1	0
0	0	0	1	0	1	0
1	1	1	1	1	1	1

(*cont.*)

Rating	Treaty name	Date	Region	Graduated steps (3 or more)	Steps of limited scope and duration
7	*Agreement between the Government of Angola and the Government of Namibia on the Establishment of the Cuvelai Watercourse Commission (CUVECOM).*	2014-09-16	Africa	0	1
5	*Agreement on Declaration of Principles between The Arab Republic of Egypt, The Federal Democratic Republic of Ethiopia And The Republic of the Sudan On The Grand Ethiopian Renaissance Dam Project (GERDP).*	2015-03-23	Africa	0	0
6	*Agreement between the Government of the Federal Republic of Germany and the Government of the Republic of Poland on common improvement of the situation on waterways in the German-Polish border area (flood control, drainage and navigation conditions).*	2015-04-27	Europe	0	0
7	*Protocol on Sediment Management to the Framework Agreement on the Sava River Basin.*	2015-07-06	Europe	1	1

Clear progression through steps	Recourse to technical expertise and decision making	A distinct technical step	A distinct diplomatic step	A distinct adjudicative step	A compulsory step	Ultimate step is binding
1	1	0	1	1	1	1
1	1	0	1	1	1	0
1	1	0	1	1	1	1
1	1	1	1	0	1	0

(*cont.*)

Rating	Treaty name	Date	Region	Graduated steps (3 or more)	Steps of limited scope and duration
2	*Cooperation Agreement between the Republic of Azerbaijan and the Islamic Republic of Iran in the field of construction of hydroelectric power stations "Khudafarin" and "Maiden Tower" on the Araz River and use of energy and water resources.*	2016-02-23	Asia	0	0
3	*Rules and Procedures for Sharing of Data Related to the Management and Development of the Zambezi Watercourse.*	2016-02-25	Africa	0	0
2	*Agreement between the Government of the Russian Federation and the Government of the Republic of Kazakhstan on the Conservation of the Ecosystem of the Transboundary Ural River Basin.*	2016-10-04	Asia	0	0
2	*Agreement between the Ministry of Agriculture and Water Economy of the Republic of Uzbekistan and the Ministry of Agriculture and Water Economy of Turkmenistan on cooperation on water issues.*	2017-03-06	Asia	0	0

Clear progression through steps	Recourse to technical expertise and decision making	A distinct technical step	A distinct diplomatic step	A distinct adjudicative step	A compulsory step	Ultimate step is binding
0	0	0	1	0	1	0
1	0	0	1	0	1	0
0	0	0	1	0	1	0
0	0	0	1	0	1	0

(*cont.*)

Rating	Treaty name	Date	Region	Graduated steps (3 or more)	Steps of limited scope and duration
2	*Agreement between the Government of the Republic of Uzbekistan and the Government of the Kyrgyz Republic on the interstate use of the Orto-Tokoi (Kasansay) reservoir in the Ala-Buka district of the Jalal-Abad region of the Kyrgyz Republic.*	2017-10-06	Asia	0	0
3	*Agreement that establishes the Binational Commission for the Integrated Management of Water Resources of Transboundary Hydrographic Basins between the Republic of Peru and the Republic of Ecuador.*	2017-10-20	South America	0	0
7	*Agreement between the Government of Romania and the Government of the Republic of Serbia regarding cooperation in the field of sustainable management of transboundary waters.*	2019-06-05	Europe	1	0
4	*Agreement between the Government of the Republic of Belarus and the Government of the Republic of Poland on cooperation in the field of protection and rational use of transboundary waters.*	2020-02-07	Europe	0	0

Clear progression through steps	Recourse to technical expertise and decision making	A distinct technical step	A distinct diplomatic step	A distinct adjudicative step	A compulsory step	Ultimate step is binding
0	0	0	1	0	1	0
0	1	0	1	0	1	0
1	1	0	1	1	1	1
1	1	0	1	0	1	0

(*cont.*)

Rating	Treaty name	Date	Region	Graduated steps (3 or more)	Steps of limited scope and duration
2	*Memorandum of Understanding under the Joint Working Group on Water Resources Cooperation of Lancang-Mekong Cooperation on the Provision of Hydrological Information of the Lancang River Throughout the Year by China to the Other Five Member Countries.*	2020-11-01	Asia	0	0
2	*Agreement between the Government of Romania and the Government of the Republic of Moldova regarding the regulation of the construction of waterworks.*	2021-05-20	Europe	0	0
2	*Agreement between the Government of the Republic of Uzbekistan and the Government of Turkmenistan on the Joint Uzbek-Turkmen Intergovernmental Commission on Water Management Issues.*	2021-05-26	Asia	0	0
7	*Agreement between the Government of the Republic of Mozambique, South Africa and the Kingdom of Eswatini on the Establishment of the Incomáti and Maputo Watercourse Commission.*	2021-11-18	Africa	0	1

Clear progression through steps	Recourse to technical expertise and decision making	A distinct technical step	A distinct diplomatic step	A distinct adjudicative step	A compulsory step	Ultimate step is binding
0	0	0	1	0	1	0
0	0	0	1	0	1	0
0	0	0	1	0	1	0
1	1	0	1	1	1	1

(*cont.*)

Rating	Treaty name	Date	Region	Graduated steps (3 or more)	Steps of limited scope and duration
2	*Agreement between the Government of Turkmenistan and the Government of the Republic of Uzbekistan on the management, protection and rational use of water resources of the Amudarya River.*	2022-07-14	Asia	0	0
2	*Agreement between the Ministry of Water Resources of the Republic of Uzbekistan and the Water Resources Service under the Ministry of Agriculture of the Kyrgyz Republic on cooperation on water management issues.*	2022-11-03	Asia	0	0
2	*Agreement between the Government of the Republic of Uzbekistan and the Cabinet of Ministers of the Kyrgyz Republic on joint management of water resources of the Andijan (Kempirabad) reservoir.*	2022-11-03	Asia	0	0

0 = No, 1 = Yes

Clear progression through steps	Recourse to technical expertise and decision making	A distinct technical step	A distinct diplomatic step	A distinct adjudicative step	A compulsory step	Ultimate step is binding
0	0	0	1	0	1	0
0	0	0	1	0	1	0
0	0	0	1	0	1	0

Appendix B: Table of Cases

Date	Case
1923	*Status of Eastern Carelia* (1923), Advisory Opinion, PCIJ (Ser B) No 5.
1924	*Case of the Mavrommatis Palestine Concessions* (*Greece v Great Britain*), *(1924) PCIJ (Ser A) No 2.*
1927	*The Donauversinkung Case* (*Württemberg and Prussia v Baden*) (1927), 4 ILR 128.
1929	*Territorial Jurisdiction of the International Commission of the River Oder* (1929) PCIJ, (Ser A) No 23.
1941	*Trail Smelter Arbitration* (*United States v Canada*) (1941), 3 RIAA 1911.
1943	*Colorado v Kansas*, 320 US 383 (1943).
1948	*Corfu Channel case* (*United Kingdom v Albania*), Order of December 17 1948, [1948] ICJ Rep 124.
1949	*Corfu Channel case* (*United Kingdom v Albania*), Judgment of April 9 1949, [1949] ICJ Rep 4.
1957	*Affaire du Lac Lanoux* (*France v Spain*) (1957), Judgment, 12 RIAA 281.
1984	*Delimitation of the Maritime Boundary in the Gulf of Maine Area* (*Canada v United States of America*), Appointment of Expert, Order of March 30 1984, [1984] ICJ Rep 165.
1997	*Gabčíkovo-Nagymaros Project* (*Hungary v Slovakia*), Judgment of September 25 1997, [1997] ICJ Rep 7.
1998	*Case concerning the land and maritime boundary between Cameroon and Nigeria* (*Cameroon v Nigeria*), [1998] ICJ Rep 275.
1999	*Case Concerning Kasikili/Sedudu Island* (*Botswana v Namibia*), Separate Opinion of Judge Oda of December 13 1999, [1999] ICJ Rep 1116.
2007	*Baglihar Hydro-electric Plant* (*Pakistan v India*), Neutral Expert Determination on the Baglihar Hydro-electric Plant dated 12 February 2007.
2008	*United States – Final Anti-Dumping Measures on Stainless Steel from Mexico* (*Complaint by Mexico*), WTO Doc WT/DS344/AB/R (Appellate Body Report), online: WTO <http://docsonline.wto.org>.
2009	*Case Concerning the Dispute Regarding Navigational and Related Rights* (*Costa Rica v Nicaragua*), Judgement of July 13 2009, [2009] ICJ Rep 213.
2010	*Case Concerning Pulp Mills on the River Uruguay* (*Argentina v Uruguay*), Judgment of April 20 2010, [2010] ICJ Rep 14.

 | DOI:10.1163/9789004736771_009

(*cont.*)

Date	Case
2010	*Case Concerning Pulp Mills on the River Uruguay (Argentina v Uruguay)*, Joint Dissenting Opinion of Judges Al-Khasawneh and Simma of April 20 2010, [2010] ICJ Rep 108.
2010	*Case Concerning Pulp Mills on the River Uruguay (Argentina v Uruguay)*, Declaration of Judge Yusef of April 20 2010, [2010] ICJ Rep 216.
2010	*Case Concerning Pulp Mills on the River Uruguay (Argentina v Uruguay)*, Separate Opinion of Judge Greenwood of April 20 2010, [2010] ICJ Rep 221.
2010	*Case Concerning Pulp Mills on the River Uruguay (Argentina v Uruguay)*, Dissenting Opinion of Judge *ad hoc* Vinuesa of April 20 2010, [2010] ICJ Rep 266.
2013	*Indus Waters Kishenganga Arbitration (Pakistan v India)* (18 February 2013), Partial Award, 31 RIAA 55, (Permanent Court of Arbitration).
2013	*Indus Waters Kishenganga Arbitration (Pakistan v India)* (20 December 2013), Final Award, 31 RIAA 309, (Permanent Court of Arbitration).
2015	*Certain Activities Carried Out by Nicaragua in the Border Area (Costa Rica v Nicaragua) and Construction of a Road Along the San Juan River (Nicaragua v Costa Rica)*, Judgment of 16 December 2015, [2015] ICJ Rep 665.
2022	*Dispute over the Status and Use of the Waters of the Silala (Chile v Bolivia)*, Judgment of 1 December 2022, [2022] ICJ 614.
2022	*Dispute over the Status and Use of the Waters of the Silala (Chile v Bolivia)*, Separate Opinion of Judge Ad Hoc Simma of 1 December 2022, [2022] ICJ 677.
2023	*Indus Waters Treaty Arbitration (Pakistan v India)* (6 July 2023), Award on the Competence of the Court, PCA Case No 2023-01, (Permanent Court of Arbitration), online: <https://pca-cpa.org/en/cases/284/>.
2023	*Indus Waters Treaty Neutral Expert Proceedings (India v Pakistan)*, PCA Case No 2023-14, (Permanent Court of Arbitration), online: <https://pca-cpa.org/en/cases/297/>.

Appendix C: Table of Treaties and Other Instruments

Whenever possible complete citations are provided.

Date	Treaty
1903	*Final working agreement relative to the Sirhind Canal between Great Britain and Patiala, Jind and Nabha*, 12 August 1903, C.U. Aitchison, A Collection of Treaties, Engagements and Sanads Relating to India and Neighbouring Countries, Volume I: Part II, 207.
1906	*Agreement between Great Britain and the Independent State of the Congo, modifying the Agreement signed at Brussels*, May 12, 1894, relating to the Spheres of Influence of Great Britain and the Independent State of the Congo in East and Central Africa, 9 May 1906, 99 BSP 173.
1908	*Agreement between the British Government and the Panna State regarding jurisdiction and other matters connected with the working of the Ken Canal*, 30 September 1908, C.U. Aitchison, A Collection of Treaties, Engagements and Sanads Relating to India and Neighbouring Countries, Volume V: Part II, 122.
1909	*Treaty Relating to Boundary Waters, and Questions Arising Between the United States and Canada, Great Britain and United States*, 11 January 1909, UKTS 1910 No 23 (*Boundary Waters Treaty*).
1915	*Convention to fix the boundary between the Colonies of Suriname and French Guiana* (*Convention en vue de fixer la limite entre les Colonies de Suriname et de la Guyane Française*), France and Netherlands, 30 September 1915, 12 Nouveau Recueil General de Traites et Autres Actes Relatifs aux Rapports de Droit International (3d ser, Heinrich Triepel, ed) 269.
1920	*Convention on certain points connected with the mandates for Syria and the Lebanon, Palestine and Mesopotamia*, Great Britain and France, 23 December 1920, XXII LNTS 353
1920	*Peace Treaty and Protocol*, Lithuania and Soviet Government of Russia, 12 July 1920, III LNTS 105.
1921	*Convention Concerning the Delimitation of the Frontier Between Austria and Czechoslovakia and Various Questions Connected Therewith*, 10 March 1921, IX LNTS 334.
1921	*Convention Instituting the Definitive Statute of the Danube*, 23 July 1921, XXVI LNTS 173.

 | DOI:10.1163/9789004736771_010

(*cont.*)

Date	Treaty
1922	*Convention instituting the Statute of Navigation of the Elbe, with Protocol of signature*, 22 February 1922, XXVI LNTS 219.
1923	*Convention Relating to the Development of Hydraulic Power Affecting More than One State*, 9 December 1923, 36 LNTS 76.
1924	*Treaty for the Regulation of the Rhine from the Confluence of the Ill to the Lake of Constance*, Austria and Switzerland, 19 November 1924, XXXIX LNTS 25, RO 41 730.
1925	*Agreement to Regulate the Level of the Lake of the Woods and Protocol relating thereto*, United States and Canada, 24 February 1925, 43 LNTS 251.
1925	*Convention concerning the International Legal Regime of the Waters of the Pasvik (Patsjoki) and the Jakobselv (Vuoremajoki), with Protocol*, 14 February 1925, Finland and Norway, XLIX LNTS 379.
1926	*Agreement between South Africa and Portugal regulating the use of the water of the Kunene River for the purposes of generating hydraulic power and inundation and irrigation in the Mandated Territory of South West Africa*, 1 July 1926, LXX LNTS 316.
1926	*Convention for the Settlement of Relations Between Switzerland and France on the Subject of Certain Clauses of the Legal Regime of the Future Derivation of Kembs, France and Switzerland* (*Convention pour le règlement des rapports entre la Suisse et la France au sujet de certaines clauses du régime juridique de la future dérivation de Kembs*), 27 August 1926, RO 44 9.
1927	*Convention between Belgium and Portugal regarding various questions of economic interest of the colonies Belgian Congo and Angola*, 20 July 1927, LXXI LNTS 436.
1927	*Convention between Spain and Portugal to regulate the hydro-electric development of the international section of the River Douro*, 11 August 1927, LXXXII LNTS 130.
1928	*Convention regarding the Maintenance and Administration of the Frontier Waterways, with Final Protocol*, Germany and Lithuania, 29 January 1928, LXXXIX LNTS 337.
1929	*Agreement Concerning the Frontier Between Germany and Belgium*, Belgium and Germany, 7 November 1929, 121 LNTS 329.
1929	*Arbitration Treaty*, Spain and France, 10 July 1929, CXLVIII LNTS 369.
1929	*Exchange of Notes Regarding the Use of Waters of the Nile for Irrigation Purposes*, Egypt and Great Britain, 7 May 1929, 93 LNTS 43.

(*cont.*)

Date	Treaty
1929	*Treaty between Chile and Peru for the settlement of the dispute regarding Tacna and Arica*, 3 June 1929, 94 LNTS 401.
1929	*Treaty of peace, friendship and of arbitration* (*Traité de Paix, d'Amitié et d'Arbitrage*), Dominican Republic and Haiti, 20 February 1929, CV LNTS 215.
1930	*Convention Between Switzerland and France on the Subject of the Concession of the Chatelot Waterfall* (*Convention Entre la Suisse et la France au Sujet de la Concession de la Chute du Châtelot*), 19 November 1930, RO 48 409.
1933	*Declaration of Montevideo concerning the industrial and agricultural use of international rivers approved by the seventh international conference of American States*, 24 December 1933, 28 American Journal of International Law 59, Pan American Union, Seventh International Conference of American States, Plenary Sessions, Minutes and antecedents, 114 (*1933 Montevideo Declaration*).
1934	*Agreement Between the United Kingdom and Belgium Regarding Water Rights on the Boundary Between Tanganyika and Ruanda-Urundi*, 22 November 1934, 190 LNTS 95.
1944	*Utilization of Waters of the Colorado and Tijuana Rivers and of the Rio Grande*, Mexico and the United States of America, 3 February 1944, 59 Stat 1219.
1945	Charter of the United Nations.
1946	*Agreement concerning the utilization of the rapids of the Uruguay River in the Salto Grande area*, Argentina and Uruguay, 30 December 1946, 671 UNTS 17.
1946	*Treaty of friendship and neighbourly relations, and six annexed protocols, signed at Ankara*, Iraq and Turkey, 29 March 1946, 37 UNTS 226.
1948	American Treaty on Pacific Settlement, 30 April 1948, 30 UNTS 55 (*Pact of Bogotá*).
1948	*Convention Regarding the Regime of Navigation on the Danube*, 18 August 1948, 33 UNTS 180.
1949	*Agreement Between Switzerland and Italy on the Subject of the Concession of Hydraulic Forces of the Reno Di Lei, with Additional Protocol* (*Accord Entre la Suisse et l'Italie au Sujet de la Concession de Forces Hydrauliques du Reno di Lei avec protocole additionnel*), 18 June 1949, RO 1955 611.
1949	*Exchange of Notes Constituting an Agreement Between the Great Britain and Egypt Regarding the Construction of the Owen Falls Dam, Uganda*, 30–31 May 1949, 226 UNTS 274.

(*cont.*)

Date	Treaty
1950	*Agreement Between the Federal Government of the Republic of Austria and the Free State of Bavaria Concerning the Osterreichisch-Bayerische Kraftwerke* AG *(Austrian Bavarian Hydroelectric Company)*, Republic of Austria and Free State of Bavaria, 16 October 1950 in United Nations Legislative Series, *Legislative Texts and Treaty Provisions Concerning the Utilization of International Rivers for Other Purposes than Navigation* (UN Doc No ST/Leg/SER.B/12, 1963) 470.
1950	*State Treaty between the Grand Duchy of Luxembourg and the Land Rhineland-Palatinate in the Federal Republic of Germany concerning the construction of a hydro-electric power plant on the Sauer (Sûre) at Rosport/ Ralingen*, Luxembourg and the Federal Republic of Germany, 25 April 1950 in United Nations Legislative Series, Legislative Texts and Treaty Provisions Concerning the Utilization of International Rivers for Other Purposes than Navigation (UN, 1963) 721 (UN Doc No ST/Leg/SER.B/12).
1950	Terms of Reference of the Helmand River Delta Commission and an Interpretative Statement Relative Thereto, Afghanistan and Iran, 7 September 1950 in United Nations Legislative Series, *Legislative Texts and Treaty Provisions Concerning the Utilization of International Rivers for Other Purposes than Navigation* (UN, 1963) 270 (UN Doc No ST/Leg/SER.B/12).
1952	*Agreement between the Government of the Republic of Austria and the Government of the Federal Republic of Germany and of the Free State of Bavaria concerning the Donaukraftwerk-Jochenstein-Aktiengesellschaft (Danube power-plant and Jochenstein joint-stock company)*, 13 February 1952 in United Nations Legislative Series, Legislative Texts and Treaty Provisions Concerning the Utilization of International Rivers for Other Purposes than Navigation (UN, 1963) 476 (UN Doc No ST/Leg/SER.B/12).
1953	*Agreement between the Republic of Syria and the Hashemite Kingdom of Jordan concerning the utilization of the Yarmuk waters*, 4 June 1953, 184 UNTS 25.
1954	*Agreement between the Government of India and Government of Nepal on the Kosi Project*, 25 April 1954, 5 INDIA Bilateral Treaties and Agreements 418.
1954	*Agreement concerning water economy questions in respect of the frontier sector of the Mura and the frontier waters of the Mura (the Mura Agreement)*, Austria and Yugoslavia, 16 December 1954, 396 UNTS 100.

(*cont.*)

Date	Treaty
1954	*Convention Concerning Water Economy Questions Relating to the Drava*, Yugoslavia and Austria, 25 May 1954, 227 UNTS 128.
1954	*Treaty between the Swiss Confederation and the Republic of Austria for the regulation of the Rhine from the mouth of the Ill to Lake Constance* (*Traité Entre la Confédération Suisse et la République d'Autriche pour la Régularisation du Rhin de l'Embouchure de l'Ill au Lac de Constance*), 10 April 1954, RO 1955 741.
1955	*Agreement between Yugoslavia and Hungary together with the statute of the Yugoslav-Hungarian water economy commission*, 8 August 1955 in United Nations Legislative Series, *Legislative Texts and Treaty Provisions Concerning the Utilization of International Rivers for Other Purposes than Navigation* (UN, 1963) 830 (UN Doc No ST/Leg/SER.B/12).
1955	*Agreement between Yugoslavia and Romania concerning questions of water control on water control systems and watercourses on or intersected by the state frontier, together with the statute of the Yugoslav-Romanian Water Control Commission*, 7 April 1955 in United Nations Legislative Series, *Legislative Texts and Treaty Provisions Concerning the Utilization of International Rivers for Other Purposes than Navigation* (UN, 1963) 928 (UN Doc No ST/Leg/SER.B/12).
1955	*Convention Between Italy and Switzerland Concerning the Regulation of Lake Lugano*, 17 September 1955, 291 UNTS 213.
1956	*Agreement concerning water economy questions, together with the statue of the Yugoslav-Albanian water economic Commission and the Protocol concerning fishing in frontier lakes and rivers, Yugoslavia and Albania, 5 December 1956 in United Nations Legislative Series, Legislative Texts and Treaty Provisions Concerning the Utilization of International Rivers for Other Purposes than Navigation* (UN, 1963) 721 (UN Doc No ST/Leg/SER.B/12).
1956	*Convention between the Federal Republic of Germany and the French Republic on the management of the upper course of the Rhine between Basel and Strasbourg and protocol annexed to the convention*, signed at Luxembourg, 27 Oct 1956, 1461 UNTS 15.
1956	*Convention between the Federal Republic of Germany, the French Republic, and the Grand-Duchy of Luxembourg on the subject of Moselle canalization*, 27 October 1956, 2375 UNTS 3.
1956	*Treaty (with annexes) concerning the regulation of water economy questions in the frontier region*, Hungary and Austria, 9 April 1956, 438 UNTS 123.

(*cont.*)

Date	Treaty
1957	*Convention between the Swiss Confederation and the Italian Republic on the subject of utilization of the hydraulic force of the Spol and additional protocol (Convention entre la Confédération suisse et la République italienne au sujet de l'utilisation de la force hydraulique du Spöl avec protocole additionnel)*, 27 May 1957, RO 1959 432.
1958	*Agreement between the government of the French Republic and the Spanish government relating to Lake Lanoux*, 12 July 1958, 796 UNTS 217.
1958	*Agreement Concerning Water Economy Questions Between Bulgaria and Yugoslavia*, 4 April 1958, 367 UNTS 104.
1958	*State Treaty between the Grand Duchy of Luxembourg and the Land Rhineland Palatinate in the Federal Republic of Germany, concerning the construction of hydroelectric power installations on the Our (with Annexes)*, Luxembourg and Germany, 10 July 1958 in United Nations Legislative Series, Legislative Texts and Treaty Provisions Concerning the Utilization of International Rivers for Other Purposes than Navigation (UN, 1963) 726 (UN Doc No ST/Leg/SER.B/12).
1959	*Agreement (with annexes) concerning the regulation of Lake Inari by means of the Kaitakoski hydroelectric power station and dam*, 29 April 1959, 346 UNTS 168.
1959	*Agreement Between Greece and Yugoslavia Concerning Hydro-economic Questions*, 18 June 1959, 363 UNTS 135.
1959	*Agreement on the Gandak Irrigation and Power Project*, Nepal and India, 4 December 1959, *in* Salman M.A. Salman & Kishor Uprety, Conflict and Cooperation on South Asia's International Rivers 361 (2002).
1959	*Indo-Pakistan Agreement (with appendices) on East Pakistan border disputes*, East Pakistan and India, 23 October 1959, 362 UNTS 3.
1960	*The Indus Waters Treaty 1960 (with annexes)*, 19 September 1960, 419 UNTS 125 (*Indus Waters Treaty*).
1960	*Treaty between the Kingdom of the Netherlands and the Federal Republic of Germany concerning the course of the common frontier, the boundary waters, real property situated near the frontier, traffic crossing the frontier on land and via inland waters, and other frontier questions*, 8 April 1960, 508 UNTS 148 (*Frontier Treaty*).
1961	*Protocol between the government of the Federal Republic of Germany, the French Republic and the Grand Duchy of Luxembourg concerning the establishment of an international commission to protect the Moselle against pollution*, 20 December 1961, 940 UNTS 217.

(*cont.*)

Date	Treaty
1961	*Protocol concerning the establishment of an international commission to protect the Saar against pollution, signed at Paris*, Germany and France, 20 December 1961,1053 UNTS 515
1961	Treaty between Canada and the United States of America relating to co-operative development of the water resources of the Columbia River Basin, 17 January 1961, 542 UNTS 246.
1963	*Act Regarding Navigation and Economic Co-operation between the States of the Niger Basin*, 26 October 1963, 587 UNTS 9.
1963	*Agreement between the Socialist Federal Republic of Yugoslavia and the Romanian People's Republic concerning the construction and operation of the Iron Gates Water Power and Navigation System on the River Danube*, 30 November 1963, 512 UNTS 42.
1963	*Charter of the Organization of African Unity*, 25 May 1963, 479 UNTS 39.
1963	*Convention between the Socialist Federal Republic of Yugoslavia and the Romanian People's Republic concerning the execution of works for the Iron Gates Water Power and Navigation System on the River Danube*, 30 November 1963, 512 UNTS 152.
1963	*Convention concerning the Émosson Hydroelectric Facility* (*with exchanges of letters*), France and Switzerland, 23 August 1963, 1248 UNTS 347.
1963	*Convention Relating to the General Development of the Senegal River Basin, Adopted* 26 July 1963, XIXth year, no 2 (April–June 1965) Rev Jurid & Pol (Paris) 299.
1963	*Exchange of notes constituting an agreement establishing a Joint Commission for the development of the Mirim Lagoon, Brazil and Uruguay*, 26 April 1963, 922 UNTS 259.
1963	*Statute of the Mixed Yugoslav-Romanian Commission for the Iron Gates*, 30 November 1963, 513 UNTS 154.
1964	*Agreement between Finland and the Soviet Union Concerning Frontier Watercourses*, 24 April 1964, 537 UNTS 252.
1964	*Agreement Concerning the Niger River Commission and the Navigation and Transport on the River Niger*, 25 November 1964, 587 UNTS 19.
1964	*Convention and Statute relating to the Development of the Chad Basin, Fort Lamy*, 22 May 1964, vol 4, no18 September 15, 1964 OJ of Cameroun, 1003, http://www.fao.org/faolex/results/details/en/c/LEX-FAOC001076/.
1964	*Convention Relating to the Statute of the Senegal River*, 7 February 1964, http://gis.nacse.org/tfdd/tfdddocs/275FRE.pdf (Adopted at Dakar).

(*cont.*)

Date	Treaty
1964	*Convention to regulate the hydroelectric development of the international sections of the river Douro and its tributaries (with additional protocol)*, Spain and Portugal, 16 July 1964, 1288 UNTS 191.
1964	*Exchange of notes (with attachment) constituting an agreement regarding sale of Canada's entitlement to downstream benefits under the Treaty relating to co-operative development of the water resources of the Columbia River Basin*, Canada and the United States of America, 22 January 1964, 542 UNTS 244.
1964	*Exchange of Notes (with attachments) constituting an agreement authorizing the Canadian Entitlement Purchase Agreement provided for under the Treaty relating to co-operative development of the water resources of the Columbia River Basin*, Canada and the United States of America, 16 September 1964, 542 UNTS 244, Can TS 1964 No 2.
1964	*Organization of African Unity: Protocol of the Commission of Mediation, Conciliation and Arbitration*, 21 July 1964, 3 ILM 6.
1966	*Agreement with Final Protocol Regulating the Withdrawal of Water from Lake Constance*, 30 April 1966, 620 UNTS 191.
1966	*Revised Agreement between the Government of India and His Majesty's Government of Nepal Concerning the Kosi Project*, India and Nepal, 19 December 1966 5 INDIA Bilateral Treaties and Agreements 352.
1967	*Franco-Italian Convention Concerning the Supply of Water to the Commune of Menton*, 28 September 1967, 940 UNTS 197.
1967	*Treaty between the Republic of Austria and the Czechoslovak Socialist Republic concerning the regulation of water management questions relating to frontier waters*, 7 December 1967, 728 UNTS 313.
1968	*African Convention on the Conservation of Nature and Natural Resources*, 15 September 1968, 1001 UNTS (Signed at Algiers).
1968	*Agreement Between the People's Republic of Bulgaria and the Republic of Turkey Concerning Cooperation in the Use of Waters of Rivers Flowing Through the Territory of Both Countries*, 23 October 1968, 807 UNTS 117.
1968	*Agreement concerning the establishment of a River Administration in the Rajka-Gönyü sector of the Danube (with exchange of letters)*, Czechoslovakia and Hungary, 27 February 1968, 640 UNTS 49.
1968	*Agreement regulating the use and development of the water resources of the international reaches of the rivers Miño, Limia, Tajo, Guadiana, and Chanza and of their tributaries (with additional protocol)*, Portugal and Spain, 29 May 1968, 1206 UNTS 24.

(*cont.*)

Date	Treaty
1969	*Convention between the French Republic and the Federal Republic of Germany concerning development of the Rhine between Strasbourg/Kehl and Lauterbourg/Neuburgweier*, 4 July 1969, 760 UNTS 305.
1969	*Vienna Convention on the Law of Treaties*, 23 May 1969, 1155 UNTS 331 (entered into force 27 January 1980).
1970	*Exchange of letters constituting an agreement amending the Agreement relating to Lake Lanoux (with arrangement concerning the lake's development) of 12 July 1958*, France and Spain, 27 January 1970, 796 UNTS 217.
1971	*Agreement between the government of the Socialist Republic of Romania and the government of the Union of Soviet Socialist Republics on the joint construction of the Stînca-Costesti hydraulic engineering scheme on the river Prut and the establishment of the conditions for its operation (with protocols)*, 16 December 1971, 890 UNTS 3.
1971	*Convention for the study of the use of the resources of the Paraá river (Convenio para el estudio del aprovechamiento de los recursos del Río Paraná)*, Paraguay and Argentina, 18 June 1971, https://www.fao.org/faolex/results/details/es/c/LEX-FAOC052664/
1972	*Agreement between the government of the Republic of Finland and the government of the Union of Soviet Socialist Republics concerning the production of electric power in the part of the Vuoksi River bounded by the Imatra and Svetogorsk hydroelectric stations*, 12 July 1972, 884 UNTS 57.
1972	*Convention establishing the Senegal River Basin Organization*, 11 March 1972, OJ of the Republic of Senegal, 26 July 1972, Law 72–71, 72–73, http://www.fao.org/faolex/results/details/en/c/LEX-FAOC016003/.
1972	*Convention relating to the Statute of the Senegal River*, 11 March 1972, *in* Basic Documents of African Regional Organizations (New York: Oceana Publishers, 1972), vol. III, http://www.fao.org/faolex/results/details/en/c/LEX-FAOC016004/.
1972	*Statute of the Indo-Bangladesh Joint Rivers Commission*, 24 November 1972, *in* Salman M.A. Salman & Kishor Uprety, Conflict and Cooperation on South Asia's International Rivers 383 (2002).
1973	*Agreement Creating a Development Fund of the Chad Basin Commission (Accord portant création d'un fonds de développement de la commission du bassin du Tchad signe a Yaoundé)*, 10 October 1973, https://www.ecolex.org/details/treaty/agreement-creating-a-development-fund-of-the-chad-basin-commission-tre-001971/?q=Chad+Basin+Commission&xdate_min=&xdate_max=.

(*cont.*)

Date	Treaty
1973	*Agreement Revising the Agreement Concerning the Niger River Commission and the Navigation and Transport on the River Niger of 25 November 1964*, 15 June 1973, 1346 UNTS 195.
1973	*Treaty Between the Federative Republic of Brazil and the Republic of Paraguay Concerning the Hydroelectric Utilization of the Water Resources of the Paraná River Owned in Condominium by the Two Countries, from and Including the Salto Grande de Sete Quedas or Salto del Guairá, to the Mouth of the Iguassu River* (*Treaty of Itaipú*), 26 April 1973, 923 UNTS 92.
1973	*Treaty of Yacyretá*, Argentina and Paraguay, 3 December 1973, 1380 UNTS 80.
1975	*Agreement between Iran and Iraq concerning the use of frontier water-courses*, 26 December 1975, 1017 UNTS 255.
1975	*Statute of the river Uruguay, signed at Salto*, Argentina and Uruguay, 26 February 1975, 1295 UNTS 339 (*Statute of the river Uruguay*).
1975	*Supplementary Convention to the Convention concerning the development of the Rhine between Strasbourg/Kehl and Lauterbourg/Neuburgweier of 4 July 1969*, France and Germany, 16 July 1975, 1025 UNTS 398.
1975	*Treaty Concerning the State Frontier and Neighbourly Relations Between Iran and Iraq*, 13 June 1975, 1017 UNTS 54.
1976	*Agreement between the government of the Federal Republic of Germany and the government of the Grand Duchy of Luxembourg concerning the maintenance, restoration and operation of the section of the Moselle common to the two States*, 14 September 1976, 1045 UNTS 277.
1976	*Convention on the Protection of the Rhine Against Chemical Pollution*, 3 December 1976, 1124 UNTS 423.
1976	*Convention on the Protection of the Rhine Against Pollution by Chlorides*, 3 December 1976, 1404 UNTS 90.
1977	*Agreement between the Government of Canada and the Government of the United States of America Concerning Transit Pipelines*, 8 January 1977, Can TS 1977 No 29.
1977	*Agreement for the Establishment of the Organization for the Management and Development of the Kagera River Basin*, 24 August 1977, 1089 UNTS 165.
1977	*Agreement on Sharing of the Ganges Waters at Farakka and on Augmenting Its Flows*, Bangladesh and India, 5 November 1977, 1066 UNTS 3.
1977	*Treaty Concerning the Construction and Operation of the Gabčíkovo-Nagymaros System of Locks*, Czechoslovak Socialist Republic and the Hungarian People's Republic, 16 September 1977, 1109 UNTS 235.

(*cont.*)

Date	Treaty
1977	*Treaty on Cooperation for the Utilization of the Natural Resources and the Development of the Mirim Lagoon Basin*, Brazil and Uruguay, 7 July 1977, 1079 UNTS 375.
1978	*Convention Concerning the Legal Status of Common Works*, 21 December 1978, *in* FAO, Treaties Concerning the Non-Navigational Uses of International Watercourses: Africa (FAO Legislative Study 61) 53–61 (1997).
1978	*Convention Relating to the Status of the River Gambia*, 30 June 1978, *in* Dep't of Tech.Co-operation for Dev., Treaties Concerning the Utilization of International Water Courses for Other Purposes than Navigation (Natural Resources/Water Series No. 13), at 39, UN Doc. ST/ESA/141, UN Sales No E/F.84.II.A.7 (1984), http://www.fao.org/faolex/results/details/en/c/LEX-FAOC015878/.
1978	*Protocol of the Agreement between the Republic of Guinea and the Republic of Guinea Bissau on the Management of the Koliba-Korubal River* (*Koliba-Korubal River Basin Protocol*), 21 October 1978, *in* FAO, Treaties Concerning the Non-Navigational Uses of International Watercourses: Africa (FAO Legislative Study 61) 164–166 (1997), http://www.fao.org/faolex/results/details/en/c/LEX-FAOC015973/.
1978	*The Convention Relating to the Creation of the Gambia River Basin Development Organization*, 30 June 1978, http://www.fao.org/faolex/results/details/en/c/LEX-FAOC015879/.
1980	*Convention between the Kingdom of Belgium and the Grand-Duchy of Luxembourg on the subject of the water of the Sûre* (*Convention entre le Royaume de Belgique et le Grand-Duché de Luxembourg au sujet des eaux de la Sûre*), 17 March 1980, 29-03-1984 Monituer Belge 3864, https://www.fao.org/faolex/results/details/en/c/LEX-FAOC018027/.
1980	*Treaty for the developing the shared water resources of the frontier sections of the Uruguay river and its tributary, the Pepiri-Guaçu* (*Pepirí-Guazú*) *River*, Brazil and Argentina, 17 May 1980,1333 UNTS 49.
1982	*Convention concerning improvement of the common River Lys between Deulemont and Menin* (*with annexes*) (*Convention au sujet de l'amélioration de la Lys mitoyenne entre Deulemont et Menin* (*avec annexes*)), France and Belgium, 3 February 1982, 1483 UNTS 239.
1982	*Convention modifying and completing the Supplementary Convention of 16 July 1975 to the Convention between the French Republic and the Federal Republic of Germany concerning development of the Rhine between Strasbourg/Kehl and Lauterbourg/Neuburgweier. Signed at Paris*

(*cont.*)

Date	Treaty
	on 4 July 1969 (with Supplementary Protocol) (Convention modifiant et complétant la Convention additionnelle du 16 Juillet 1975 à la Convention entre la République française et la République fédérale d'Allemagne au sujet de l'aménagement du Rhin entre Strasbourg/Kehl et Lauterbourg/ Neuburgweier. Signee a Paris le 4 juillet 1969 (avec protocole additionnel)), France and Germany, 6 December 1982, 1482 UNTS 268.
1982	*Indo-Bangladesh memorandum of understanding on the sharing of Ganga waters at Farakka*, Bangladesh and India, 7 October 1982, https://www.fao.org/faolex/results/details/en/c/LEX-FAOC017926/.
1982	*United Nations Convention on the Law of the Sea*, 10 December 1982, 1833 UNTS 397.
1984	*Treaty relating to the Skagit River and Ross Lake, and the Seven Mile Reservoir on the Pend d'Oreille River*, Canada and the United States of America, 2 April 1984, 1469 UNTS 309.
1986	*Convention between the government of the French Republic and the government of the Grand Duchy of Luxembourg for the realization and exploitation of certain industrial settlements on the Moselle (Convention entre le Gouvernement de la Republique francaise et le Gouvernement du Grand-Duche de Luxembourg pour la realisation et l'exploitatlon de certaines implantations industrielles sur la Moselle)*, 12 March 1986, Journal Official de la République Française (JO) No 298 of 24 Décembre 1986, 15543.
1986	*Treaty on the Lesotho Highlands Water Project between the Government of the Kingdom of Lesotho and the Government of the Republic of South Africa*, 24 October 1986, https://www.fao.org/faolex/results/details/en/c/LEX-FAOC015909/.
1987	*Agreement between the Federal Republic of Germany and the European Economic Community, on the one hand, and the Republic of Austria, on the other, on cooperation on management of water resources in the Danube Basin*, 1 December 1987, Official Journal of the European Communities, 1990, L90, 20.
1987	*Agreement between the Republic of Syria and the Hashemite Kingdom of Jordan concerning the utilization of the Yarmuk waters*, 3 September 1987, 1870 UNTS 285.
1987	*Agreement Between the Republic of Zimbabwe and the Republic of Zambia Concerning the Utilization of the Zambesi River*, 28 July 1987, http://gis.nacse.org/tfdd/tfdddocs/458ENG.pdf.

(*cont.*)

Date	Treaty
1987	*Revised convention Pertaining to the Creation of the Niger Basin Authority* (*Convention Révisée Portant Création de L'Autorité du Bassin du Niger*), 29 October 1987, http://gis.nacse.org/tfdd/tfdddocs/462FRE.pdf (signed at N'Djamena).
1988	*Exchange of notes constituting an agreement concerning the construction of a joint ring levee* (*with plan*), Canada and the United States of America, 30 August 1988, 1852 UNTS 63.
1989	*Agreement between the Government of Canada and the Government of the United States of America for Water Supply and Flood Control in the Souris River Basin*, 23 October 1989, Can TS 1986 No 36.
1989	*Agreement concerning the establishment of the Regional Coordination Committee on drinking water and sanitation institutions of Central America, Panama and the Dominican Republic*, 23 October 1989, 1654 UNTS 323.
1989	*Agreement concerning the regulations governing Lake Saimaa and the Vuoksi River* (*with annexes*), Finland and Union of Soviet Socialist Republics, 26 October 1989, 1663 UNTS 325.
1990	*Agreement Between the Federal Republic of Nigeria and the Republic of Niger Concerning the Equitable Sharing in the Development, Conservation and Use of their Common Water Resources*, 18 July 1990, https://www.fao.org/faolex/results/details/en/c/LEX-FAOC016750/.
1990	*Agreement Between the Government of Botswana and the Republic of Namibia on the Establishment of a Joint Water Commission*, 13 November 1990, http://gis.nacse.org/tfdd/tfdddocs/487ENG.pdf (signed at Windhoek).
1991	*Protocol IV to the treaty on the Lesotho Highlands Water Project – supplementary arrangements regarding phase IA*, 19 November 1991, http://gis.nacse.org/tfdd/tfdddocs/498ENG.pdf.
1992	*Agreement between the government of the Republic of Namibia and the government of the Republic of South Africa on the establishment of a permanent water commission*, 14 September 1992, http://gis.nacse.org/tfdd/tfdddocs/511ENG.pdf.
1992	*Agreement Between the Republic of Kazakhstan, the Kyrgyz Republic, the Republic of Tajikistan, Turkmenistan, and the Republic of Uzbekistan on Cooperation in the Field of Joint Management of the Use and Conservation of Water Resources of Interstate Sources* (*Almaty Agreement*), 18 February 1992, http://cawater-info.net/library/eng/l/ca_cooperation.pdf.

(*cont.*)

Date	Treaty
1992	*Agreement on the development and utilisation of the water resources of the Komati River Basin between the government of the Republic of South Africa and the government of KaNgwane*, 7 October 1992 http://gis.nacse.org/tfdd/tfdddocs/512ENG.pdf.
1992	*Ancillary agreement to the deed of undertaking and relevant agreements entered into between the Lesotho Highlands Development Authority and the government of the Republic of South Africa*, 31 August 1992, http://gis.nacse.org/tfdd/tfdddocs/510ENG.pdf.
1992	*Convention on the Protection and Use of Transboundary Watercourses and International Lakes*, 17 March 1992, 1936 UNTS 269 (*UNECE Water Convention*).
1992	*Convention on the Protection of the Marine Environment of the Baltic Sea Area*, 9 April 1992, Official Journal of the European Communities, 1994, L73, 20.
1992	*Treaty between the Czech Republic Government and the Slovak Republic Government on mutual relations and principles of cooperation in agriculture, food industry, forestry, and water economy under the conditions of the customs union*, 23 November 1992, https://www.fao.org/faolex/results/details/ru/c/LEX-FAOC023131/.
1992	*Treaty on the Development and Utilization of the Water Resources of the Komati River Basin Between the Government of the Kingdom of Swaziland and the Government of the Republic of South Africa*, 13 March 1992, http://www.fao.org/docrep/W7414B/w7414b14.htm.
1992	*Treaty on the Establishment and Functioning of the Joint Water Commission Between the Government of the Kingdom of Swaziland and the Government of the Republic of South Africa*, 13 March 1992, http://www.fao.org/faolex/results/details/en/c/LEX-FAOC017391/.
1993	*Agreement Concerning the Establishment of a Border Environment Cooperation Commission and a North American Development Bank*, Mexico and the United States, 16–18 November 1993, 32 ILM 1545.
1993	*Exchange of Notes relating to the creation of the Binational Autonomous Authority of the Basin of the Lake Titicaca System, Desaguadero River, Lake Poopó, Salar de Coipasa (TDPS) (Notas Reversales relacionadas con la creación de la Autoridad Binacional Autónoma de la Cuenca del Sistema Lago Titicaca, Río Desaguadero, Lago Poopó, Salar de Coipasa (TDPS))*, Bolivia and Peru, 21 June 1993, https://www.fao.org/faolex/results/details/en/c/LEX-FAOC017672/.

(*cont.*)

Date	Treaty
1994	*Agreement between Lebanon and Syria on the distribution of water of Al-Asi River rising in Lebanon*, 20 September 1994, https://www.fao.org/faolex/results/details/en/c/LEX-FAOC037703.
1994	*Agreement between the Federal Ministry for the Environment, Nature Conservation and Nuclear Safety of the Federal Republic of Germany and the Ministry of the Environment of the Czech Republic on the implementation of the joint environmental protection pilot project "Municipal Wastewater Treatment Plants North Bohemia" (Abkommen zwischen dem Bundesministerium für Umwelt, Naturschutz und Reaktorsicherheit der Bundesrepublik Deutschland und dem Ministerium für Umwelt der Tschechischen Republik über die Durchführung des gemeinsamen Umweltschutzpilotprojekts "Kommunale Abwasserbehandlungsanlagen Nordböhmen")*, 19 December 1994, 1995 Part II Bundesgesetzblatt Nr 3, https://www.fao.org/faolex/results/details/en/c/LEX-FAOC007479.
1994	*Agreement between the government of the People's Republic of China and the government of Mongolia on the protection and utilization of transboundary waters*, 29 April 1994, https://www.fao.org/faolex/results/details/en/c/LEX-FAOC017921/.
1994	*Agreement Between the Governments of the Republic of Angola, the Republic of Botswana and the Republic of Namibia on the Establishment of a Permanent Okavango River Basin Water Commission (OKACOM)*, 15 September 1994, http://www.fao.org/faolex/results/details/en/?details=LEX-FAOC017435.
1994	*Agreement by exchange of notes between the Republic of Argentina and the Republic of Paraguay adopting the statute of the binational commission administering the lower basin of the Pilcomayo river (Acuerdo por canje de notas por el que se adopta el Estatuto de la Comisión Binacional Administradora de la Cuenca Inferior del Río Pilcomayo, entre la República Argentina y la República del Paraguay)*, 5 August 1994, https://www.fao.org/faolex/results/details/en/c/LEX-FAOC043346/.[a]

a Another version with a preamble is available on the government of Paraguay website: *Agreement by Exchange of Notes between the Republic of Argentina and the Republic of Paraguay Relating to the Adoption of the Statute of the Binational Commission Administering the Lower Basin of the Pilcomayo River (Acuerdo por canje de notas reversales relativo a la adopcion del estatuto de la comision binacional administradora de la cuenca inferior del rio Pilcomayo)*, 5 August 1994, https://www.bacn.gov.py/archivos/11125/ley+5431995.pdf.

(*cont.*)

Date	Treaty
1994	*Convention for the Establishment of the Lake Victoria Fisheries Organization with Annex and Final Act*, 30 June 1994, https://www.ecolex.org/details/treaty/convention-for-the-establishment-of-the-lake-victoria-fisheries-organization-tre-001239/?q=lake+victoria (as amended by the council of Ministers at its second session, 12 November 1998)
1994	*Convention on Cooperation for the Protection and Sustainable Use of the River Danube*, 29 June 1994, 1997 OJ (L342) 19.
1994	*Treaty of peace between the state of Israel and the Hashemite Kingdom of Jordan (with annexes, agreed minutes and maps)*, Israel and Jordan, 26 October 1994, 2042 UNTS 351.
1994	*Understanding on Rules and Procedures Governing the Settlement of Disputes, Marrakesh Agreement Establishing the World Trade Organization, Annex 2*, 15 April 1994, 1869 UNTS 401.
1995	*Agreement between the government of Hellenic Republic and the government of the Republic of Bulgaria for the use of the Nestos River waters*, 22 December 1995, https://www.fao.org/faolex/results/details/en/c/LEX-FAOC030368/.
1995	*Agreement constituting the trilateral commission for the development of the Pilcomayo river basin (Acuerdo Constitutivo de la comision trinacional para el desarrollo de la cuenca del rio Pilcomayo)*, 9 February 1995, https://www.fao.org/faolex/results/details/en/c/LEX-FAOC016756/.
1995	*Agreement for the multiple use of the resources of the upper basin of the Bermejo River Basin and of the Río Grande de Tarija: creation of the binational commission*, Argentina and Bolivia, 9 June 1995, Reg No 57038 UNTS.
1995	*Agreement on the Cooperation for the Sustainable Development of the Mekong River Basin*, 5 April 1995, 2069 UNTS 3.
1995	*Israeli-Palestine Liberation Organization: Interim agreement on the West Bank and the Gaza Strip, with selected Annexes*, Israel and Palestine, 28 September 1995, 36 ILM 551.
1995	*Protocol on Shared Watercourse Systems in the Southern African Development Community (SADC) Region*, 28 August 1995, http://www.fao.org/faolex/results/details/en/c/LEX-FAOC035640/.
1996	*Convention concerning the collection, storage and discharge of waste from ships navigating along the Rhine and other inland waters (Convention relative à la collecte, au dépôt et à la reception des déchets survenantt en navigation rhenane et intériieure)*, 9 September 1996, https://www.fao.org/faolex/results/details/en/c/LEX-FAOC017474/.

(*cont.*)

Date	Treaty
1996	*Joint Water Commission terms of reference*, Mozambique and South Africa, 1996, https://www.fao.org/faolex/results/details/en/c/LEX-FAOC215958/.
1996	*Treaty Concerning the Integrated Development of the Mahakali River including Sarada Barrage, Tanakpur Barrage and Pancheshwar Project*, India and Nepal, 12 February 1996, 36 ILM 531.
1996	*Treaty on Sharing of the Ganga/Ganges Waters at Farakka*, Bangladesh and India, 12 December 1996, https://www.fao.org/faolex/results/details/en/c/LEX-FAOC017351/.
1997	*Agreement between the Government of Romania and the Government of Ukraine on cooperation in the field of border water management*, 30 September 1997, https://www.fao.org/faolex/results/details/en/c/LEX-FAOC217065.
1997	*Agreement Between the Government of the Russian Federation and the Government of the Republic of Estonia Concerning Cooperation in the Protection and Rational Use of Transboundary Waters*, 20 August 1997, https://www.fao.org/faolex/results/details/en/c/LEX-FAOC032669/.
1997	*Agreement between the Republic of Turkey and the Republic of Bulgaria on determination of the boundary in the mouth area of the Mutludere/Rezovska River and delimitation of the maritime areas between the two States in the Black Sea*, 4 December 1997, https://www.fao.org/faolex/results/details/en/c/LEX-FAOC017355/.
1997	*Convention on the Law of Non-Navigational Uses of International Watercourses*, 21 May 1997, 2999 UNTS 77, 36 ILM 700 (*UN Watercourses Convention*) (entered into force 17 August 2014).
1997	*International Plant Protection Convention* (*new revised text*), 17 November 1997, 2367 UNTS 223 (entered into force 2 October 2005).
1997	*Treaty between the Republics of El Salvador, Guatemala and Honduras for the execution of the Trifinio Plan* (*Tratado entre las Repúblicas de El Salvador, Guatemala y Honduras para la ejecución del Plan Trifinio*), 31 October 1997, https://www.fao.org/faolex/results/details/en/c/LEX-FAOC215577.
1998	*Agreement between the government of the Republic of Kazakhstan, the government of the Kyrgyz Republic and the government of the Republic of Uzbekistan on cooperation in the area of environment and rational nature use*, 17 March 1998, https://www.fao.org/faolex/results/details/en/c/LEX-FAOC054532/.

(*cont.*)

Date	Treaty
1998	*Agreement between the Governments of the Republic of Kazakhstan, the Kyrgyz Republic, and the Republic of Uzbekistan on the Use of Water and Energy Resources of the Syr Darya Basin*, 17 March 1998, http://www.fao.org/faolex/results/details/en/c/LEX-FAOC054530/ (Tajikistan joined in 1999).
1998	*Agreement on Cooperation for the Protection and Sustainable Use of the Waters of the Spanish-Portuguese Hydrographic Basins*, Spain and Portugal, 30 November 1998, 2099 UNTS 275.
1998	*Regulations for the administration of the Zarumiilla canal and the use of its waters* (*Reglamento para la Administracion del Canal de Zarumilla y la utilizacion de sus aguas*), Ecuador and Peru, 26 October 1998, https://www.fao.org/faolex/results/details/en/c/LEX-FAOC017680/.
1999	*Convention on the Protection of the Rhine*, 12 April 1999, 2000 OJ (L289) 31, https://www.fao.org/faolex/results/details/en/c/LEX-FAOC017477/.
1999	*Protocol VI to the Treaty on the Lesotho Highlands Water Project Supplementary Arrangements Regarding the System of Governance for the Project*, Lesotho and South Africa, 4 June 1999, https://www.fao.org/faolex/results/details/en/c/LEX-FAOC216572.
1999	*Treaty for the establishment of the East African Community*, 30 November 1999, 2144 UNTS 255 (signed at Arusha).
2000	*Agreement between the Government of the Republic of Kazakhstan and the Government of the Kyrgyz Republic on utilization of the water facilities of interstate use on the Chu and Talas Rivers*, 11 February 2000, https://www.fao.org/faolex/results/details/en/c/LEX-FAOC054535.
2000	*Agreement Between the Governments of the Republic of Botswana, the Kingdom of Lesotho, the Republic of Namibia, and the Republic of South Africa on the Establishment of the Orange-Senqu River Commission*, 3 November 2000, http://wis.orasecom.org/content/study/ORASECOM/general/Documents/Legal/ORASECOM_Agreement_Reprint%20August%202012.pdf.
2000	*Revised Protocol on Shared Watercourses in the Southern African Development Community* (*SADC*), 7 August 2000, 40 ILM 321.
2001	*Agreement between the Government of the Republic of Kazakhstan and the Government of the People's Republic of China on Cooperation in the Use and Protection of Transboundary Rivers*, 12 September 2001, http://www.fao.org/faolex/results/details/en/c/LEX-FAOC065815/.

(*cont.*)

Date	Treaty
2002	*Agreement for the sharing of the Great Southern River Basin waters and the building of a joint dam on it*, Syria and Lebanon, 20 April 2002, https://www.fao.org/faolex/results/details/en/c/LEX-FAOC035726/.
2002	*Framework Agreement on the Sava River Basin Between Bosnia and Herzegovina, Croatia, Slovenia and the Federal Republic of Yugoslavia*, 3 December 2002, 2366 UNTS 479.
2002	*International Treaty for the Meuse* (*Accord International sur la Meuse*), 3 December 2002, Journal Official de la République Française (JO) No 0198 of 27 Août 201 texte No 6 sur 136, La Commission Internationale de la Meuse (CIM), http://www.meuse-maas.be/CIM/media/ACCORDS/accord-gand_f.pdf, 198.
2002	*Protocol on the Navigation Regime to the Framework Agreement on the Sava River Basin*, 3 December 2002, https://www.iea.ulaval.ca/en/agreements/4311.
2002	*Tripartite Interim Agreement for Cooperation on the Protection and Sustainable Utilization of the Water Resources of the Incomati and Maputo Watercourses* (*IIMA*), 29 August 2002, http://www.fao.org/faolex/results/details/en/c/LEX-FAOC034943/.
2002	*Water Charter of the Senegal River* (*Charte des Eaux du Fleuve Sénégal*), 28 May 2002, https://www.ecolex.org/details/treaty/charter-of-waters-of-the-senegal-river-tre-153511/.
2003	*African Convention on the Conservation of Nature and Natural Resources*, 11 July 2003, https://www.ecolex.org/details/treaty/african-convention-on-the-conservation-of-nature-and-natural-resources-revised-version-tre-001395/? (Revised Version).
2003	*Agreement between the Government of the Hellenic Republic and the Government of the Republic of Albania on the establishment of the permanent Greek-Albanian commission on transboundary freshwater issues*, 3 April 2003, https://www.fao.org/faolex/results/details/en/c/LEX-FAOC063938/.
2003	*Amendments to Articles 25 and 26 of the Convention on the Protection and use of Transboundary Watercourses and International Lakes*, 28 November 2003, 2897 UNTS 92 (entered into force 6 February 2013).
2003	*Convention on the Sustainable Management of Lake Tanganyika*, 12 June 2003, http://www.fao.org/faolex/results/details/en/c/LEX-FAOC045450/.
2003	*Framework Convention of the protection and sustainable development of the Carpathians*, 22 May 2003, No 56390 UNTS, https://www.fao.org/faolex/results/details/en/c/LEX-FAOC045448.

(*cont.*)

Date	Treaty
2003	*Protocol for Sustainable Development of Lake Victoria Basin*, 29 November 2003, http://www.fao.org/faolex/results/details/en/c/LEX-FAOC041042/.
2004	*Agreement between the council of ministers of the Republic of Albania and the Government of the Republic of Macedonia for the protection and sustainable development of Lake Ohrid and its watershed*, 17 June 2004, https://www.fao.org/faolex/results/details/en/c/LEX-FAOC069075/.
2004	*Agreement on the Establishment of the Zambezi Watercourse Commission*, 13 July 2004, https://www.fao.org/faolex/results/details/en/c/LEX-FAOC180628/.
2004	*Memorandum of Understanding between the Republic of Niger and the Republic of Mali relating to the construction of the Taoussa dams in Mali and Kandadji dams in Niger* (*Protocole d'accord entre la République du Niger et la République du Mali relatif à la réalisation des barrages de Taoussa au Mali et de Kandadji au Niger*), 6 June 2004, https://www.fao.org/faolex/results/details/en/c/LEX-FAOC050442/.
2007	*Convention on the Status of the Volta River and Establishment of the Volta Basin Authority*, 19 January 2007, https://www.fao.org/faolex/results/details/en/c/LEX-FAOC180705/.
2008	*Niger Basin Water Charter* (*La Charte de L'eau du Bassin du Niger*), 30 April 2008, http://www.abn.ne/images/documents/Charte_Eau/niger_basin_water_charter_certified_copy.pdf.
2009	*Agreement between Finland and Sweden Concerning Transboundary Rivers*, 11 November 2009, https://www.fao.org/faolex/results/details/en/c/LEX-FAOC215421.
2009	*Agreement for the Establishment of the Binational Commission for the Integrated Mangement of Water Resources of the Transboundary Hydrographic Basin of the Zarumilla River*, Ecuador and Peru, 22 October 2009, https://www.fao.org/faolex/results/details/en/c/LEX-FAOC098810.
2009	*Memorandum of Understanding between the Government of Turkey and the Government of the Syrian Arab Republic on establishment of a pumping station for withdrawal of water from Tigris River*, 23 December 2009, https://www.fao.org/faolex/results/details/en/c/LEX-FAOC103283.
2009	*Memorandum of Understanding in the field of remediation of water quality between the Government of the Republic of Turkey and the Government of the Syrian Arab Republic*, 23 December 2009, https://www.fao.org/faolex/results/details/en/c/LEX-FAOC103198.

(*cont.*)

Date	Treaty
2009	*Protocol on Prevention of the Water Pollution Caused by Navigation to the Framework Agreement on the Sava River Basin*, 1 June 2009, https://www.savacommission.org/en/protocols-to-the-fasrb-257/257.
2010	*Agreement between the Government of the Republic of South Africa and the Government of the Kingdom of Swaziland on water supply across the border between South Africa and Swaziland*, 23 July 2010, 2765 UNTS 407.
2010	*Agreement between the Government of the Republic of Tajikistan and the Government of the Islamic Republic of Afghanistan on cooperation in the development and management of water resources of the Pyanj and Amu Darya rivers*, 25 October 2010, https://www.fao.org/faolex/results/details/en/c/LEX-FAOC215068.
2010	*Agreement between the Government of the Russian Federation and the Government of the Republic of Azerbaijan on the Rational Management and Protection of the Water Resources of the Transboundary River Samur*, 3 September 2010, https://www.fao.org/faolex/results/details/en/c/LEX-FAOC110898/.
2010	*Agreement between the Government of the Russian Federation and the Government of the Republic of Kazakhstan on joint management of transboundary waterbodies*, 7 September 2010, https://www.fao.org/faolex/results/details/en/c/LEX-FAOC110899.
2010	*Agreement on the Nile Basin Cooperative Framework*, 14 May 2010, https://www.fao.org/faolex/results/details/en/c/LEX-FAOC203276/.
2010	*Agreement on the Protection and Sustainable Development of the Prespa Park Area*, 2 February 2010, https://www.fao.org/faolex/results/details/en/c/LEX-FAOC106015.
2010	*Guarani Aquifer Agreement* (*Acuerdo sobre el Acuífero Guaraní*), 2 August 2010, http://www.fao.org/faolex/results/details/en/c/LEX-FAOC143888/.
2010	*Memorandum of Understanding between the Government of the Republic of Turkey and the Government of the Islamic Republic of Iran on Natural Resources and Watershed Management*, 29 September 2010, https://www.fao.org/faolex/results/details/en/c/LEX-FAOC151210.
2010	*Protocol on Flood Protection to the Framework Agreement on the Sava River Basin*, 1 June 2010, https://www.iea.ulaval.ca/en/agreements/4939.
2010	*Statute of the Binational Commission for the Integrated Management of Water Resources of the Transboundary Hydrographic Basin of the Zarumilla River*, Ecuador and Peru, 5 November 2010, https://www.fao.org/faolex/results/details/en/c/LEX-FAOC099503.

(*cont.*)

Date	Treaty
2011	*Agreement between the Government of the Republic of Kazakhstan and the People's Republic of China on water quality protection of transboundary waters*, 22 February 2011, https://www.fao.org/faolex/results/details/en/c/LEX-FAOC110874.
2012	*Agreement between the Cabinet of Ministers of Ukraine and the Government of the Republic of Moldova on cooperation in the sphere of protection and sustainable development of the Dniester river basin*, 29 November 2012, https://www.fao.org/faolex/results/details/en/c/LEX-FAOC175782.
2012	*Agreement on cooperation between the Republic of Portugal and the Kingdom of Spain related to the International Park of Tagus River*, 9 May 2012, https://www.fao.org/faolex/results/details/en/c/LEX-FAOC124290.
2012	*Water Charter for the Lake Chad Basin* (*Charte de l'Eau du Bassin du Lac Tchad*), 30 April 2012, https://www.fao.org/faolex/results/details/en/c/LEX-FAOC203691; https://cblt.org/technical-documents/.
2013	*Agreement between Norway and Finland on a Norwegian-Finnish Water District*, 30 October 2013, https://www.fao.org/faolex/results/details/en/c/LEX-FAOC215506.
2014	*Agreement between the Government of Angola and the Government of Namibia on the Establishment of the Cuvelai Watercourse Commission* (*CUVECOM*), 16 September 2014, https://www.fao.org/faolex/results/details/en/c/LEX-FAOC156656.
2014	*Memorandum of Understanding for the establishment of a Consultation Mechanism for the Integrated Management of the Water Resources of the Iullemeden, Taoudeni/Tanezrouft Aquifer Systems* (*ITAS*), 28 March 2014, https://www.fao.org/faolex/results/details/en/c/LEX-FAOC135180.
2015	*Agreement between the Government of the Federal Republic of Germany and the Government of the Republic of Poland on common improvement of the situation on waterways in the German-Polish border area* (*flood control, drainage and navigation conditions*), 27 April 2015, https://www.fao.org/faolex/results/details/en/c/LEX-FAOC146490.
2015	*Agreement on Declaration of Principles between The Arab Republic of Egypt, The Federal Democratic Republic of Ethiopia And The Republic of the Sudan On The Grand Ethiopian Renaissance Dam Project* (*GERDP*), 23 March 2015, https://www.fao.org/faolex/results/details/en/c/LEX-FAOC203275.

(*cont.*)

Date	Treaty
2015	*Protocol on Sediment Management to the Framework Agreement on the Sava River Basin*, 6 July 2015, https://www.iea.ulaval.ca/en/agreements/5071.
2016	*Agreement between the Government of the Russian Federation and the Government of the Republic of Kazakhstan on the Conservation of the Ecosystem of the Transboundary Ural River Basin*, 4 October 2016, https://www.fao.org/faolex/results/details/en/c/LEX-FAOC172770.
2016	*Cooperation Agreement between the Republic of Azerbaijan and the Islamic Republic of Iran in the field of construction of hydroelectric power stations "Khudafarin" and "Maiden Tower" on the Araz River and use of energy and water resources*, 23 February 2016, https://www.fao.org/faolex/results/details/en/c/LEX-FAOC173805.
2016	*Rules and Procedures for Sharing of Data Related to the Management and Development of the Zambezi Watercourse*, 25 February 2016, https://www.fao.org/faolex/results/details/en/c/LEX-FAOC210267.
2017	*Agreement between the Government of the Republic of Uzbekistan and the Government of the Kyrgyz Republic on the interstate use of the Orto-Tokoi (Kasansay) reservoir in the Ala-Buka district of the Jalal-Abad region of the Kyrgyz Republic*, 6 October 2017, https://www.fao.org/faolex/results/details/en/c/LEX-FAOC215061.
2017	*Agreement between the Ministry of Agriculture and Water Economy of the Republic of Uzbekistan and the Ministry of Agriculture and Water Economy of Turkmenistan on cooperation on water issues*, 6 March 2017, https://www.fao.org/faolex/results/details/en/c/LEX-FAOC175286.
2017	*Agreement that establishes the Binational Commission for the Integrated Management of Water Resources of Transboundary Hydrographic Basins between the Republic of Peru and the Republic of Ecuador*, 20 October 2017, https://www.fao.org/faolex/results/details/en/c/LEX-FAOC199805.
2019	*Agreement between the Government of Romania and the Government of the Republic of Serbia regarding cooperation in the field of sustainable management of transboundary waters*, 5 June 2019, https://www.fao.org/faolex/results/details/en/c/LEX-FAOC215970.
2020	*Agreement between the Government of the Republic of Belarus and the Government of the Republic of Poland on cooperation in the field of protection and rational use of transboundary waters*, 7 February 2020, https://www.fao.org/faolex/results/details/en/c/LEX-FAOC215073.

(*cont.*)

Date	Treaty
2020	*Memorandum of Understanding under the Joint Working Group on Water Resources Cooperation of Lancang-Mekong Cooperation on the Provision of Hydrological Information of the Lancang River Throughout the Year by China to the Other Five Member Countries*, 1 November 2020, https://www.fao.org/faolex/results/details/en/c/LEX-FAOC215424.
2021	*Agreement between the Government of Romania and the Government of the Republic of Moldova regarding the regulation of the construction of waterworks*, 20 May 2021, https://www.fao.org/faolex/results/details/en/c/LEX-FAOC215967.
2021	*Agreement between the Government of the Republic of Mozambique, South Africa and the Kingdom of Eswatini on the Establishment of the Incomáti and Maputo Watercourse Commission*, 18 November 2021, https://www.fao.org/faolex/results/details/en/c/LEX-FAOC215181.
2021	*Agreement between the Government of the Republic of Uzbekistan and the Government of Turkmenistan on the Joint Uzbek-Turkmen Intergovernmental Commission on Water Management Issues*, 26 May 2021, https://www.fao.org/faolex/results/details/en/c/LEX-FAOC215058.
2022	*Agreement between the Government of the Republic of Uzbekistan and the Cabinet of Ministers of the Kyrgyz Republic on joint management of water resources of the Andijan (Kempirabad) reservoir*, 3 November 2022, https://www.fao.org/faolex/results/details/en/c/LEX-FAOC215056.
2022	*Agreement between the Government of Turkmenistan and the Government of the Republic of Uzbekistan on the management, protection and rational use of water resources of the Amudarya River*, 14 July 2022, https://www.fao.org/faolex/results/details/en/c/LEX-FAOC215059.
2022	*Agreement between the Ministry of Water Resources of the Republic of Uzbekistan and the Water Resources Service under the Ministry of Agriculture of the Kyrgyz Republic on cooperation on water management issues*, 3 November 2022, https://www.fao.org/faolex/results/details/en/c/LEX-FAOC215060.

Bibliography

Books

Bankes, Nigel and Barbara Cosens, *The Future of the Columbia River Treaty* (Munk School of Global Affairs University of Toronto, October 2012).

Bankes, Nigel and Barbara Cosens, *Protocols for Adaptive Water Governance: The Future of the Columbia River Treaty* (Munk School of Global Affairs University of Toronto, October 2014).

Beach, Heather L. et al, *Transboundary freshwater dispute resolution: Theory, practice, and annotated references* (United Nations University Press, 2000).

Berber, Friedrich J., *Rivers in International Law* translated by R.K. Batstone (1959).

Boisson de Chazournes, Laurence, *Fresh Water in International Law*, 2nd ed (Oxford University Press, 2021).

Chapman, J.D., ed, *The International River Basin: Proceedings of a Seminar on the Development and Administration of the International River Basin*, held under the auspices of the Regional Training Centre for United Nations Fellows (University of British Columbia, 1963).

Chauhan, B.R., *Settlement of International Water Law Disputes in International Drainage Basins* (Erich Schmidt, 1981).

Collier, John and Vaughan Lowe, *The Settlement of Disputes in International Law* (Oxford University Press, 1999).

Crawford, James, *Brownlie's Principles of Public International Law*, 9th ed (Oxford University Press, 2019).

The International Bureau of the Permanent Court of Arbitration, ed, *The Permanent Court of Arbitration/Peace Palace Papers Resolution of International Water Disputes* (Kluwer Law International, 2003).

Kittikhoun, Anoulak and Susanne Schmeier, eds, *River Basin Organizations in Water Diplomacy* (Routledge, 2021).

Leb, Christina, *Cooperation in the Law of Transboundary Water Resources* (Cambridge University Press, 2013).

Mackenzie, Ruth et al, *The Manual on International Courts and Tribunals*, 2nd ed (Oxford University Press, 2010).

Makene Moïse Mbengue and Rukmini Das, *Use of Experts in International Freshwater Disputes* (Brill Research Perspectives in International Water Law, 2019).

McCaffrey, Stephen C., "International Watercourses" in R-J Dupuy ed, *Hague Academy of International Law, A Handbook on International organizations*, 2d ed (Martinus Nijhoff, 1998).

McCaffrey, Stephen C., *The Law of International Watercourses,* 2nd ed (Oxford University Press, 2007).

McCaffrey, Stephen C., *The Law of International Watercourses,* 3rd ed (Oxford University Press, 2019).

Muckleston, Keith W., *International Management in the Columbia River System* (UNESCO-IHP, PCCP Series, 2003).

Organisation for Economic Co-operation and Development (OECD), *Environmental Outlook to 2050* (OECD Publishing, 2012).

Panel of Experts on the Legal and Institutional Aspects of International Water Resources Development, *Management of International Water Resources: Institutional and Legal Aspects, Natural Resources/Water* Series No 1 (UN, 1975).

Salman, Salman M.A., *The World Bank Policy for Projects on International Waterways: An Historical and Legal Analysis* (World Bank, 2009).

Schmeier, Susanne, *Governing International Watercourses: River Basin Organizations and the sustainable governance of internationally shared rivers and lakes* (Earthscan, 2013).

Smith, H.A., *The Economic Uses of International Rivers* (P.K. King and Son, 1931).

Tanzi, Attila, *The Economic Commission for Europe Water Convention and the United Nations Watercourses Convention: An analysis of their harmonized contribution to international water law,* Water Series No 6 (UN, 2015).

United Nations, *Handbook on the Peaceful Settlement of Disputes* (UN, 1992).

United Nations Children's Fund (UNICEF) and World Health Organization (WHO), *Progress on household drinking water, sanitation and hygiene 2000–2017: Special focus on inequalities* (UNICEF and WHO, 2019).

United Nations Department of Economic and Social Affairs, Population Division, *World Population Prospects 2019: Highlights* (UN, 2019).

United Nations Environment Programme (UNEP), *Atlas of International Freshwater Agreements* (UNEP, 2002).

United Nations Educational, Scientific and Cultural Organization (UNESCO) and United Nations Economic Commission for Europe (UNECE), *Progress on Transboundary Water Cooperation, Global Baseline for SDG Indicator 6.5.2* (UNESCO, 2018).

United Nations, Legislative Series, *Legislative Texts and Treaty Provisions Concerning the Utilization of International Rivers for Other Purposes than Navigation* (UN, 1963) (UN Doc No ST/Leg/SER.B/12).

Vinogradov, Sergei, et al, *Transforming Potential Conflict into Cooperation Potential: The Role of International Water Law* (UNESCO-IHP, PCCP, 2003).

Periodicals

Anderson, David, "Negotiation and Dispute Settlement" in Malcom Evans, ed, *Remedies in International Law: The Institutional Dilemma* (Hart Publishing, 1998) chapter 6.

Andrassy, M. Juraj, "Utilisation des eaux internationals non maritimes (en dehors de la navigation) (Neuvième Commission) Rapport provisoire" in *Annuaire de L'Institut de Droit International*, vol 48:1 (1959) 131.

Boisson de Chazournes, Laurence, "The Settlement of Disputes through Judicial Means (Article 33(10) and Annex on Arbitratin)" in Laurence Boisson de Chazournes et al eds, *The UN Convention on the Law of the Non-Navigational Uses of International Watercourses: A Commentary* (Oxford University Press, 2018) 364.

Bourne, C.B., "Mediation, Conciliation and Adjudication in the Settlement of International Drainage Basin Disputes" (1971) 9 Canadian Yearbook of International Law 114.

von Bar, L., "Deuxième rapport de M.L. von Bar, rapporteur, et contre-propositions de Mr Kaufmann" in *Annuaire de L'Institut de Droit International 1911*, vol 24 (1911) 168.

Caflisch, L., "La convention du 21 mai 1997 sur l'utilisation des cours d'eau internationaux à des fins autres que la navigation" (1997) 43 Annuaire français de droit international 793.

Clagett, Brice McAdoo, "Survey of Agreements Providing for Third-Party Resolution of International Waters Disputes" (1961) 55:3 The American Journal of International Law 645.

Evensen, Jens, "First report on the law of the non-navigational uses of international watercourses" (UN Doc A/CN.4/367) in *Yearbook of the International Law Commission 1983*, vol 2, part 1 (1985) 155 (UN Doc A/CN.4/SER.A/1983/Add.1 (Part 1)).

Gleick, Peter H., "An introduction to global fresh water issues" in Peter H. Gleick, ed, *Water in Crisis A Guide to the World's Fresh Water Resources* (Oxford University Press, 1993) 3.

van den Hout, Tjaco T., "Introduction" in The International Bureau of the Permanent Court of Arbitration, ed, *The Permanent Court of Arbitration/Peace Palace Papers Resolution of International Water Disputes* (Kluwer Law International, 2003) xi.

L'Institut de Droit International/Institute of International Law, "Texte des Résolutions adoptees enc e qui concerne la Règlementation international de l'usage des cours d'eau internationaux" in *Annuaire de L'Institut de Droit International 1911*, vol 24 (1911) 365 at 367.

L'Institut de Droit International/Institute of International Law, "Utilization of Non-Maritime International Waters (Except for Navigation)" ("Salzburg Resolution") in *Annuaire de L'Institut de Droit International*, vol 40 (1961) 381.

The International Law Association, "Uses of the Waters of International Rivers" in *Report of the Forty-Eighth Conference of the International Law Association Held at New York, September 1–7, 1958*, vol 48 (1958) 28.

The International Law Association, "Helsinki Rules on the Uses of the Waters of International Rivers" ("Helsinki Rules") in *Report of the Fifty-Second Conference of the International Law Association Held at Helsinki, August 14–20, 1966*, vol 52 (1967) 484.

The International Law Commission, "Report of the Commission to the General Assembly on the work of its forty-third session" (UN Doc A/46/10) in *Yearbook of the International Law Commission 1991* vol 2 part 2 (1994) 1 (UN Doc A/CN.4/SER.A/1991/Add.1 (Part 2)).

The International Law Commission, "2188th meeting Friday, 6 July 1990, at 10.05 a.m." in *Yearbook of the International Law Commission 1990* vol 1 (1993) 287 at 293 para 77 (UN Doc A/CN.4/SER.A/1990).

The International Law Commission, "2311th Meeting Thursday, 24 June 1993, at 10.10 a.m." in *Yearbook of the International Law Commission 1993* vol 1 (1995) 93 at 94 para 10 (UN Doc A/CN.4/SER.A/1993).

The International Law Commission, Comment by Mr. Yamada, "2312th Meeting Friday, 25 June 1993, at 10.05 a.m." in *Yearbook of the International Law Commission 1993* vol 1 (1995) 96 at 98 para 13 (UN Doc A/CN.4/SER.A/1993).

The International Law Commission, Comment by Mr. Sreenivasa RAO, "2313th Meeting Friday, 29 June 1993, at 10.10 a.m." in *Yearbook of the International Law Commission 1993* vol 1 (1995) 104 at 110 para 40 (UN Doc A/CN.4/SER.A/1993).

The International Law Commission, "2353rd Meeting Tuesday, 21 June 1994, at 10.10 a.m." in *Yearbook of the International Law Commission 1994* vol 1 (1996) 158 at 171 para 93 (UN Doc A/CN.4/SER.A/1994).

The International Law Commission, "Report of the Commission to the General Assembly on the work of its forty-sixth session" (UN Doc A/49/10) in *Yearbook of the International Law Commission 1994* vol 2 part 2 (1997) 1 (UN Doc A/CN.4/SER.A/1994/Add.1 (Part 2)).

Jennings, Robert, "Keynote Address" in The International Bureau of the Permanent Court of Arbitration, ed, *The Permanent Court of Arbitration/Peace Palace Papers Resolution of International Water Disputes* (Kluwer Law International, 2003) 23.

Jiménez Cisneros, Blanca E. et al, "Freshwater Resources" in IPCC, Christopher B Field et al eds, *Climate Change 2014: Impacts, Adaptation, and Vulnerability Part A: Global and Sectoral Aspects Contribution of Working Group II to the Fifth Assessment Report of the Intergovernmental Panel on Climate Change* (Cambridge University Press, 2014) 229.

Kittikhoun, Anoulak and Susanne Schmeier, "Do river basin organizations make a difference in water diplomacy and conflict management" in Anoulak Kittikhoun and Susanne Schmeier, eds, *River Basin Organizations in Water Diplomacy* (Routledge, 2021) 1.

Kohen, Marcelo G., "Interaction between Diplomatic and Judicial Means at the Initiation of Proceedings" in Laurence Boisson de Chazournes et al, eds, *Diplomatic and Judicial Means of Dispute Settlement* (Martinus Nijhoff Publishers, 2013) 13.

McCaffrey, Stephen C., "Sixth report on the law of the non-navigational uses of international watercourses" (UN Doc A/CN.4/427 and Add.1) in *Yearbook of the International Law Commission 1990*, vol 2, part 1 (1993) 41 (UN Doc A/CN.4/SER.A/1990/Add.1 (Part 1)).

McCaffrey, Stephen, "The UN Convention on the law of the Non-Navigational Uses of International Watercourses: Prospects and Pitfalls" in Salman M.A. Salman and Laurence Boisson de Chazournes, eds, *International Watercourses: Enhancing Cooperation and Managing Conflict, Proceedings of a World Bank Seminar, World Bank Technical Paper No 414* (The World Bank, 1998) 17.

McCaffrey, Stephen, "The contribution of the UN Convention on the law of the non-navigational uses of international watercourses" (2001) 1:3/4 International Journal of Global Environmental Issues 250.

McCaffrey, Stephen C., "Water Disputes Defined: Characteristics and Trends for Resolving Them" in The International Bureau of the Permanent Court of Arbitration, ed, *The Permanent Court of Arbitration/Peace Palace Papers Resolution of International Water Disputes* (Kluwer Law International, 2003) 49.

McCracken, Melisa and Aaron T. Wolf, "Updating the Register of International River Basins of the world" (2019) 35: 5 International Journal of Water Resource Development 732.

Moy, Richard and Jonathan O'Riordan, "The International Joint Commission's Unique and Colourful Role in Three Projects in the Pacific Northwest" in Daniel Macfarlane and Murray Clemen, eds, *The First Century of the International Joint Commission* (University of Calgary Press, 2020) 239.

Petersen-Perlman, Jacob D. et al, "International water conflict and cooperation: challenges and opportunities" (2017) 42:2 Water International 105.

Rosenstock, Robert, "Second report on the law of the non-navigational uses of international watercourses" (UN Doc A/CN.4/462) in *Year Book of the International Law Commission 1994* vol 2 part 1 (2001) 113 (UN Doc A/CN.4/SER.A/1994/Add.1 (Part 1)).

Salman, Salman M.A., "Good Offices and Mediation and International Water Disputes" in The International Bureau of the Permanent Court of Arbitration, ed, *The Permanent Court of Arbitration/Peace Palace Papers Resolution of International Water Disputes* (Kluwer Law International, 2003) 155.

Salman, Salman, "Evolution and Context of International Water Resources Law" in Laurence Boisson de Chazournes and Salman Slaman, eds, *Les resources en eau et le droit international – Water resources and International Law* (Martinus Nijhoff Publishers, 2005) 45.

Samboly Ba, Abdoul & Makane Moïse Mbengue, "Le Régime Juridique du Fleuve Sénégal: Aspects du Droit des Cours d'Eau dans un Contexte Régional," in *African Yearbook of International Law*, Volume 12, Issue 1 (2004) 322.

Sands, Philippe, Q.C., "Water and international law: science and evidence in international litigation" (2010) 22 Environmental Law & Management 151.

Schwebel, Stephen M., "Third report on the law of the non-navigational uses of international watercourses" (UN Doc A/CN.4/348) in *Year Book of the International Law Commission 1982* vol 2 part 1 (1984) 65 (UN Doc A/CN.4/SER.A/1982/Add.1(Part 1)).

Shiklomanov, Igor A., *World Water Resources a New Appraisal and Assessment for the 21st Century* (UNESCO, 1998).

Smith, H.A., "The Waters of the Jordan: A Problem of International Water Control" (1949) 25 International Affairs 415.

Subedi, S.P., "Challenges for the 21st Century" in The International Bureau of the Permanent Court of Arbitration, ed, *Resolution of International Water Disputes* (The Permanent Court of Arbitration/Peace Palace Papers, 2003) 33.

Tanzi, Attila and Maria Farnelli, "The Settlement of Disputes through Non-Judicial Means (Article 33(1)-33(9))" in Laurence Boisson de Chazournes et al eds, *The UN Convention on the Law of the Non-Navigational Uses of International Watercourses: A Commentary* (Oxford University Press, 2018) 349.

United Nations, Secretary-General, "Long-Term Programme of Work, Including: Consideration of Recommendation Concerning Commencing the Work on the Law of Non-Navigational Uses of International Watercourses" (UN Doc A/5409) in *Year Book of the International Law Commission 1974* vol 2 part 2 (1974) 33 (UN Doc A/CN.4/SER.A/1974/Add.1(Part 2)).

Wolf, Aaron T., "Shared Waters: Conflict and Cooperation" (2007) 32 Annual Review of Environment and Resources 241.

Wouters, Patricia K., "Allocation of the Non-Navigational Uses of International Watercourses: Efforts at Codification and the Experience of Canada and the United States" (1992) 30 Canadian Yearbook of International Law/Annuaire Canadien de Droit International 43.

Wouters, Patricia, "Universal and Regional Approaches to Resolving International Water Disputes: What Lessons Learned from State Practice?" in The International Bureau of the Permanent Court of Arbitration, ed, *The Permanent Court of Arbitration/Peace Palace Papers Resolution of International Water Disputes* (Kluwer Law International, 2003) 111.

Online

Boyle, Alan, "Environmental Dispute Settlement" (last updated 2009), online: *Max Planck Encyclopedias of International Law* <https://opil.ouplaw.com/home/mpil>.

Hakapää, Kari, "Negotiation" (last updated 2013), online: *Max Planck Encyclopedias of International Law* <https://opil.ouplaw.com/home/mpil>.

IGRAC (International Groundwater Resources Assessment Centre), UNESCO-IHP (UNESCO International Hydrological Programme), "Transboundary Aquifers of the World Map 2015 1:50 000 000" (Map Special Edition for the 7th World Water Forum 2015) (IGRAC, 2015), <https://www.un-igrac.org/resource/transboundary-aquifers-world-map-2015>.

NASA, "freshwater availability" (8 September 2021), online: *NASA Earthdata open access for open science* <earthdata.nasa.gov/learn/toolkits/freshwater-availability>.

Oregon State University: International River Basin Organization (RBO) Database, International River Basin Organization (RBO) Database: Home (last visited 7 May 2025), online: International Freshwater Treaties Database <https://transboundarywaters.ceoas.oregonstate.edu/international-river-basin-organization-database>.

Oregon State University: Transboundary Freshwater Disputes Database, International Freshwater Treaties Database: Home (last visited 13 November 2021), online: International Freshwater Treaties Database <transboundarywaters.science.oregonstate.edu/content/international-freshwater-treaties-database>.

Oregon State University: Transboundary Freshwater Disputes Database, "International Freshwater Treaties Database – Codebook and Description for Excel" (Updated January 2023), online: International Freshwater Treaties Database <https://transboundarywaters.ceoas.oregonstate.edu/sites/transboundarywaters.ceoas.oregonstate.edu/files/2024-02/TreatyCodeBook_v29%20%281%29.pdf>.

United Nations, Press Release, SG/SM/8139-OBV/262, "World's Water Problems Can be 'Catalyst for Cooperation' says Secretary-General in Message on World Water Day" (26 February 2002) online: UN Meetings Coverage and Press Releases <https://www.un.org/press/en/2002/sgsm8139.doc.htm>.

United Nations, Secretary-General, *UN Convention on the Law of the Non-Navigational Uses of International Watercourses, Entry into Force*, UN Doc C.N.271.2014. TREATIES-XXVII.12 (Depository Notification), 21 May 1997, (last visited November 15, 2021) Online: United Nations Treaty Collection <treaties.un.org/doc/Publication/CN/2014/CN.271.2014-Eng.pdf>.

Legislation

United Kingdom *Government of India Act*, 1935 (UK), 26 Geo V, c 2.

United Nations General Assembly *Manila Declaration on the Peaceful Settlement of International Disputes*, GA Res 37/10, UNGAOR, 37th Sess, SUPP NO 51, UN Doc A/37/51, (1982) 261.

Decisions and Reports of Joint Bodies or International Organizations

Indus (Rau) Commission, *Report of the Indus (Rau) Commission and Printed Proceedings* 10 (1950).

International Joint Commission, *Impacts of a Proposed Coal Mine in the Flathead River Basin*, (December 1988), online: <https://www.ijc.org/en/impacts-proposed-coal-mine-flathead-river-basin> (accessed 8 May 2025).

United Nations Economic Commission for Europe Meeting of the Parties to the Convention on the Protection and Use of Transboundary Watercourses and International Lakes, *Decision VI/1 Support to implementation and compliance*, UNECOSOCOR, 2012, ECE/MP.WAT/37/Add.2 (2013) 2.

United Nations General Assembly, *Progressive development and codification of the rules of international law relating to international water courses*, GA Res 2669 (XXV), UNGAOR, 25th Sess, Supp No 28, UN Doc A/8028 (1970) 127.

United Nations General Assembly, 51st Sess, 62nd Mtg, UN Doc A/C.6/51/SR.62 (1997).

United Nations General Assembly, 51st Sess, 99th Plen Mtg, UN Doc A/51/PV.99 (1997).

Index

Index (Treaties)

www.ingramcontent.com/pod-product-compliance
Lightning Source LLC
Chambersburg PA
CBHW051357240926
51852CB00001B/51
9789004736764